RESILIENCY IN ACTION

Practical Ideas for Overcoming Risks and Building Strengths

in youth, families, & communities

Nan Henderson, Bonnie Benard, Nancy Sharp-Light

Editors

Foreword by Peter L. Benson

Published by
Resiliency In Action, Inc.

ACKNOWLEDGEMENTS

We owe much to so many who have contributed to the life of the journal, *Resiliency In Action*, and to the birth of this book. We especially want to thank:

Emmy Werner, Peter Benson, Steve and Sybil Wolin, Dennis Saleeby, and Glenn Richardson for their encouragement and support, their scholarship and wisdom, and—especially—for having the courage to follow where the research leads.

Art Bernstein, Debra DeSantis, Tim Duffey, Donna Duffey, Don Henderson, Kelsey Henderson, Janice Janecki, Bill Lofquist, Craig Noonan, Sue Mahoney, Rich Ott, and Peter Seidman for their contributions of time, energy, talent, and advice, and for providing us personally with much "caring and support."

Ann and Dennis Holmes, Bob Francis, Brenda Holben, Barbara Keller, Kathy Marshall, Carol Klopp, Michael Lahti, Mary Miller, Betsy Thompson, Sally Shields, Mary VanderWall, and all our other early subscribers, whose pioneering spirit in organizations and communities truly demonstrate Resiliency In Action.

*Dedicated to the subscribers
of* Resiliency In Action *across
the U.S. and around the
world, without whom this
book would not exist.*

Preface

This book challenges a widely accepted myth about people, especially young people, who experience risks, stress, trauma, and adversity in their lives. Contrary to popular opinion, the majority of these individuals do, over time, bounce back from their problems and do well. There is a growing body of scientific research from several fields that documents this fact and yields important information as to what can be done to facilitate this process of overcoming.

In 1996, a middle school teacher and two social workers, convinced that the extensive national focus on risks, deficits, and pathologies obscured this truth took one of the biggest risks of their professional lives. With only a few hundred dollars, but a wealth of conviction about the need to publicize and make practical the research findings of the self-righting capacity within all, Nancy Sharp-Light, Bonnie Benard, and I founded what has become a leading publication on moving youth, families, and communities from risk to resiliency. Little did we realize that within three short years the journal we began, *Resiliency In Action: Bouncing Back from Risk and Adversity—Ideas for Youth Families, and Communities* would gain an audience of subscribers in almost every state in the country, as well as in Puerto Rico, Canada, Argentina, Australia, New Zealand, Malaysia, Samoa, Israel, and Portugal.

This book is a direct result of the enthusiastic response the journal received. Rather than meet the requests of our readers for reprints of many single issues of *Resiliency In Action*, we decided to compile a book of "the best" of all the issues.

Our goal in starting the journal, and reprinting it in a book format, was a simple one: Share the results of the dozens of scientific studies that have emerged in the past decade showing specifically how people, families, and even organizations overcome risk, trauma, and adversity to go on to life success, in a practical, reader-friendly format. We wanted to make the researchers themselves human through one-to-one interviews that included their heart-to-heart advice as to how to best foster resiliency. We also wanted to spotlight the many individuals and schools and community groups we knew that were integrating the results of this research and finding significant improvements in emotional, behavioral, and academic outcomes. Finally, we wanted to highlight the lives of young people whose personal stories demonstrate the reality of resilient overcoming.

In short, we learned so much about how to help foster this process of resilient overcoming by studying the research documenting exactly *how* it happens and talking with people and organizations making it happen, we wanted everyone who cares about kids, families, and communities to know what we had learned. Of course in the process of making our goal a reality, we have learned—along with, and from, our readers—much more.

The hopeful information about the capacity for resiliency and how to foster it has been publicized in several other leading publications since we began *Resiliency In Action*. It was the cover story in the November 11, 1996 issue of *U.S. News and World Report*, the November, 1997 issue of *Principal Magazine*, and the June, 1998 *Psychology Today*. Extensive examination of the resiliency framework has also appeared in journals for psychologists, social workers, family therapist, and other youth-serving professionals during this time. In 1998, Martin Seligman, Ph.D., a resiliency researcher and then President of the American Psychological Association, stated that the entire field of psychology is moving away from the deficit approach to a strengths-based model.

The reason for the growing popularity of the resiliency approach to viewing and helping others is, I believe, an increasing awareness best expressed to me by a resilient young man who had spent most of his life in dozens of foster homes enduring tremendous risk, trauma, and adversity. What helped the most, he told me, were those people along the way who gave him the message, "What is right with you is more powerful than anything that is wrong with you."

The truth of this message, which has often been missing in the deficit-based models of the past, is at the heart of the growing support for the resiliency approach. *Resiliency In Action* is dedicated to showing how to recognize, nurture, and utilize the "power of what is right" to transform the lives of children and youth, families, and communities.

Nan Henderson
San Diego CA
January, 1999

Foreword

As life zips by too quickly, I have decided to set certain boundaries about time. One of them is to seek to connect with people, places, and ideas dedicated to transformation. The transformation I care the most about is deep change in how American culture—through its systems, rituals, symbols, and norms—embraces and promotes the healthy development of *all* children and adolescents.

Such transformation will require a massive flow of human energy and spirit directed to naming and growing the inherent strengths found in each human life *and* unleashing the capacity of individuals, organizations, and institutions to create places and settings of support and growth. The change process begins with a transformation in human consciousness and understanding.

Resiliency is one of those consciousness-changing ideas. Grounded in decades of research and practice, the concept of resiliency causes us to think differently. With its accents on the processes of human development, the internal and external forces that promote positive growth, and conceptual and practical dimensions of change-making, resiliency becomes a way of thinking and being which changes lives. Accordingly, it is about hope and possibility.

Resiliency in Action: Practical Ideas for Overcoming Risks and Building Strengths makes this growing body of knowledge and understanding more accessible. And it does so by creating a wonderful balance of theory and practice, of head and heart. It is a unique and important compilation of core material, drawing on the work of major thinkers, writers, and practitioners. That it does so is really a testament to the quality of the *Resiliency In Action* journal from which these articles are gleaned.

This work and the ideas it conveys should be consumed and discussed by many—not just by the professionals who work with young people in schools, congregations, youth organizations, and agencies, but also by those who carry no formal portfolio for human development. For it may be that it is the people of our communities who have the most capacity to trigger and sustain the transformation we need.

Peter L. Benson, Ph.D.
President
Search Institute
Minneapolis, MN

CONTENTS

PART ONE

The Foundations of Resiliency

From the Editors

Join Us in a National Promotion of Resiliency

Welcome to _Resiliency In Action_! We believe that the time has come for a publishing company dedicated solely to the exciting, hopeful, and very real concept of resiliency—the ability of children, youth, adults, organizations, and communities to bounce back from stress and risk and adversity.

In working with this paradigm for several years, we have learned: Resiliency is more prevalent and more powerful than "risk." Everyone, every day, bounces back in little ways from the stresses of life, and most people have bounced back from significant losses or traumas. Resilient kids are real. More kids bounce back than do not. More kids are doing well than are doing poorly. Life is, in fact, "resiliency in action."

One purpose of this book is to spread the news of resiliency, through sharing research and theory from the various disciplines from which resiliency has emerged, including psychology, sociology, psychiatry, education, prevention, addiction studies, and community development. On page 11, you will find the words of the preeminent resiliency researcher in this country, Dr. Emmy Werner, summarizing from a scientific perspective what is, and isn't, known about resiliency. Bonnie Benard also shares the research foundations of the paradigm on page 5, in "From Research to Practice."

A second purpose of this book is to facilitate the practical application and evaluation of the resiliency paradigm. Following Emmy Werner's exhortation that evaluation is critical for the growth and acceptance of the concept, we invite any practitioner who is involved in program evaluation or practitioner research showing how people bounce back from stress, risk, and adversity to submit their work for publication. Finally, we have included in this issue an up-to-date list of resources and events related to resiliency.

Resiliency In Action was also started to challenge the prevalent message of doom and gloom about "at risk" children and adults in our culture. As Dr. Werner reports, most teenage welfare mothers and youth offenders do not wind up as adults dependent on welfare, or in the adult criminal population. On page 21, Nan Henderson has profiled two young people who put faces to the concept of resiliency. We believe identifying and publicizing resilient young people are some of the most important actions any of us can take. "The Faces of Resiliency" are included throughout this book. In working on this feature, we have learned what you may already know—resilient kids and resilient overcomings of all kinds are _everywhere_!

Join us in putting "resiliency in action." We sincerely hope this forum will further motivate and aid you in fostering resiliency in yourself and others, and in spreading the word: Resiliency is real and we can help ourselves and others become more resilient.

Nan Henderson, M.S.W.,

Bonnie Benard, M.S.W.,
Editors

Nancy Sharp-Light

From Research To Practice

The Foundations of the Resiliency Paradigm

by Bonnie Benard, M.S.W.

Welcome to all of you in our new mutual venture, Resiliency In Action! *We hope that this publication will serve as one vehicle for spreading the Good Word about resiliency research and practice and for networking all of us trying to live and work from a paradigm of empowerment that still remains the exception in our schools and other youth-serving organizations and in our workplaces. We do invite you to make* RIA *yours by sending us your suggestions, comments, and articles describing your resiliency work and to connect with the folks you read about in these pages. We know an axiom of working from a resiliency perspective is "walking the talk!" so we want this journal to be a forum for reflection and dialog, for relationship-building, and for mutual support.*

As the Research Editor I will continue my 13-year "tradition" (beginning in 1983 at Illinois Prevention Resource Center and continuing from 1990 until 1996 at the Western Center for Drug-Free Schools and Communities) of providing research synthesis and policy recommendations to the prevention, education, and youth development fields. In addition, for future issues I plan on conducting brief interviews with some of the wonderful researchers and practitioners contributing to the advancement of the resiliency paradigm. I am excited and hope to hear from you as we venture on this new journey together! In this introductory column, I thought a background summary of just what resiliency research is and what it has contributed to the prevention, education, and youth development fields—as well as the promise it offers to transform our existing institutions—is in order.

Resiliency Background

In the strictest sense, resiliency research refers to a body of international cross-cultural, lifespan developmental studies that followed children born into seriously high-risk conditions such as families where parents were mentally ill, alcoholic, abusive, or criminal, or in communities that were poverty-stricken or war-torn. The astoun-ding finding from these long term studies was that at least 50%—and often closer to 70%—of youth growing up in these "high risk" conditions did develop social competence despite exposure to severe stress and did overcome the odds to lead successful lives. Furthermore, these studies not only identified the characteristics of these "resilient" youth, several documented the characteristics of the environments—of the families, schools, and communities—that facilitated the manifestation of resilience.

> **"We are all born with innate resiliency."**

Resiliency Capacities

At the most fundamental level, resiliency research validates prior research and theory in human development that has clearly established the biological imperative for growth and development that exists in the human organism—that is part of our genetic makeup—and which unfolds naturally in the presence of certain environmental attributes. We are *all* born with innate resiliency, with the capacity to develop the traits commonly found in resilient survivors:

social competence (responsiveness, cultural flexibility, empathy, caring, communication skills, and a sense of humor); *problem-solving* (planning, help-seeking, critical and creative thinking); *autonomy* (sense of identity, self-efficacy, self-awareness, task-mastery, and adaptive distancing from negative messages and conditions); and *a sense of purpose and belief in*

> **"Resilience is not a genetic trait that only a few 'superkids' possess."**

a bright future (goal direction, educational aspirations, optimism, faith, and spiritual connectedness) (Benard, 1991). The major point here is that resilience is not a genetic trait that only a few "superkids" possess, as some journalistic accounts (and even several researchers!) would have us believe. Rather, it is our inborn capacity for self-righting (Werner & Smith, 1992) and for transformation and change (Lifton, 1993).

Environmental Protective Factors

Resiliency research, supported by research on child development, family dynamics, school effectiveness, community development, and ethnographic studies capturing the voices of youth themselves, documents clearly the characteristics of family, school, and community environments that elicit and foster the natural resiliency in children. These "protective factors," the term referring to the characteristics of environments that appear to alter—or even reverse—potential negative outcomes and enable individuals to transform adversity and develop resilience despite risk, comprise three broad categories. *Caring relationships* convey compassion, understanding, respect, and interest, are grounded in listening, and establish safety and basic trust. *High expectation messages* communicate not only firm guidance, structure, and challenge but, and most importantly, convey a belief in the youth's innate resilience and look for strengths and assets as opposed to problems and deficits. Lastly, *opportunities for meaningful participation and contribution* include having opportunities for valued responsibilities, for making decisions, for giving voice and being heard, and for contributing one's talents to the community (Benard, 1991).

Knowledge Base For Practice

Resiliency research clearly provides the prevention, education, and youth development fields with nothing less than a fundamentally different knowledge base and paradigm for research and practice, one offering the promise of transforming interventions in the human arena. It situates risk in the broader social context of racism, war, and poverty—not in individuals, families, and communities—and asks how it is that youth successfully develop in the face of such stressors. It provides a powerful rationale for moving our narrow focus in the social and behavioral sciences from a risk, deficit, and pathology focus to an examination of the strengths youths, their families, their schools, and their communities have brought to bear in promoting healing and health. The examination of these strengths

> **"Resiliency research clearly provides...nothing less than a fundamentally different knowledge base and paradigm for research and practice."**

and the acknowledgment that everyone has strengths and the capacity for transformation gives the prevention, education, and youth development fields not only a clear sense of direction—informing us about "what works!"—but also mandates we move beyond our obsession with risk identification, a statistically weaker practice that has harmfully labeled and stigmatized youth, their families, and their communities as "at risk" and "high risk", a practice that perpetuates

> **"The knowledge that everyone has innate resilience grounds practice in optimism and possibility."**

stereotyping and racism. Most importantly, the knowledge that everyone has innate resilience grounds practice in optimism and possibility, essential components in building motivation. Not only does this prevent the burn-out of practitioners working with seriously troubled youth but it provides one of the major protective factors—positive expectations—that when internalized by youth motivate and enable them to overcome risks and adversity.

> **"At the core of each of these approaches is an assumption of the biological imperative for growth and development (i.e., the self-righting nature of the human organism) which unfolds naturally in the presence of certain environmental attributes."**

Focus on Human Development

Resiliency research also offers the prevention, education, and youth development fields solid research evidence for placing human development at the center of everything we do. "Studies of resilience suggest that nature has provided powerful protective mechanisms for human development" (Maston, 1994) that "appear to transcend ethnic, social class, geographical, and historical boundaries" (Werner & Smith, 1992). This is precisely because they address our common, shared humanity. They meet our basic human needs for love and connectedness; for respect, challenge, and structure; and for meaningful involvement, belonging, power, and, ultimately, meaning. The development of resilience is none other than the process of healthy human development—a dynamic process in which personality and environmental influences interact in a reciprocal, transactional relationship. Resiliency research validates prior theoretical models of human development, including those of Erik Erikson, Urie Bronfenbrenner, Jean Piaget, Lawrence Kohlberg, Carol Gilligan, Rudolf Steiner, Abraham Maslow, and Joseph Chilton Pierce. While focused on different components of human development—psycho/social, moral, spiritual, and cognitive—at the core of each of these approaches is an assumption of the biological imperative for growth and development (i.e., the self-righting nature of the human organism) which unfolds naturally in the presence of certain environmental attributes. Stated simply by Maston, "When adversity is relieved and basic human needs are restored, then resilience has a chance to emerge" (1994). The major implication from resiliency research for practice is that if we hope to create socially competent people who have a sense of their own identity and efficacy, who are able to make decisions, set goals, and believe in their future, then meeting their basic human needs for caring, connectedness, respect, challenge, power, and meaning must be the *primary* focus of any prevention, education, and youth development effort.

Emphasis on Process—Not Program!

Resiliency research has clearly shown that fostering resilience, i.e., promoting human development, is a process and not a program. In fact, Rutter encourages the use of the term protective *processes* which captures the dynamic nature of resilience instead of the commonly used protective *factors*: "The search is not for broadly defined factors but, rather, for the developmental and situational mechanisms involved in protective processes" (1987). Resiliency research thus promises to move the prevention, education, and youth development fields beyond their focus on program and *what* we do, to an emphasis on process and *how* we do what we do; to move beyond our fixation with content to a focus on *context*. The fostering

> **"Fostering resilience is a process and not a program."**

of resilience operates at a deep structural, systemic, human level: at the level of relationships, beliefs, and opportunities for participation and power that are a part of every interaction, every intervention no matter what the focus. As McLaughlin and her colleagues found in their extensive study of inner-city youth-serving neighborhood organizations, the organizations that engaged youth and facilitated their successful development had total diversity in program focus and content, organizational structure, and physical environment. What they shared was an emphasis on meeting the needs of the youth—over programmatic concerns—a belief in the potential of each youth, a focus on listening, and providing opportunities for real responsibility and real work. These researchers state, "We questioned the assumption that what works has to be a particular program. Our research shows that a variety of neighborhood-based programs work as long as there is an interaction between the program and its youth that results in those youths treating the program as a personal resource and a bridge to a hopeful future" (1994). Schorr's earlier exploration of successful prevention programs came to similar conclusions: child-centered programs based on the establishment of mutual relationships of care, respect, and trust between clients and professionals were the critical components in program effectiveness (1988).

> *"Resiliency research thus promises to move the prevention, education, and youth development fields beyond their focus on program and what we do, to an emphasis on process and how we do what we do."*

Summary

The voices of those who have overcome adversity—be they in longitudinal studies or some of the more recent ethnographic explorations—tell us loud and clear that ultimately resilience is a process of *connectedness*, of linking to people, to interests, and ultimately to life itself. Rutter states that, "Development is a question of linkages that happen within you as a person and also in the environment in which you live. Our hope lies in doing something to alter these linkages, to see that kids who start in a bad environment don't go on having bad environments and develop a sense of impotency" (Pines, 1984). Similarly, James Coleman claims the most fundamental task for parents, educators, and policy makers is linking children into our social fabric. Our task is "to look at the whole fabric of our society and say, 'Where and how can children be lodged in this society? Where can we find a stable psychological home for children where people will pay attention to them?'" (Olson, 1987). Resiliency research shows the field that the blueprint for building this sense of home and place in the cosmos lies in relationships. To Werner and Smith, effective interventions must reinforce within every arena, the natural social bonds—between young and old, between siblings, between friends—"that give meaning to one's life and a reason for commitment and caring" (1982). Ultimately, research on resilience challenges the field to build this connectedness, this sense of belonging, by transforming our families, schools, and communities to become "psychological homes" wherein youth can find mutually caring and respectful relationships and opportunities for meaningful involvement. Ex-gang member Tito sums up most insightfully the message of resiliency research: "Kids can walk around trouble,

if there is some place to walk to, and someone to walk with" (McLaughlin et al., 1994).

To create these places and to be that "someone," we must, first and foremost, support our own resilience. Building community and creating belonging for youth means we must also do this for ourselves. As Sergiovanni writes, "The need for community is universal. A sense of belonging, of continuity, of being connected to others and to ideas and values that make ourselves meaningful and significant—these needs are shared by all of us" (1993). We, too, need the protective factors of caring and respectful relationships and opportunities to make decisions; without these, we cannot create them for youth.

> *"Resiliency research shows the field that the blueprint for building this sense of home and place in the cosmos lies in relationships."*

We see learning as primarily a process of modeling; thus walking our talk is a basic operating principle of resilience work. We acknowledge this is a major challenge for educators and youth workers given we live in a society that doesn't place a high priority on children and youth nor on meeting the basic human needs of its people. This makes our work as caregivers of youth not only a challenge but a vital necessity.

> *"Ultimately, resiliency research provides a mandate for social change."*

Ultimately, resiliency research provides a mandate for social change—it is a clarion call for creating these relationships and opportunities in all human systems throughout the lifespan. Changing the status quo in our society means changing paradigms, both personally and professionally, from risk to resilience, from control to participation, from problem-solving to positive development, from Eurocentrism to multiculturalism, from seeing youth as problems to seeing them as resources, from institution-building to community-building, and so on. Personally, fostering resilience is an inside-out, deep structure process of changing our own belief systems to see resources and not problems in youth, their families, and their cultures. However, fostering resilience also requires working on the policy level for educational, social, and economic justice. Ultimately, it means transforming not only our families, schools, and communities but creating a society premised on meeting the needs of its citizens, young and old. Our greatest hope for doing just this lies with our youth and begins with our belief in them. We must know in our hearts that when we create communities wherever we are with youth that respect and care for them as individuals and invite their participation—their critical inquiry, dialogue, reflection, and action—we are creating the conditions that allow their innate potential for social competence, problem-solving, sense of identity and efficacy, and hope for the future to unfold. And, in the process, we are building a critical mass of future citizens who will, indeed, rescind the mean-spirited, greed-based, control-driven social policies we now have and recreate a social covenant grounded in social and economic justice. ☺

References

Benard, B. (1991). *Fostering resiliency in kids: Protective factors in the family, school, and community.* Portland, OR: Western Center for Drug-Free Schools and Communities.

Lifton, R. J. (1993). *The protean self: Human resilience in an age of transformation.* New York, NY: Basic Books.

Maston, A. (1994). *Resilience in individual development: Successful adaptation despite risk and adversity.* In Wang, M. & Gordon, E. (eds.). *Educational resilience in inner-city America: Challenges and prospects.* Hillsdale, NJ: Lawrence Erlbaum Associates.

McLaughlin, M., et al. (1994). *Urban sanctuaries: Neighborhood organizations in the lives and futures of inner-city youth.* San Francisco, CA: Jossey-Bass.

Olson, L. (1987). A prominent boat rocker rejoins the fray. *Education Week,* January 14, 14-17.

Pines, M. (1984). Resilient children: Why some disadvantaged children overcome their environments, and how we can help. *Psychology Today,* March.

Rutter, M. (1987). Psychosocial resilience and protective mechanisms. *American Journal of Orthopsychiatry 57,* 316-331.

Schorr, L. (1988). *Within our reach: Breaking the cycle of disadvantage.* New York, NY: Doubleday.

Sergiovanni, T. (1993). *Building community in schools.* San Francisco, CA: Jossey-Bass.

Werner, E., & Smith, R. (1982, 1989). *Vulnerable but invincible: A longitudinal study of resilient children and youth.* New York, NY: Adams, Bannister, and Cox.

Werner, E., & Smith, R. (1992). *Overcoming the odds: High-risk children from birth to adulthood.* New York, NY: Cornell University Press.

Bonnie Benard, M.S.W., has authored numerous articles and papers on resiliency and provides speeches and training on resiliency throughout the country. She can be reached at Resiliency Associates, 1238 Josephine, Berkeley, CA 94703 (510-528-4344), or by e-mail: (bbenard@flash.net).

Special Feature

How Children Become Resilient: Observations and Cautions

by Emmy Werner, Ph.D.

Dr. Emmy Werner is Research Professor of Human Development at the University of California, Davis. She is known—in the words of Dr. Norman Garmezy—as "Mother Resilience" for her decades of longitudinal research on the island of Kauai that has provided a foundation for the emerging resiliency paradigm in prevention, intervention, and education, and for her understanding and discussion of the body of resiliency-focused research.

On January 27, 1995, Emmy Werner keynoted a conference in Albuquerque, New Mexico, sponsored by the Albuquerque Public Schools Team Action for Student Assistance and the U.S. Center for Substance Abuse Prevention. In her presentation, excerpted below (and edited by Dr. Werner), she offers her observations about what is known about fostering resiliency, what is yet to be learned, and the urgent need for program evaluation to move the concept forward. She also offers some advice for practitioners in the field who want to foster resiliency in children and youth.

>>=<+>=<<

I want to offer a few observations in the light of my experience with a longitudinal study that I have been associated with over the past 30 years. Let me hasten to say I also have worked with other children in "at risk" situations. I spent a lot of time working for UNICEF in Southeast Asia, both during the Vietnamese war, then during the Indian Pakistani War. I've worked in Israel, Egypt, and in East Africa. So my concern with issues of resiliency really has cut across different cultures and ethnic groups, but also different contexts. I want to emphasize today which of those constellation of factors that we first found in our Kauai study we can now say seem to be universal, whether you apply it to children of African American heritage, Asian American heritage, Hispanic heritage, or Native American heritage here in this country, or [to] children in developing countries. Which of these buffers seem to help them even under extraordinarily trying circumstances?

Before I summarize these factors, I want to say something about the concept of "resilience." As evidenced by this and many other conferences and workshops—and I have to tell you I'm called upon to attend workshops on resilience in the learning

> *"We've got to be really careful whenever we talk about fostering resiliency in our own particular neck of the woods [to] say what it is really that we want to do."*

disabled, resilience in Alzheimer patients, resilience in children of teen-age mothers—the concept has probably become too popular for it's own sake. Because if something becomes very, very popular, it loses its meaning. I'm not a politician; I'm trying to be a scientist. We've got to be really careful whenever we talk about fostering resiliency in our own particular neck of the woods [to] say what it is really that we want to do: specifically in this school system, in the primary grades, in Albuquerque [for example], for children from these kinds of backgrounds.

I think the reason why the concept took off was it is so quintessentially American. I see in spite of all the dire newspaper headlines this wonderful optimism of this country that forever and ever and ever is hoping to live up to the Horatio Algiers stories. Maybe some of you have heard of them. Way back in the nineteenth century the theme was: "Go West young man, and you'll make it." I'm not saying that we shouldn't help children make it, whatever that "it" is. But we need to be specific about objectives. It bears remembering that the research base that undergirds your attempts at doing something for these children is based mostly on studies of children who did it themselves, with some informal help by kith and kin.

A Caution About Putting Children "in Boxes"

There are actually relatively few long-term longitudinal studies of "resilient" individuals. Most studies of resiliency focus on a couple of years, mostly in middle childhood or in adolescence. We need to look and see what researchers found in the first place. They found that there was an *interplay* of individual, environmental, and situational factors. It wasn't just that the children behavioral scientists studied were empty boxes into which someone poured "resiliency." First we used the term—and we still do—"at risk" or

> **"We find that 'resiliency' is not something fixed, concrete."**

"high risk" children to describe youngsters with the odds against them. I always [got] this uncomfortable feeling that a child who was considered "at risk" was a nice little box in our diagnostic manuals or in our behavioral evaluations. Then, once we had him or her classified, we knew what we knew. Then we could check him or her up and that was it. Right? Some of you must have had that experience.

My sense has been that certainly all of you who are concerned with "at risk" children have hoped to get these kids out of those boxes and to look at their strengths instead. But in that process—I just want to put in a little warning—make sure that you don't get

boxed in again and say "if they attend this workshop or if they've been in the system for three years in a program called 'Fostering Resiliency' we automatically shift them from 'at risk' to 'resilient'." They attended the program or their trainers went for so many hours learning how to teach life skills, so they *must be* resilient now, by definition.

> **"Let's not get boxed in again and suddenly call everyone 'resilient' when they may be today as a child in a certain context, and they may not be ten years later, and then they may become again resilient in adulthood."**

We tend to get into this new box maybe too frequently, with our enthusiasm now about this concept. Because certainly if we look at studies, and especially in our study [done] over a long time, we find that "resiliency" is not something fixed, concrete. The very definition, which comes from engineering, has to do with bouncing back, right? If it was fixed, a bridge would collapse in an earthquake or hurricane. It's the going back and forth from vulnerability to resiliency that's actually the essence of the phenomenon. Look it up in Webster's dictionary! So, just a little note of warning: Let's not get boxed in again and suddenly call everyone "resilient" when they may be today as a child in a certain context, and they may not be ten years later, and then they may become again resilient in adulthood. But my words of caution should not dampen your enthusiasm!

The Kauai Longitudinal Study

So what we have learned—you may want to look at the last one of the four books [we have written] on the children of Kauai, *Overcoming the Odds: High Risk Children from Birth to Adulthood*—is based on a group of children that represent a great number of different ethnic groups. Some certainly would be considered offspring of what you here in the Southwest or the Canadians call "First Nations" because the Hawaiians really were there in the first place, just like the Navajo and the Pueblo Indians were here in the first place before other immigrants came to settle. We have a fairly large proportion of [these] children and also children whose parents intermarried with the newcomers like the Japanese, Chinese, Filipino, and

Portuguese. And we have a fairly wide range of socioeconomic classes in our study. But more than half of the children have grown up in very restricted circumstances, if you just judge by where they came from: They were born and [were] reared in chronic poverty. They had parents who did not graduate from high school. Many parents had less than eight grades of education. Many had parents who had either physical handicaps or signs of psychopathology, including substance abuse. And the children themselves that were "high risk" oftentimes also had birth complications and suffered from perinatal stress. The presence of four or more such risk factors made us judge these children to be at especially "high risk" when we started our study at birth.

We looked at about 700 people over time for more than three decades; about one-third had grown up in this "high risk" context. When we first reported these findings, I thought there was something unusual with our findings because we were working in an exotic island. [It] may look good to you when you come to visit and you stay in hotels; [it] does not look good when you live there. Even today, the average income on Kauai is somewhere [around] $11,000, which I think, in California at least, qualifies for poverty level.

After we reported our findings, pretty soon other researchers who looked at cohorts (cohort means a whole group of people all born together at a certain time, [no one] selected out) of children in many communities in the United States [found] much the same—that about one-third or so, mostly in urban areas, but also in rural areas, were "at risk" because of those background factors [of] chronic poverty, poor parental educational level, and other issues, especially parental substance abuse and psychopathology.

Limits to "Fostering Resiliency"

I spent a quarter at the Kavolinska Institute in Stockholm this fall. I thought the Swedes who do everything for their children would have a much lower proportion of what we call "at risk" children. Then, I was interviewed by someone from the major Swedish newspaper and he asked right at the beginning, "What should we Swedes do about the one-third of our Swedes that we have written off?" And I said, "What? You've written them off? You who provide prenatal care free, postnatal care free, free housing, free subsidized day care, two years paid parental leave for both parents. You've written off one-third of all the Swedes?"

This is something we need to ponder, folks. Countries that have tried very hard to commit themselves to caring for their children from birth on by tremendous expenditures of taxpayers' money as the Swedes and the Danes do, when you look over time you still find that one out of three in a given community in these countries today is considered as "high risk"—mostly because of antisocial behavior, substance abuse, or mental illness. It means there may just be certain limits to what we can accomplish to foster resiliency against such odds. That doesn't mean we should stop trying. The Swedes and the Danes have much lower infant mortality rates than we have. They have much lower prematurity and low birth weight rates than we do. They have much less morbidity and mortality among preschool children. So in consequence they must have cut down on the number of children who might be hyperactive or might have a learning disability, right? They succeeded there. They have a longer life span than we have. So they must be doing something right about health. But even these countries, after two generations of solid commitment to supporting their children and their grown-ups too—from the cradle to the grave—we find that there is a residue in their community of people whom they consider "at risk."

> "There may just be certain limits to what we can accomplish to foster resiliency....That doesn't mean we should stop trying."

Believing that we can push everyone into being the "perfect" person, that may just be a little bit too much. The Navajo in your state I am told weave one little error in the rugs they make because they do not want to be considered gods. Only gods are perfect. We have to watch that our attempt at fostering resiliency isn't becoming an enterprise that might later just disappoint us a little bit because we're putting our promises so high up without quite knowing whether we really will be able to deliver down the whole long road. You may get down a little bit [of] the road but maybe not the whole road. And that's fine. Each step counts.

Protective Factors Transcend Ethnicity

What we know from research (and I ask you to look at Benard's paper) is that protective buffers—the ones I'm going to talk about—appear to transcend ethnic, social class, and geographical boundaries. We can agree that they seem to be helpful to us [as] members of the human race, no matter what our ethnic background is. We also know that these protective factors appear to make a more profound impact on the life course of individuals who grow up and overcome adversity than do specific risk factors. There are some buffers within the individual, in the extended family, in the community that really do seem to cut across us as humankind, regardless of the stress and strains that we are individually exposed to. So those are the ones that we need to nurture most of all.

> *"Protective factors appear to make a more profound impact on the life course of individuals who grow up and overcome adversity than do specific risk factors."*

One of the first things we learned from studying children quite early—and ours is probably the only study that really started with "children who became resilient in spite of high risks at birth"—is it is easier for children who have an easy temperament and the ability to actively recruit competent adult caregivers to attract support from the extended family, the school, and the community at large. I'm not trying to say shy children or withdrawn children won't ever be successful candidates for any program to foster resiliency. I'm trying to say, and I think we forget this sometimes, that fostering resiliency isn't just putting stuff into an empty box by the teacher, or elder, or whatever else. It's based on countless interactions between the individual child or adolescent or adult and the opportunities [in their] world and the challenges they face.

Individual Differences

People do seem to differ—there's just no if, but, when about it—in their ability to make lemonade out of lemons. I think we sometimes forget this when we talk about programs for fostering resiliency for everyone. Of course, we can do something for everyone. But maybe for some we can do more things faster and

in more areas of competency than for others. And that's just something we need to accept. I think we need to keep *individual variability* in mind all along when we talk about fostering resiliency. The whole concept came really from the idea that there are individual differences in response to risk factors. By the same token, there will be individual differences

> *"Fostering resiliency isn't just putting stuff into an empty box by the teacher, or elder, or whatever else. It's based on countless interactions between the individual child or adolescent or adult and the opportunities [in their] world and the challenges they face."*

in response to programs that try to introduce protective factors into their lives. Not [just] our study but others [have shown] that the "at risk" children who seem to come through unscathed by the trouble in their background and are competent, caring, and confident, at a minimum have some skills in communication and problem-solving. We know that. [The children] on Kauai were not especially gifted. But on the average they had at least the sort of skills that didn't make them problem readers, for instance. Most all of the resilient children that have ever been studied had at least competence in reading skills, basic reading skills.

Reading is Essential

You might say, "Well this doesn't sound very dramatic, and this is sort of dreary. Why does she talk about reading? We want resiliency." Right? "We want something that really grabs us. [We] can preach about it." But reading is a skill that is essential to survive and in a sense essential to fostering resiliency in a society like ours that does depend on that written word.

In my home state of California right now, one out of three—this is the magic number again—of children by the fourth grade are already behind in reading. One out of three. So, of course, those are the kids that are the first ones to never say no to experiments with drugs. Those are the ones that slowly but surely by the time they get to be in the fifth or sixth grade are the first to be truant and to do a couple of delinquent acts that may eventually set them on the road to disaster. Those are the ones that may eventually be teenage parents—the few who actually stay on the welfare roles because they don't have that skill. (The majority get off, by the way [as] I will mention in a moment.) We need to keep in mind that cognitive competence is one of the hallmarks of resiliency. So if we want to do something about fostering resiliency, let's remember that reading skills are all-important.

We do find, indeed, that most resilient children over time develop a positive self-confidence. But that comes from some competence. It comes from competence in reading and problem-solving skills. It comes from having a special hobby. It comes from some talent or gift that they can be proud of, that they can [use to] be accepted by their peers, and that can also provide them [with] solace when things fall apart in their home. That is certainly a very important buffer found in many, many studies, including ours.

> **"Reading is a skill that is essential to survive and in a sense essential to fostering resiliency in a society like ours that does depend on that written word."**

A lot of emphasis [is placed] on high expectations in trying to foster resiliency. I want to sound a word of caution about high expectations. I would say what the research on resiliency shows is *realistically* high expectations. There is a difference. We've got to have realistically high expectations. It's like saying, "Black is beautiful. White is beautiful. Native American is beautiful." Yes, it's beautiful to be a human being no matter what your color or creed, but you've got to learn how to read.

A Close Bond is Critical

Other buffers that we do know seem to cut across different cultures, creeds, and races: There's no doubt about it, a close bond with a competent, emotionally stable caregiver seems to be essential in the lives of children who overcome great adversities. As we know from studies of resilient children a lot of this nurturing can come from substitute parents, such as

grandparents, aunts, uncles, older siblings. I'm sure that this is nothing new to the Native Americans in this group. We, as lonesome Caucasians, have to learn that lesson over again, that really a family and parents need not be just your biological father or mother. There are other folk who can step in, but one of them at least needs to be available and stable. A change of nannies in the most affluent families doesn't help, necessarily, if you have to relearn their names every two weeks or so. A stable, competent person needs to be around at the beginning of your life.

> **"Cognitive competence is one of the hallmarks of resiliency."**

The other thing that we found in our study that has been replicated (and the reason why scientists are so eager to at least say we need to repeat it once is to see if it was really so) in the Berkeley studies of ego-resilient children is a particular kind of childrearing orientation that appears to promote resiliency a little bit different in boys than girls. I haven't noticed reference to that much in talks and workshops on resiliency. What we found with our mostly Pacific Asian children, and what the people in Berkeley found with mostly Caucasian and African American children, is that resilient boys who overcome great adversities tend to come from households where there [are] structure and rules [and] a male who serves as a model of identification. But, again, it need not be the father. It could be a grandfather. It could be an older brother. It could be an uncle. There is also some encouragement of emotional expressiveness. For the girls, it's almost the flip-flop. The resilient girls tend to come from households that combine an emphasis on risk-taking and independence, with reliable support from the female caregiver. If it's not the mother [then] a grandmother, an aunt, an older sister.

Getting Away from Sex Role Typing

So, what you see at work here is a process of getting away from sex role typing in childrearing. The ones who held up the best over time in great adversities were boys and girls who could be assertive but also nurturant, emotionally expressive, but also willing to take a risk. It is apparently easier to overcome great odds if you have learned early that you don't have to fit into a prescribed role of the dependent female who cries or the macho male who can't cry. It helps to have both of these characteristics. That's something that we continue to observe in our study as we look at these resilient children in adulthood. Now as parents in

> *"A close bond with a competent, emotionally stable caregiver seems to be essential in the lives of children who overcome great adversities."*

mid-life, they very much take those same roles. They are nurturant fathers but also assertive fathers. And they are certainly caring mothers, but they're also mothers who want independence and autonomy in their children.

One of the characteristics that we find in our own and a number of other studies that you need to think about when you look at children you want to work with, is how good are they at actively recruiting substitute parents. It really is amazing what individual differences you find among children even in the worst situations. It's amazing the difference you see among [some] young children's ability to reach out and make friends with everyone around the room versus others who shy back and cling only to their mothers. This ability is something I think really needs to be fostered because it was something these children actively practiced not only as toddlers but also in middle childhood and adolescence. In other words, they *looked* for the people who could give them the help they needed. They didn't passively wait until someone came and said, "I'm going to enroll you in a program that fosters resiliency."

"Giving Something Back" as Children and Adults

The interesting thing we found and they're beginning to find in other studies is that these children, by the time they got to middle childhood, also gave something back. They had learned to give something back to their family or neighborhood. Psychologists, who are good at inventing words, call this "required helpfulness." What they mean is these children really were part of a household, whether an extended family or even just a single parent family, where their input mattered, where they contributed to caring for another sibling, or taking over the household when a mother was incapacitated, or doing something for an elder, a grandparent, an older

aunt, to make her life a bit easier. This sort of required helpfulness again seems to be a characteristic that in turn carries over into the adult lives of these children. As adults, no matter how poor they still may be and how busy they may be with the world of work and their own children, they do contribute something to their community as volunteers in church, in school, in their children's sports activities, as Big Brothers and Sisters— you name it.

As you may have seen, we're beginning to incorporate "required helpfulness" into service learning programs. I don't know if they do it here but in California slowly we're teaching kindergartners and first and second and third graders not to always say, "I, I, I," but to do something for other folks. You can do this even if you're five, six, seven years old.

I have a student in my classroom from Ethiopia who at age seven during the civil war took care of four other brothers and sisters and fled with them at night across the Sahara desert to safety, the youngest being one year old. She is now a person who is going to go back to Erithrea, the part that's split from Ethiopia, as a medical doctor. It's people like her who learn this required helpfulness early who usually practice it later on. You don't have to tell them to do it, they [just] do it.

The Importance of Faith

One of the major themes we found [that] has sometimes been shortchanged in scientific studies is that these children had some faith that gave meaning to their lives. When I speak of faith, I don't mean necessarily a narrow denominational faith. We found in our study that regardless of whether you were Catholic, or Lutheran, or mainstream Protestant, or belonged to

> *"The ones who held up the best over time in great adversities were boys and girls who could be assertive but also nurturant, emotionally expressive, but also willing to take a risk."*

Jehovah's Witnesses, or were a Latter Day Saint, or practiced the old original Hawaiian religion, or whether you were Buddhist because Buddhism is the major religion in Kauai—the ones who were able to use this faith to overcome adversity were the ones that saw meaning in their lives, even in pain and suffering. It wasn't church attendance but it was a belief that life, despite everything, made sense and that even the pain they experienced could ultimately be transformed. Very young children—children of age ten—could actually verbalize that. That helped them not to be bitter later on when they confronted parents that may have gone astray, who constantly were in and out of hospitals, and were alcoholic and suicidal or were physically and emotionally abusive.

We do know, and you know now, that there are other sources in the community that also are buffers for children in adversity. All of the children in our study—and [this] comes through in other studies in North America—were good at making and keeping a few good friends. They didn't have to be popular or "in with the crowd" or admired by lots of boyfriends. [It was] just that as they were good at picking substitute

> **"These children really remember one or two teachers who made the difference."**

parents, they were good at picking a couple of friends that were with them and stayed with them, from kindergarten to middle age. Often in Kauai, they would pick these friends from neighbors' families where they might go to get some sense of stability. Many eventually got married to the sons and daughters of their neighbors. They now have a very good relationship with their in-laws because they first started recruiting them as their substitute parents in the neighborhood.

How Schools Make a Difference

We also know that school can make a difference. But it's not the trappings of the school—the building, the bricks, the resource rooms. It seems to be the model of adults that they find within the schools. That comes right back to you, whether you are a teacher, or a counselor, or a school nurse, or whatever. One of the wonderful things we see now in adulthood is that these children really remember one or two teachers who made the difference. And they mourn these teachers when they die. They mourn some of those teachers more than they do their own family members because what went out of their life was a person who looked beyond outward experience, their behavior, their unkempt—oftentimes—appearance and saw the promise. That could happen anywhere along the way.

It could happen in Headstart. It could happen in kindergarten. It happened a lot in the first three grades. It also happened in high school and even in community college for those who dropped out and went back later on.

> **"The ones who were able to use this faith to overcome adversity were the ones that saw meaning in their lives, even in pain and suffering."**

Participation in meaningful community activities that foster cooperation was [also] a very important protective buffer in the lives of these children. I don't mean "make believe" activities. It didn't need to be a costly enterprise like the theater, the ballet, or whatever. It included activities where you join a cooperative enterprise. On Kauai, it was mostly 4H or the Y or being a Big Brother or Big Sister to someone else, or being active in a youth group in church. But whatever it was, it was an activity where you were not just a passive recipient, but where you were called upon to help someone else and you grew up in the process.

The Long Term Perspective

These are certainly some of the protective factors that we know cut across many different studies and that we can hope to foster in whatever setting we're in. I want to also say something about the fact that resiliency or being "at risk" doesn't stop by the time you get through high school. One of the wonderful things we found as we're looking at these people now in adulthood is that there is a great deal of potential for recovering among "at risk" kids who have problems in childhood and adolescence. Among the group [of "high risk" children—one-third of the study's total cohort] in our study, two-thirds actually did develop problems in the first two decades of life. They did have problems in school, and they had behavior problems in adolescence. They [became] teenage parents. They [became] delinquents. They [had] mental health problems. But when we looked at them in their 30s and now at 40 we found that even out of this group, *the majority staged a recovery.*

I think right now teenage parents and the delinquents are among the most misunderstood. [They] are the object of a lot of vindictiveness in our society. When I speak of vindictiveness, I mean vindictiveness on the state *and* federal level including the press. Most magazine articles and newspapers talk about teenage parents as being a permanent welfare dependent, right? That's the image they portray but it does not jibe with reality.

> *"There is a great deal of potential for recovering among 'at risk' kids who have problems in childhood and adolescence."*

Most Teenage Mothers Do Get Off Welfare

The fact is that most teenage mothers do not end up permanently taking Aid For Families of Dependent Children. Very few people have bothered to study them over time. They make good headlines when they just had their second child, maybe the first at 14 and the other at 16. They've dropped out of high school, and they are on AFDC. But there are only three studies right now that have looked at these teenage mothers *in later life.* One is our study with Asian American children, one is a study in Baltimore with African American children, and one is a study in New Orleans with Caucasian and African Americans. There's three studies in three very different contexts— one in the Pacific West, one in the inner city ghetto of Baltimore, and another in the Deep South. All show the same trends—over time, teenage mothers do work themselves out of the dependency on AFDC, given two things: one, access to continued education, and the other, access to child care.

> *"Over time, teenage mothers do work themselves out of the dependency on AFDC, given two things: one, access to continued education, and the other, access to child care."*

Of the teenage mothers in our sample only two with preschool children—that was less than five percent— were still on some kind of government support, when we saw them in their mid 30s. All the others had finished the equivalent of high school. If they didn't go back, then they got the GED or they went to community colleges. They then moved up the socioeconomic ladder as they got more education and more vocational skills, and were in their mid-thirties people who had pretty decent and well-paying jobs. The key was access to education and child care. I think that's the message you have to give everywhere at every level [and] to every governor. They're not lost causes at all, but they do need that kind of assistance.

Most Delinquents Don't Become Adult Criminals

Also, most delinquents in our study and in other longitudinal studies, both with African American and with Caucasian youngsters, actually do *not* turn out to become hardened criminals. In my state we now have the "three strikes against you and you are out" law. We no longer practice prevention but containment. We will spend much more money on prisons than we will in education. The money spent on prisons might save the UC system of higher education, once the pride of the nation. But we're building prison after prison after prison instead!

> *"The message you have to give everywhere at every level [and] to every governor... they're not lost causes at all."*

Three out of four of the delinquent males in our study and nine out of ten delinquent females, *did not go on* to become adult criminals. The difference between those who desisted and those who did go on depended on the people who saw to it that these youngsters got help—again, with reading skills because many of those kids were way below the third grade level in reading when they became delinquent. It lay in the presence of a foster grandparent, mother, or father who sat down and helped them in remedial work. It lay with probation officers who really cared and with a case load that was low enough so they could do something for the youth, not just check off a box. And it lay with the concern of other family members—if the father was absent then with other elders—who saw to it that someone helped this youngster go straight. We really need to look at the differences between the lives of young people who are only passing through a delinquent phase because of peer pressure and the really hardened criminal for whom we do need more serious measures. Those two groups do get confused in our attempts at so-called "violence prevention."

The Help of Good Friends

Finally, let me say something about the people who had serious mental health problems in our group. Again, we find that just with the help of good friends, I guess it was a Beatles' song, "I Get By With A Little Help From My Friends", two out of three in that group got by—because no one [else] helped them. They were

> *"Most delinquents in our study and in other longitudinal studies ... actually do not turn out to become hardened criminals."*

diagnosed and filed away. What *did* help many was the presence of a strong church community. A number of youngsters in this group who [had] mental health problems in adolescence converted to a community that gave them structure and stability. Jehovah's Witnesses are a remarkably disciplined group that has helped many of the kids who had serious mental health problems on the island. So did the Latter Day Saints. Those groups that attracted teenagers who had mental health problems did something for them that often takes many years of psychotherapy and $100,000 to accomplish. They gave them a sense of self. They gave them a sense of community. And [the church organizations] gave them some sense of a mission. I think the presence of a concerned church group should certainly not be underrated.

The Shifting Balance Between Vulnerability and Resiliency

I started out [by saying] we should not look at resiliency as something that's clad in concrete. Certainly, one of the trends we saw over time is that with each passing decade one gender was a bit more vulnerable than the other. In the first decade, we found more boys who were "at risk," who had problems. In the second decade, especially toward the end of adolescence, it was the girls. In the third decade, the pendulum swung back again. I think a lot of that has to do with the expectations we have for each gender at each of

these stages. We need to think about programs with these expectations in mind. Protective factors did not always have the same impact at each stage of life. What mattered in early childhood were protective factors that had to do with a caring, stable adult, that had to do with good health, with helping a child who had health problems, and that had to do with allowing him or her the opportunity to reach out to others, not just his own small family. Protective factors that worked well in middle childhood were building competency, problem-solving skills, concerned teachers, and responsible friends. Protective factors in adolescence had more to do with the building of self-esteem, an internal locus of control, and providing a sense of meaning for a youngster's life. As you look at the literature on resiliency you must look a little closer to see whether some of the things you are doing could possibly be focused a bit more on the needs of children at different stages of their lives and be tailored more toward those processes that are most effective at each particular stage. In adulthood what seemed to matter was the support of a close friend or mate, personal competence, and finally—again—faith that their world/life mattered.

"Where's the Beef?"—The Need to Evaluate

Let me say something about [what] was addressed admirably this morning, [the need for research]. Some of you may remember a commercial that was on television when Walter Mondale ran for the presidency against Ronald Reagan. It pictured a little old lady looking at a gaping hole in a hamburger. Remember that? She ask plaintively, "Where's the beef?" I haven't seen her lately, but I thought that was a wonderful commercial. I ask the same question really [in regards] to all the programs that have been discussed at the workshops at this conference.

> *"Protective factors did not always have the same impact at each stage of life."*

I do not doubt the sincerity in commitment of the individuals [here]. But as a scientist I must ask, like the little old lady, for the *hard evidence* that these programs actually effect lasting positive changes in the behaviors of the individuals, not just in your hearts. You'll feel good after two and a half days of this [conference focused on resiliency]. But when you go back and do whatever you do, please try and find a way to see if it *does* make a difference in the lives of people you are trying to help that's beyond saying, "I feel good." We need to move from what I would consider almost an evangelistic fervor about resilience to evaluation because in Washington and the state houses, they [say not only,] "Where's the beef?" but they say, "Let's do away with the pork." Right?

> **"When you go back and do whatever you do, please try and find a way to see if it does make a difference in the lives of people you are trying to help that's beyond saying, 'I feel good'."**

All of you may need outside money or seed money to start your programs. But those who are in charge of grants are going to ask much more now from you—not just how many people attended workshops, the thing that's called "bean counting," or how many processes you actually covered in your handouts in your program. You've got to show that it did make some measurable difference in the lives of youngsters you worked with. And they and the nation as a whole have a right to ask this question.

I was thinking of the "fostering resiliency" program in Albuquerque, which is wonderful, inspirational—according to the video you prepared and showed at this conference. It stops now, as of today. This is the end now, right? Now we've got to find out how many principals are going to continue this program without money from the "Feds." Programs that foster resiliency as far as I'm concerned will not actually really foster resiliency unless they function without outside money. It's got to come from the community. UNICEF does a much better thing. They go into communities where they know that whatever problems they start [solving], their programs will be taken over by the community. They have only ten cents to spend for *each* of the two billion children in the world.

Even in this program in Albuquerque, if it could be shown that reading scores increased or fewer people had reading problems at grade four after they participated, or there was less absenteeism, or in the best of all possible worlds there was a lower drop-out rate, or fewer teenage pregnancies. Or did it make any difference at all? You've got to—in the end—present these hard data, not just a videotape. Because [otherwise] I would predict by the end of the millennium resiliency will be a concept that will be long forgotten. If you [just] use it as a buzzword to get grants or as a kind of power—oxygen at the end of a conference—it won't be enough.

You Can Foster Resiliency Wherever You Are

Having said this doesn't mean that we should despair. It is important to evaluate the effectiveness of your programs. That's *absolutely necessary* no matter how big or little your program is—preferably little, one step at a time, as kids grow up. But this doesn't mean that you personally wherever you are cannot foster resiliency in an individual child. It doesn't take any money from anywhere. It needs time for care and caring.

One of the most useful things [is what we have learned from] the life stories of the resilient youngsters we have studied, who are now adults. We've learned from them that competence and confidence and caring can flourish, even under adverse circumstances. If children encounter persons who provide them with a secure basis for the development of trust, autonomy, initiative, and competence they can successfully overcome the odds. That success brings hope, *realistic hope*. And that is a gift each of us can share. You can share that gift with a child at home, in a classroom, on the playground, or in the neighborhood. The rediscovery of the healing powers of hope may be the most precious harvest you can glean in the work you do—for yourself and for the youngsters whose lives you touch. ✪

21

The Faces Of Resiliency

by Nan Henderson, M.S.W.

A year ago I decided to go into my community and find young people whose lives demonstrate "resiliency in action." I found that resilient kids are everywhere, that secondary teachers, college and university professors, youth agency workers, community and church youth workers, even my friends and neighbors all knew young people whose lives put faces on the concept of resiliency. I plan to include these faces each issue, sharing the specific stories and words of these resilient young people. I hope you will do the same—identify and publicize the many young people in your community who are resilient—as one way to challenge the prevalent but inaccurate stereotypes of kids from "risk" environments.

Two such young people are profiled below. In interviewing them, I asked open-ended questions about their lives and their overcoming of adversity and about advice they wanted to share with others. The themes that emerged from the young people themselves were right out of the research on resiliency, as well as the research on drop-out prevention and gang prevention.

Leslie Krug's story documents the critical need for caring and high expectations in schools, as well as the power of one person—in her case, her mother—who will not give up on a child. She also testifies as to the powerful influence of friends who themselves have bounced back and are doing well.

Phil Canamar's story shows the importance of caring adults outside the family. As he lists all the people who have contributed to his resiliency we see the power of these other "surrogates" in a young person's community to make a difference, validating the research of Gina O'Connell Higgins (1994) and other resiliency researchers. His message confirms much of what is known about why young people get into gangs and offers inspiration about how they can leave. He also comments on the critical components of effective schools that so many kids—those who drop out and those who don't—note as missing in traditional high schools. Finally, he demonstrates, as Emmy Werner so beautifully describes, the importance of spiritual faith for many of those who are resilient.

Leslie Krug: "I've Been In So Much Trouble and I'm Still Here"

Leslie Krug went through ninth grade in a traditional high school three times. A lot of her problems, she said, began in sixth grade when her dad died, which "hurt a lot." Though she was sent to counseling, seventh through ninth grade were years of skipping school, drinking, and using drugs.

Her message now: "I've been in so much trouble and I'm still here." Today, at age 16, Leslie is back in school and doing well. She was one of two students selected, in fact, by the school staff of the alternative school she now attends to be featured as a "face of resiliency." She is no longer using drugs, and is contemplating a future as a small business owner.

When asked who helped her bounce back Leslie credited her mom, her friends, her boyfriend's parents, and the school she now attends. She gave most of the credit to her mom. "She just kept making me go to school. She wouldn't let me drop out," Leslie said. She reports that during her years of skipping school and "hanging out" her mom got mad at her for her behavior, but she never gave up on her. No matter what, Leslie said, her mom "was just always there."

Leslie's advice to adults trying to help kids succeed is, "Show that they care. They've got to care."

An absence of caring was a main reason Leslie struggled in traditional school. One teacher, she said, told her friends that one day they would be driving Mercedes and BMWs and Leslie would be working the window at McDonald's.

And, she reported, "there is so many drugs" around traditional schools. If a student is doing drugs, she added, "you're not going to do them at school." So that is another reason she skipped.

Leslie stopped doing drugs because of the influence of her friends, especially one, who stopped. Seeing him stop, she said, made her realize that it could be done. And seeing other friends going to school and doing well provided motivation for her to do the same.

She also gives credit to the Albuquerque alternative school she attends, School on Wheels. Leslie said she feels that the teachers at this school really care. "They're not here because it's their job. They want to teach." She added, "They treat you like things aren't just going to happen for you. You've got to work."

"They make you responsible and the teachers care," are two main reasons Leslie said she is doing well in school now. She also learns things "useful for my life." One example is discussions about racism in school curriculum. "All you learn about is George Washington" in traditional classrooms, Leslie said. "Here they teach you more about Hispanic heroes"— information about her culture she didn't get in school before. She said classrooms work as teams, with cooperation emphasized. And she gets a chance to pursue one of her main interests—art.

Leslie looks forward to finishing her high school credits at the local community college, through an arrangement between her alternative school and the college. "When we are 17 we can go to TVI and get our credits," she said. Through attending TVI, she hopes to pursue her goal of one day owning a small business.

Phil Canamar: "I Feel the Pain and Anger in Everybody's Heart that Joins a Gang"

Phil Canamar, 18, just wrote a grant proposal to Honeywell asking the company for $80,000 to help "ten multicultural youth, to train them in the logistics of making videos." Besides attending school, he works in a local organization dedicated to getting youth involved in their own businesses, funded by grants from the state of New Mexico. He is looking forward to graduating from high school next year, and pursuing his passion of video production at the college level.

Phil has come a long way since he began using drugs in middle school, robbed houses with his friends in ninth grade, joined a gang at age 16, dropped out of school, and ran away from home.

Phil said he has never known his father, whom his mother divorced when he was three. He lived until he was seven with his mother and grandfather. Then, his grandfather died. His mother had two other children, too, and had to work full-time. He remembers a childhood of being "treated like an adult... cooking for myself, cleaning for myself... and trying to be the father" for his brother and sister.

Eventually, about the time he was in middle school, "I started hanging out with the wrong friends and got into trouble." At first, Phil reported, it was telling teachers off and smoking. Then he began using drugs, partially because he was hanging out with his older sister's friends. He drank a lot, and used marijuana, LSD, and heroin. Then he began the house robberies with his friends. Getting caught, Phil said, taught him a lesson—"never do that again."

Phil dropped out of school in tenth grade. He said a lot of teachers had the attitude when he left of, "Well...see you later, bye." "Some of them did care," Phil said. But "many of them didn't want to help." They thought, "Well, he deserved it." After he dropped out, he hung around the house for about a year, "a bum, just doing nothing. I was looking for a job but no one would hire me. I was only 16 and I had dropped out of school."

He and his mom eventually got into an argument, during which she said, " 'Go ahead. Go on. Go out on your own.' So I packed my stuff. I left." At age 16, Phil walked 40 miles into Albuquerque.

Phil moved in with a friend he had met years before whose mom told him he could always come there if he ever had problems. For awhile he and his friend hung around, "smoking weed, drinking beer." Then his friend's mom started pressuring the boys to get jobs, but "no one would hire us because we weren't in school.

"Finally, I said, 'I'm going to go try School on Wheels'," Phil said. He had heard about the alternative school from his sister years before. He and his friend both decided to give it a try. From his first encounter with the school principal, Phil said his life began to change. "He said, 'Hey I remember you. You used to go to my church. We'll see what we can do about getting you in here because I know you are a good kid.'" The principal told Phil to call every day until there was an opening at the school. "I called for three or four weeks before I got in," Phil remembered.

Phil began attending the school and moved in with a man who had been a friend for years. "My mom met him when I was nine at the State Fair. She was always looking for a father image for me and my brother. She said to him, 'Can you help me with my kids...take them here or there or something?' and he said sure, 'I love kids, especially boys. I always wished I had a boy.'" This man, whom Phil calls Joe, has been an important part of Phil's life since that time.

He joined a gang, in fact, during a time when his mom wouldn't let him see Joe anymore, due to a misunderstanding. "It was at that point in time when I said, 'No one is here for me, you know. I'm sick of it.' And I turned toward the gang to find support.

"That's the pain and anger I feel in everybody's heart that joins a gang. They want to feel accepted, you know, because they don't have that going on in their home life. The mother or father isn't there."

Phil left the gang when he moved to Albuquerque. It was helpful, he said, that "that gang isn't here" though "everyone here in Albuquerque says 'Oh, you're Chicano, you must be in a gang.' Now," Phil said, "I just look at them. I have a lot of love." And, he tells them, "I'm here in peace."

In addition to Joe and Joe's parents, whom Phil calls "his elders" that give him care and support, he credits School on Wheels for his resiliency. "It was the structure here, then the environment, then third, but not least, Kathryn, my teacher. She always gave me encouragement to take it one day at a time."

> *"Phil has come a long way since he began using drugs in middle school, robbed houses with his friends in ninth grade, joined a gang at age 16, dropped out of school, and ran away from home."*

Phil likes the team work, cooperation, the fact he has just one teacher, the experiential activities, and the caring he feels at School on Wheels. His advice to traditional schools: "Interview teachers to see if they do care about the students. And hire one principal. Most schools have four principals and they all have their own opinion of how to run the school. All they're doing is making chaos."

Finally, Phil credits his Christian faith with helping him through his difficulties. He said that while many people have helped him along the way, "God told me, 'Take something of them. Don't take the bad part. Take the good part you like in them...take them with you.'" Phil added, "They've all given me a little piece, something that makes me grow. The major one is Joe, then my teacher, Kathy, my other teacher, Ron, my teacher now, Ed. The school has helped a lot. And where I'm working now. We're trying to get "at risk" youth involved in their own businesses."

Phil said he wrote the grant to Honeywell so he can offer something to other kids like himself. His goal is his own video production staff. He wants to give other kids this invitation: "Hey are you guys bored? Are you guys tired of gangs? Come over here. I'll teach you about video, let's make a video or a movie...let's make a music video." The purpose of the organization, Phil said, is "to give them meaningful stuff to do."

Phil's advice to other kids like himself is, "Don't drop out of school. Find an alternative." And his advice to adults trying to help kids is, "Take time out to see what they need. Try to provide what they need. I'm not sure if there is anything else to do." ℮

Nan Henderson, M.S.W., is a national and international speaker and consultant on fostering resiliency and wellness, alcohol and other drug issues, and on organizational change. She has co-authored/edited five books about resiliency, and is the president of Resiliency In Action. *She can be reached at Nan Henderson and Associates, 5130 La Jolla Blvd., #2K, San Diego, CA 92109, p/f (858-488-5034), or by e-mail: (nanh@connectnet.com).*

A Resiliency Resource Primer:

Foundations of Resiliency

by Nan Henderson, M.S.W., and Bonnie Benard, M.S.W.

Benard, Bonnie. ***Fostering Resiliency in Kids: Protective Factors in the Family, School, and Community***. Portland, OR: Western Regional Center for Drug-Free Schools and Communities. 1991. *This seminal publication on resiliency synthesizes more than 100 resiliency-related studies, books, and articles.*

Benard, Bonnie. ***Turning the Corner: From Risk to Resiliency***. Portland, OR: Western Regional Center for Drug-Free Schools and Communities. 1994. *This publication is a compilation of several shorter articles published between 1991 and 1993, which provide an update on Benard's 1991 work and address resiliency in several contexts.*

Bendtro, Larry, Brokenleg, Martin, and Van Bockern, Steve. ***Reclaiming Youth at Risk: Our Hope for the Future***. Bloomington, IN: National Educational Services. 1990. *While not based on resiliency research, this book presents arguments and general approaches for "reclaiming" youth from risks to resilience.*

Benson, Peter L. ***The Troubled Journey: A Profile of American Youth***. Minneapolis: Respecteen. 1992. *This free reader-friendly report details research on asset-building and healthy youth development, which correlates high levels of assets with avoidance of risk behaviors and other types of life success for youth, currently being conducted by the Search Institute. It also offers recommendations based on the research for schools, families, and community organizations.*

Benson, Peter, Galbraith, Judy, and Espeland, Pamela. ***What Kids Need to Succeed***. Minneapolis: Free Spirit. 1994. *In this book, the authors offer dozens of practical suggestions about how families, communities, and schools can build assets in youth. They include an informal asset assessment which parents can fill out and give to their children.*

Botvin, Gilbert J. ***Life Skills Training: Promoting Health and Personal Development***. Cornell University Medical Center, New York, NY: Smithfield Press, Inc. 1990. *This is the most thoroughly evaluated "skills curriculum" available, designed for a middle or junior high school level. Longitudinal research has shown significant long-term reductions in ATOD use among youth who received this training as it is designed.*

Burns, Timothy. ***From Risk to Resilience***. Dallas, TX: The Marco Polo Group. 1994. *This book weaves the findings of cognitive science, child development research, and other resiliency-focused studies and theory into an easily understood primer on developing resiliency in children.*

Haggerty, Robert, Sherrod, Lonnie, Garmezy, Norman, and Rutter, Michael (eds.). ***Stress, Risk, and Resilience in Children and Adolescents***. Rochester, NY: Cambridge University Press. 1994. *This book is a series of articles by major researchers which furthers the study of the phenomenon of resiliency. It was developed as a follow-up to the seminal volume, **Stress, Coping, and Development in Childhood** edited by Garmezy and Rutter in 1983.*

Henderson, Nan, and Milstein, Mike. **Resiliency in Schools: Making It Happen for Students and Educators**. Thousand Oaks, CA: Corwin Press (1996). *The authors provide an overview of resiliency research and theory, detail how schools build resiliency in students, extend the findings to educators, and provide a step-by-step plan for changing schools into more effective resiliency-building organizations. All the information included can be adapted to other organizations and settings.*

Higgins, Gina O'Connell. **Resilient Adults: Overcoming a Cruel Past**. San Francisco: Jossey-Bass. 1994. *This book is based on the author's research on 40 adults who survived horrendous childhoods, winding up resilient in adulthood by their own report and by several psychological tests. Their stories provide specific information on how resiliency develops in people of all ages and "advice from the resilient."*

Jessor, Richard. "Successful adolescent development among youth in high-risk settings." In **American Psychologist, 48**, 117. 1993. *This article describes an ideal model of comprehensive research based on a resiliency (positive developmental) paradigm. The "Successful Adolescent Development in High Risk Settings" consortium examines from a multidisciplinary perspective the nature of environmental contexts that promote resiliency despite risks.*

Lifton, Robert J. **The Protean Self: Human Resilience in an Age of Transformation**. New York: Basic Books. 1993. *Drawing on interviews with several disparate groups (social activists, civic leaders, poor African Americans, and Christian fundamentalists) Lifton documents in this book the incredible power of humans to transform "discontinuity and pain." Lifton challenges readers to use this capacity to transform this market-driven, greed-oriented society to the "more humane global values of a civil society."*

Mills, Roger. **Realizing Mental Health**. New York: Sulzburger and Graham. 1994. *The Health Realization approach described by its developer offers a promising explanation of how resiliency is developed—of how environmental protective factors interact with self-agency and internal self-righting. This model especially sheds light on the dynamic nature of resilience.*

Muller, Wayne. **Legacy of the Heart: The Spiritual Advantages of a Painful Childhood**. New York: Simon and Schuster. 1992. *This beautiful book written by a counselor and theologian invites anyone who experienced a hurtful childhood—or anyone who works with children growing up in troubled families—to look at the strengths, i.e. resilience, their suffering fostered. The author provides a guided path "to awaken what is already wise and strong, to claim what is deep and true...to find inner balance and to reaffirm [one's] intrinsic wholeness."*

Richardson, Glenn E., et al., "The resiliency model." **Health Education, 21** (6), 33. November/December, 1990. *This article is another seminal work on resiliency, synthesizing a number of perspectives into an excellent model of how resiliency develops in individuals.*

Seligman, Martin. **Learned Optimism: How to Change Your Mind and Your Life**. New York: Simon and Schuster. 1990. *A precursor to **The Optimistic Child** (reviewed in this journal), this foundational work documents not only the power of optimism as a protective factor, but also how to work personally, with other adults, and with youth to transform negative, hopeless, explanatory styles to positive, optimistic ones. For readers wanting a skills-focused approach to resiliency, this book is a must.*

Werner, Emmy. "Protective factors and individual resilience." In Meisels, S. and Shonkoff, J. (eds.) **Handbook of Early Childhood Intervention**. New York: Cambridge University Press. 1990. *This article is a literature review of protective factors and individual resiliency, filled with citations from the literature in several fields that relates to resiliency. Written by "Mother Resilience" herself, it is a must read for those wanting a thorough overview resiliency.*

Werner, Emmy, and Smith, Ruth. ***Vulnerable but Invincible: A Longitudinal Study of Resilient Children and Youth***. New York: Adams, Bannister, and Cox. 1982, 1989. *The authors detail lessons from children born with several significant risk factors who developed no observable problems as they moved from infancy to childhood, and through adolescence to adulthood.*

Werner, Emmy, and Smith, Ruth. ***Overcoming the Odds: High Risk Children from Birth to Adulthood***. New York: Cornell University Press. 1992. *This book documents in reader-friendly detail the results of the authors' forty year longitudinal study. It includes chapters on how teen mothers, delinquents, and children and youth with mental health problems bounced back, and ties the research findings to similar studies in the U.S. and elsewhere.*

Wolin, Steven, and Sybil. ***The Resilient Self: How Survivors of Troubled Families Rise Above Adversity***. New York: Villard. 1993. *The Wolins challenge the popular culture's emphasis on victimization, describe seven "resiliencies" they have found in "survivors" of adversity, and emphasize the importance of moving from a "Damage Model" to a "Challenge Model" of viewing adversity.*

Wolin, Steven, and Sybil. ***Survivor's Pride: Building Resilience in Youth At Risk*** (video). Vernona, Wisconsin: Attainment Co., Inc. 1994. *The Wolins' describe the "seven resiliencies" in the first part of this video, as well as the difference between the "Damage Model" and the "Challenge Model." Most of the tape, however, is in-depth interviews with resilient young people, documenting the Wolins' findings.* ☯

PART TWO
Resiliency and Schools

Special Feature

Resilient Youth: A Resiliency-Fostering Curriculum For Secondary Schools

by Glenn Richardson, Ph.D., and Don Gray, Ph.D.

In 1990 we introduced a theory-based resiliency model suggesting that resiliency is a human experience process that involves ongoing cycles of disruption and reintegration (Richardson et al., 1990). Through this process people have the opportunity to grow from the adversity and challenges of life by strengthening protective factors and developing a healthy integration of mind, body, and spirit. Since that time, we have been systematically testing variations of the model within diverse populations (Caserta, 1992; Gray, 1995). Our tests have provided substantial evidence to validate the resiliency model (Dunn, 1995, Neiger, 1991, Walker, 1996).

During the past few years, we have been exploring ways to assist educators and youth workers to successfully guide young people through the process of becoming more resilient.

We have defined resiliency as *the process and experience of adapting to disruptive, opportunistic, stressful, challenging, or informative life prompts in a way that provides the individual with more protective and coping skills and knowledge than prior to the disruption* (Richardson, 1995). Preliminary evaluation of a school-based resiliency program suggests that the application of the model has the potential to assist people in adopting and maintaining healthy and enriching responses to the challenges of life.

In addition to implementing our *Resilient Youth* program with secondary students, we have worked with military personnel, women's groups, white and blue collar business employees, and university students to develop effective resiliency training strategies that can help people to increase many protective factors (i.e., self-esteem, self-efficacy, creativity, confidence, flexibility, and purpose in life) which are the products of the resiliency process. Work in our school-based *Resilient Youth* program with urban youth to replace destructive gang activity and other "high risk" behaviors with more positive social behaviors has been especially exciting and rewarding.

We briefly describe here:
1) the key elements of the *Resilient Youth* program;
2) our experiences in pilot testing the program's curriculum; and
3) our ongoing program planning, research, and evaluation activities.

Key Elements of the *Resilient Youth* Program

The *Resilient Youth* program builds upon the existing structure, resources, and unique needs of schools and other youth-serving organizations to help young people explore their potentials, create a dream, and learn the skills that will help them live the dream. The program incorporates the following elements:

Resilient Schools/Youth Organizations Training
A 30 hour training program provides administrators, faculty, and/or agency staff with opportunities to explore personal resiliency, resilient relationships, and a resiliency practicum. The practicum provides strategies for teachers to infuse resiliency skills training into their teaching, regardless of the subject, and for counselors to infuse resiliency into their counseling. University credit and certification are available to participants.

Resilient Families Training
Resiliency training for parents and families involves youth as trainers to increase family support and involvement. Youth-produced videos, productions, and other innovative activities are designed to increase communications within families and provide active support for resiliency development. Seminars are also available to parent organizations. Since these organizations are not often attended by the populations that most need the instruction, the primary emphasis is on youth training their own families.

Resilient Youth Club
A multicultural campus club involving a mixture of youth in "high risk" situations and "mainstream" youth provides academic tutoring and support, personal and group enrichment activities, campus and community service projects, and big brother-big sister programs for younger students. A youth-directed summer retreat is a key annual event.

Resilient Youth Curriculum
The 33 module secondary curriculum based on seven topic areas (see next page) provides guidelines to initially work through protected youth exteriors, touch hearts, establish trust, and facilitate the process of building resiliency. Youth develop ownership of the program by participating in planning, shaping, and implementing each of the components of the overall program. The curriculum is designed to be flexible and responsive to the unique needs and resources available to youth and adult facilitators.

Resilient Youth Curriculum Topics

1. **Understanding the Resiliency Process**—Youth capture the meaning of the resiliency model and personalize the resiliency process.

2. **Discovering Your Resilient Nature**—Youth explore their own personal gifts, talents, and strengths. They explore the resilient nature of their own body, mind, and heart based on recent advances in mind-body medicine and other disciplines.

3. **Foundations of Resilient Relationships**—Youth learn skills to build solid friendships, family bonds, nurturing communities, and resilient schools. They discover ways of building trust, communicating more effectively, and holding themselves and others in high esteem without regard to outward appearances. They also learn relationship skills and strategies to jointly, with other students, make an impact upon their social environment.

4. **The Power of the Dream**—Youth learn that true power involves a combination of discovering their resilient potentials and then creating a passion for life through identifying and working towards their personal dream. The dream simplifies life and makes it manageable. It puts meaning to goals. Youth learn to take the dream beyond themselves and collaborate with others in a common cause. Together students practice and teach resiliency principles by writing and performing assemblies, producing videos or other media presentations, teaching younger students from feeder schools, writing newsletters, or engaging in other activities that they generate.

5. **The Resiliency Paradigms**—Paradigm is a concept used in the business world to reflect personal "world views" or perceptions. Resiliency paradigms—based on healthy perspectives for living—are explored to help youth live within their personally chosen moral framework, appreciate disruptive moments, "seize the day," build upon their strengths, and examine other paradigms.

6. **The Resiliency Skills**—Youth learn to approach solutions to problems creatively, deal with undesirable habits in creative yet effective ways, and learn about the mental conditioning it takes to control their own destiny.

7. **The Resilient Path with Heart**—At some point in the curriculum, youth actually change the way they have been living life and learn to adapt to the reality of life long change. Youth learn to impact others around them so that the way they want to live is possible. Youth experience enrichment from other cultures and traditions. They design life plans and live those plans.

Resilient Youth in Action

In our original resiliency model (Richardson, et. al, 1990), we used academic terms to describe the disruptive-reintegrative processes of resiliency. Although youth in our pilot program readily understood the concepts of the resiliency process, more user-friendly terms were needed. Thus, for example, in describing the concepts to youth we substituted "comfort zone" for the term "biopsychospiritual homeostasis." Using examples from the youths' own experiences, we explored the components of the resiliency experience (see Figure 1), emphasizing the following:

- The resiliency model is really a map of the human experience in this roller coaster called life, a map that shows how people experience and grow through change in their lives.
- Individuals often live, or try to live, in a comfort zone where life is stable and predictable; but many times each day we all experience adversity, challenges, and opportunities that prompt us to leave the comfort zone.
- People will be disrupted by these events if they have not successfully dealt with them in the past, if it is a new life event, or if the individual makes the choice not to be concerned with or affected by the life effect (i.e., ignores it).
- Individuals have both inherited characteristics and learned protective skills that may help or hinder their success in dealing with these events.
- A person can choose to 1) engage the disruption but feel defeated in the encounter and experience reintegration with loss; 2) deal with the disruption just to heal, recover, and return to the comfort zone; or 3) learn and grow from the experience for resilient reintegration.
- This disruption-reintegration process may last for months with highly significant disruptions (for example, the death of a loved one) or it may only take a few seconds when the disruption is relatively insignificant.

Figure 1:
Modified Resiliency Process Model as Presented to Students

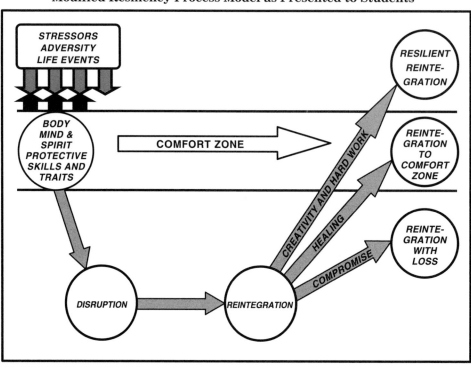

When the youth demonstrated that they understood the model's concepts and processes, they developed their own version of the model (see Figure 2).

Figure 2:
Student Version of the Resiliency Model with Experience Descriptive Blanks

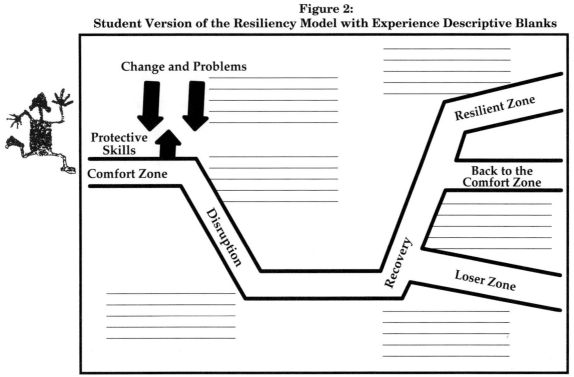

The youth then worked with the resiliency model, *as they envisioned it*, to describe and plot the resiliency process as it works in their own lives, and plan how they could apply the model in the future to become more resilient. Understanding the process, young people were then able to integrate resiliency concepts and the "how to's" of building resiliency.

Consciously choosing how one responds to life experiences is key to instilling and finding control in life and assists in resilient integration of these experiences. We explained that when individuals experience any disruption, they can choose to act in one of three ways:

1. Engage the stressor or challenge; feel defeated, helpless, or hopeless; then reintegrate with loss.
2. Deal with the disruption just to get past it and return to their comfort zones.
3. Learn and grow from the experience. Find the benefit in all experiences.

Once youth in our pilot project demonstrated comfort with and understanding of the resiliency process they defined resiliency in a way that they could see how resiliency worked in their everyday lives. Perhaps one of the students said it best: "*Resiliency is about choosing to bounce back from problems and stuff with more power and smarts.*"

We have only highlighted here some of the concepts and emphases in the *Resilient Youth* program through which youth learn to successfully adapt and grow from the adversity, challenges, and opportunities of life.

Results of the *Resilient Youth* Program

The $40,000 pilot study of the *Resilient Youth* program was funded by Utah State Department of Education gang prevention funds. Though it was conducted at Clayton Middle School and East High School in Salt Lake City, Utah, the *Resilient Youth* curriculum described here was implemented and evaluated only at the high school. Results reported below reflect that population. Administrators at East High School set up a special 15 week class and selected students to participate, with parental permission, in the class. Students attended the class and most participated in the extra-curricular Resilient Youth Of Today (RYOT) club (the name was selected by students) during the time of the study. Currently, more intensive long-term evaluation of the *Resilient Youth* program is being conducted involving two high schools and three junior high schools. Students in all schools are receiving the full curriculum and are being evaluated with pre and post program measures. These measures include sense of purpose in life, locus of control, religiosity, creativity, social competence, problem-solving skills, self-esteem, and self-efficacy. Behavioral outcomes, including school attendance, grades, and incidences of problem behaviors, are also being measured.

Preliminary results from the pilot evaluation of high school students participating in the *Resilient Youth* program indicate that the program appropriately incorporates the behavior change theories and strategies that current research suggests have the best chance to succeed with youth. The program directly involves youth in planning, implementing, and evaluating activities; and it provides repeated opportunities for participants to choose and practice desirable alternatives to self-defeating behaviors. The program's emphasis on inclusion, responsiveness, and participant ownership ensured that it directly addressed the needs and interests of participants, while enhancing participants' roles as resources in teaching the resiliency process to others.

Nineteen faculty respondents to an anonymous survey all reported that the program had strengthened their school. Faculty observed that the students involved were "more connected" to the school community, had a higher level of self-esteem, and had developed more leadership qualities and abilities. All 27 core participating youth reported that they had personally benefitted from their participation in the *Resilient Youth* program. Participants' comments included:

> *"I like the way they teach you that you can recover from any problem and be resilient."*
> *"It helped me to see the positive things within myself, to be independent and dependable."*
> *"Learning about different cultures and finding out everyone has their second chance."*
> *"The way we got together and worked with one another."*

Self-evaluation results indicated that of the 27 youth who fully participated in the *Resilient Youth* program curriculum:

- 87.0% reported having developed a sense of self-awareness related to their actions as a result of the resiliency training classes.
- 91.3% reported having more self-esteem as a result of the resiliency training classes.
- 95.6% reported having better decision-making skills as a result of the resiliency training classes.
- 100% reported being more confident in their ability to make the right choices in life.
- 56.5% reported that they were doing better in school as a result of the resiliency training classes.
- 73.9% reported that they were less involved with gang activities as a result of the resiliency training classes.

While these results are preliminary and should not be generalized to youth in other settings, it appears that there is merit in providing youth with repeated opportunities to learn and practice the resiliency process. The next step will be credible evidence about the success of resiliency training for youth obtained through evaluation using rigorous research methods.

The Resiliency Research Agenda

We have taken a systematic approach to the development of resiliency-based programs (see Figure 3), beginning by outlining a theory of resiliency in our original article (Richardson, 1990).

We then proceeded to test and validate the model in a variety of settings and with differing populations. We are currently refining and evaluating components of the *Resilient Youth* program, including exploring ways the program can be conducted in other community youth-serving organizations. We are also developing similar programs for adults. We continue to refine university courses based on *The Resiliency Training Manual* (Richardson, 1995). We are in the process of conducting additional evaluations of the *Resilient Youth* program to develop believable evidence of its success in helping youth to adopt and maintain healthy responses to the challenges of life. ☺

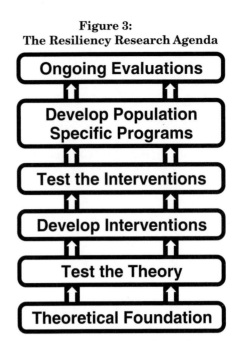

Figure 3:
The Resiliency Research Agenda

- Ongoing Evaluations
- Develop Population Specific Programs
- Test the Interventions
- Develop Interventions
- Test the Theory
- Theoretical Foundation

©1996 T.H.E. Institute - All Rights Reserved

The Resilient Youth *curriculum and training packages are being produced by The Human Experience (T.H.E.) Foundation and will be available for purchase in the fall of 1996. The curriculum and training package will include three days of comprehensive training that will provide site licenses and resiliency facilitator certification, the* Resilient Youth Curriculum Guide *and support materials, and* Resilient Youth Workbooks. *For more information contact Glenn Richardson at the University of Utah (801-581-8039), or by e-mail: (grichard@phth.health.utah.edu).*

References

Caserta, M.S. (1992). *Resiliency resources and the effectiveness of self-help groups for bereaved older adults.* Doctoral dissertation, University of Utah, Salt Lake City, UT.

Dunn, D.L. (1994). *Resilient reintegration of married women with dependent children: Employed and unemployed.* Doctoral dissertation, University of Utah, Salt Lake City, UT.

Gray, Donald Z. (1995). *Evaluation report: 1994-1995 East Clayton gang prevention and intervention project.* Research and Evaluation Program, Health Education Department, University of Utah, Salt Lake City, UT.

Neiger, B.L. (1991). *Resilient reintegration: Use of structural equations modeling.* Doctoral dissertation, University of Utah, Salt Lake City, UT.

Richardson, Glenn E.(1995). *The resiliency training manual.* Dubuque, IA: Brown and Benchmark Publishers.

Richardson, Glenn E.; Neiger, Brad L.; Jensen, Susan; and Kumpfer, Karol (1990). The resiliency model. *Health Education, 21* (6), 33.

Walker, R.L. (1996). *Resilient reintegration of children of substance abusing parents.* Doctoral dissertation, University of Utah, Salt Lake City, UT.

Glenn Richardson, Ph.D., is a full professor in the Department of Health Education at the University of Utah and Executive Director of T.H.E. Institute. He is the author of six books, including The Resiliency Training Manual, *and over 50 peer reviewed journal articles. He has also made hundreds of presentations related to optimal mental health and resiliency to local, state, national, and international organizations.*

Don Gray, Ph.D., is Director of the Research and Evaluation Program in the Department of Health Education at the University of Utah. He has been involved in planning, implementing, and evaluating innovative programs that encourage youth to adopt healthy behaviors.

Reflections From a Pioneer in Prevention, Positive Youth Development, and Education Reform: An Interview with Jeanne Gibbs

by Bonnie Benard, M.S.W.

Creating educational systems that promote and support human development has been the focus of the *Tribes* process for social development and cooperative learning for over 20 years. *Tribes* was conceived by Jeanne Gibbs in the early 1970s, when the predominant responses to problems like substance abuse were "scary films, talks by former addicts, and information on the perils of drug use." This visionary intuited that, "Building positive environments within schools and families not only would be preventive, but could be significant in promoting academic learning and social development" (1995, p. 399). Since then the *Tribes* small group process has spread nationally and internationally and has been used not only in schools but in alcohol recovery centers, juvenile facilities, convalescent homes, daycare centers, and in peer helping and recreational programs. Gibbs' latest edition of the *Tribes* manual incorporates resiliency research, stating that, "The primary mission of *Tribes*...is to assure the healthy development of every child in the school community so that each has the knowledge, skills, and resilience to be successful in our rapidly changing world." According to Gibbs, "This can happen when schools engage all teachers, administrators, students, and families in working together as a learning community—a community dedicated to caring and support, active participation, and positive expectations for all of the young people in their circle of concern" (1995, p. 402).

BB: You have been a real visionary in the prevention and education fields. How did you come to your human development perspective—which often now is called youth development or resiliency?

JG: We were actually just talking "drug education" in the mid-70s. When I became the drug education coordinator for a county health services department in California, I was appalled that what our 18 school districts expected us to do was to run around with pharmacology kits to tell kids about drugs! Now several things—besides my intuition!—led me to believe this wasn't the way to go. First of all, my own common sense as a mother: When I walked into my kids' classrooms there was often an essence of caring

and interest that told me they would be okay. This got me interested in the whole issue of school climate, which started my search for research.

Also, as my children were growing up, I was a very active volunteer both in the school and in youth organizations like the scouts. It was there that I discovered how the leader's management style affected the participation of the group. In schools, I saw a lot of weary teachers! Also my husband was a business-man who was talking to me about the management research on group and team development. This led me not only into the research on group and organizational development, but also into personally participating in a management training group for a year. At the close of the year, I realized that I was changing. In fact, all the members of the group began to talk about the changes we saw in ourselves: Some of the brash leader types had become considerate, and were listening and caring. Those who were on the quiet side, like myself, had actually become leaders. I was fascinated, and hooked on human and group development! Then I had the opportunity to take an educational training consultant course at the National Training Laboratory in Maine for three weeks one summer. It was an intensive course on how you apply participatory and team management to education. I wondered why we were not using such a process in education.

One last major influence moving me to develop the *Tribes* process was my discovery of Urie Bronfenbrenner's books. His *Two Worlds of Childhood* contrasted the extensive use of group learning in Russian schools with the highly individualized, competitive nature of education in the U.S. It also made clear to me the importance of children learning interpersonal skills.

When Bronfenbrenner published *Ecology and Human Development*, which discussed how positive human development moves from micro to macro systems and outward to the world, I was a fan for life. It shifted my whole focus from trying to shape up kids to improving the ecology around them, the environmental systems that impact their lives. I saw that the definition of macro systems have that capacity. Think of our political situation. We don't dare to stop action enough, and say to the American public, "Is this good for us? What's going on? What can we change?" This is a critical skill that has to be taught and practiced. It has always been an essential element of *Tribes*.

BB: It seems to me that the human development approach—the very idea that prevention and education should be focused on creating environments that meet youth's developmental needs for belonging, respect, power, and meaning—has always been somewhat counter cultural in the U.S. Do you see any signs that it is moving more to the mainstream of prevention and education?

JG: I think that we're coming close to it now. If we can weave all of the knowledge, all of the great research we now have—and didn't have in the 1970s—about human development, brain compatible learning, cooperative learning, multiple intelligences, and resiliency, into creating ideal learning environments, then we will finally be able to improve American education. We know from brain compatible learning research that kids cannot learn when in fear, when not feeling safe, when feeling mistrustful. The brain down shifts. We have too many classrooms that do not have an environment of safety, trust, and kindness. Yet we know from resiliency research that no matter where a youngster comes from, whatever the family or neighborhood situation, if a youth can walk into a school and feel safe and cared for, he or she will learn. Our brains shift from that reptilian place upward to where the mind can think clearly.

The primary mission of **Tribes** *is to assure the healthy development of every child in the school community so that each has the knowledge, skills, and resilience to be successful in our rapidly changing world."*

In *Tribes*, we train teachers to help students make this shift. A community circle begins every day, so that everyone gets to share, "Something special has happened for me," or "Something was exciting", or "What I hope and dream is....." It's very important to know that's how learning happens, that if we have controlling environments—expecting kids to memorize, regurgitate, and compete in an individualistic type of way—they will not achieve. It is that supportive environment that conditions taking in information and being able to think it through constructively and critically. It's very exciting to hear kids learn to give appreciation to others in their group—when they can tell others what special gifts they gave the group in order for them to work together. By appreciating the uniqueness of each individual within a group, we're building the strengths—rather than focusing on weaknesses or criticism—that help kids soar.

BB: Tell us a little about some of the international applications of *Tribes*.

JG: One of the most unique is in Slovakia, in Bratislava, at the demonstration school at the Slovak Academy of Sciences. They discovered *Tribes* when they sent two professors over about five years ago. They believed that they could not establish democracy in a state system that's been totalitarian for 40 years unless they, as instructors, knew what democracy is. These two beautiful women professors sat there and said, "We ourselves were not permitted to make decisions. How can we, then, help a new population do that?" We assisted in translating *Tribes* in 1987, and then they got a small grant from the Sauros Foundation so one of our trainers could train a cadre of their teachers.

In Scotland, for about the last four years, there's been an effort to move from regimented education to more of an emphasis on human development and caring systems. An educator from Scotland went through one of our training sessions, went back and has *Tribes* going well in the Northern Isles of Scotland.

The *Tribes* process is also being used by the Ojibwa Nation of Ontario and Manitoba, Canada. Before Laura Horton, a beautiful Ojibwa educator, took *Tribes* to her people she consulted with one of the Elders, Anne Wilson, "What do you think? Would this be appropriate for our people?" Anne responded, "We have lost this in our children. It's the Old Ways—the old ways of caring, of being there, of being concerned and taking care of each other." It is about community.

BB: Well, Jeanne, you are certainly a respected Elder in this field. Since you told me last year that you have finally given up the idea of retirement and are going "to work to create systems change in schools," you must have hope that change is possible and worth continuing to work for.

JG: It is happening, Bonnie, it is absolutely happening. Every school in Honolulu is moving this way. The Superintendent of the Department of Education of Hawaii has created a "Success Compact" which shifts the focus to instruction in relationships and community. We think at some point, every school in Hawaii will be a *Tribes* school.

Yes, people are finally saying we have to turn to a whole different sort of approach and philosophy of youth development. I am very hopeful and even confident that education will change.

BB: It is certainly a testament to your vision and the compelling work you've done for 20 years—work for which all of us who believe in human development and resiliency feel extremely grateful to you. Thank you for shining your light on the path! ☯

Jeanne Gibbs' 1995 edition of Tribes: A New Way of Learning and Being Together *(432 pages) is available through CenterSource Systems, 305 Tesconi Circle, Santa Rosa, CA 95401. Phone: 707-577-8233. Fax: 707-526-6587. E-mail:(centrsrc@aol.com). For information on training, phone 415-289-1700.*

An Introduction to Program Evaluation: A Step-by-Step Guide to Getting Started

by Craig Noonan, Ph.D., M.S.W., and Nan Henderson, M.S.W.

> *"The most savage controversies are about those matters as to which there is no good evidence either way."* –Bertrand Russell
>
> *"It is not enough to aim, you must hit."* –Italian proverb

There's an old joke about a drunk man who leaves a bar one evening and is followed outside by a friend who is concerned about him trying to drive home. He finds his drunken friend accross the street, under the street lamp, on hands and knees, searching for something and asks him what he is looking for. The inebriated friend answers: "Dropped m' keysh." His friend comes over to help look and asks him where he lost them. The drunk man says: "Over by the door." The friend is puzzled and asks: "If you lost them accross the street, why are you looking for them here?" The reply: "Becaush the light ish better."

This story reminds us of the attitude that is often taken towards program evaluation in school settings. Often a mandate from the administration or the funding source to evaluate a program initiates the evaluation process and something is thrown together to satisfy the requirement—but doesn't provide very useful information. Unfortunately, the time and energy necessary to produce a meaningless evaluation could just as easily be used to produce one that is useful to both the "powers that be" and the program being evaluated.

Educators and other helping professionals often experience resistance to program evaluation based on several fears and misconceptions. Some think they need to be trained researchers and/or statisticians to do a proper job, and feel inadequate. Others think it will take too much time to conduct an evaluation and fear becoming overwhelmed. Another fear is that the program and/or jobs may be terminated due to a negative evaluation. Finally, some have the misconception that evaluation is unnecessary because the program or curriculum being used has already been evaluated.

These fears and misconceptions are far from true. The essential ingredient for a good evaluation is familiarity with and knowledge of the program. Researchers and statisticians can be consulted to fine tune evaluation projects, often for little or no expense. Many well designed and useful evaluations are conducted every day by staff who have very little formal training in research design and statistics. The time necessary for an evaluation is always a trade off between practical limitations and needed information. (A better evaluation is always possible if more time, money, and resources are available.) The true creativity of a good evaluation lies in answering the desired questions using the fewest resources. Many of the best evaluation projects use data that are already being collected.

It is important to evaluate every program, even if it has already been evaluated and found effective (and the reality is that most drug and violence prevention programs and curriculum have not been evaluated). A previously evaluated program does not guarantee effectiveness because it was not evaluated in a specific school with specific students and staff. Effective programs require a combination of factors such as the appropriate intervention, the right dose, the proper duration, and a high quality of service delivery to be successful. Any one of these components could be less than adequate in a specific setting for specific students. Evaluating various aspects of the program to improve and fine tune it for the best results in each school should be a regular ongoing endeavor.

Evaluation as an ongoing process for program improvement is consistent with the way people naturally (every day!) evaluate their environment and behavior to make adjustments for optimal functioning. They use the information from this evaluation to improve their lives. In the same way, the best and most appropriate use of program evaluation is not to terminate programs and jobs but to help school staff, students, and administrators simply do what is better for them in their specific environments. Teachers, other educational practitioners, and some university researchers are advocating that an ongoing spiral of evaluation become the norm for staff development in education (see Figure 1) for this very reason—the benefits of improved programs for students and the sense of self-efficacy and self-empowerment for the educators actively engaged in systematic problem solving (Anderson, Herr, Nihlen, 1994).

Figure 1: The Action Research Cycle

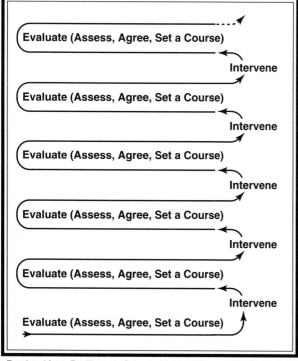

Reprinted from *Resiliency in Schools: Making It Happen For Students and Educators* (1996) by NanHenderson and Mike Milstein, published by Corwin Press, Thousand Oaks, CA

Reasons for Program Evaluation

There are other reasons for evaluating programs but we think two are most important. The first is an ethical responsibility. The programs put in place in schools may affect the lives of young people in profound and long lasting ways. The intention is that these programs will have positive effects but that may not always be the case. Drug education seemed like a good idea in the 1970s but some types of education have been shown to actually increase drug use by desensitizing young people to a previously unknown

and scary behavior. Educators have a professional responsibility to *do no harm*. The only way to insure this is to evaluate even the most well-intentioned and well-thought-out programs.

The other important reason for program evaluation is to find out if programs and curriculums are making a difference. Why waste professional time and energy on programs that aren't accomplishing what needs to be done? There are also degrees of "making a difference." Educators all want to make the biggest difference with the least amount of effort. The time and resources that are saved can be put to other good uses. Program evaluation can indicate if programs are working, but more importantly, it can indicate how they can be improved. In other words, evaluation is the key to fine tuning any program to do the best job possible with specific students, at a specific school, and at a specific time.

Program Evaluation: Step by Step

Program evaluation can be as simple or as complicated as those doing the evaluation wish to make it. Some people drive VW Bugs and some drive Cadillacs. As with automobiles, the complexity of the evaluation model will depend upon specific needs and the kinds of questions that are being asked. *Summative* evaluation questions ask about outcome: Does a program "work?" *Formative* evaluation asks how well a program is working. It provides information about program consumers (how many, attitudes about program, demographics, etc.), resources expended for program delivery, whether the program is meeting the needs of the school community, and how efficiently the program is functioning. In other words, formative evaluation provides data to fine tune the outcome and efficiency of a program. It may even provide useful information about why a program is not working. It is often useful to combine both types of evaluation— formative information often provides the context necessary to understand summative data.

Nine steps for conducting a simple program evaluation are outlined below. Erudite volumes have been written on the topic and there are many excellent manuals that go through it, step by step (see bibliography). This brief guide is designed to get educators started in answering a few simple questions or to interest them in acquiring and using a manual. At several points, consultation with an evaluation design or statistics expert is recommended for those who don't have one already working with them. A second opinion is always helpful and can avoid a disaster when something is inadvertently overlooked. Most school districts, universities, or funding sources have such individuals either formally or informally available. Educators should find an evaluator who speaks their native language and have them review all evaluation plans. It is also useful if this consultant is willing to provide a practical education so the novice evaluator will eventually become an expert too. Before beginning, be aware of the old adage: "Be careful what you ask for." Once evaluators get answers to their initial questions, they will probably want to ask many more. Program evaluation is habit forming and contagious! It also is a natural fit into the vocation of education, which has as its central purpose finding ways to improve student learning, social development, and overall life success.

Step One: Identify Questions and Involve Others

The first step is to identify the questions that need answering and to involve as many others as possible in the process. What questions will provide the most useful information for making a program as effective as possible? What information would be useful to others (administrators, parents, teachers, students)? Worksheet 1 provides a series of questions that will help clarify important questions to ask. Enlist others in filling out this worksheet to get several perspectives. Use a brainstorming process for each of these questions, keeping in mind that the key to good brainstorming is to let the creative juices flow. Don't evaluate the importance or feasibility of answering specific questions, just get them all down on paper. It also is useful to brainstorm potential barriers (both personnel and systemic) to the project as well as possible remedies for these hindrances.

Include as many other school staff and students in the process of developing and choosing evaluation questions as feasible. This gives others some ownership of the project. If they don't decide to help, they will probably at least get out of the way. Get key people involved at an early stage and allay their fears about the project. Emphasize how the project will benefit them, the school, and the students. De-emphasize the evaluation of individual work and stress the evaluation of an entire program. Invite the biggest critic of the project to be part of the evaluation. He or she will help counteract biases. Also, try to include some staff who are knowledgeable about research design and statistics and some consumers of

the program (especially students) on the evaluation team. They are worth their weight in gold for the mistakes they will prevent from happening.

**Worksheet 1:
Clarifying Evaluation Questions**

1. What reasons are there for program evaluation in our school? What purposes could it serve?
2. What are the goals of the program(s) that we might want to evaluate?
3. If we had unlimited resources, what would we like to know about our program?
4. What would we like to know about the population we serve?
5. What have we wondered about, or what questions would we like answered?
6. What are our biggest concerns and frustrations in our work? Do these suggest any evaluation questions?
7. In what ways would we like to see our services improved?
8. Is there anything we are considering adding or dropping from our program? Do these suggest any evaluation questions?
9. What is especially different about our program? Does this suggest any evaluation questions?
10. What is especially effective about our program? Does this suggest any evaluation questions?

Step Two: Prioritize Questions

The next step is to narrow the questions that have been identified down to a few that are most important. The more questions an evaluation tries to answer, the more complicated the project will get. Keep it simple is an important rule, especially for those just getting started with evaluation. Other questions can always be answered in the next evaluation project.

For summative evaluations, Worksheet 2, at the top of page 46, may be helpful in moving from the goals of the program to specific behaviors and the indicators that may measure those behaviors. Evaluating knowledge and attitudes can be useful, but don't stop there. Funding sources are interested in results and that means behavior change. Measure these outcomes as well.

Worksheet 2: Defining and Measuring Program Goals			
What are the goals of our program?	What are the changes we expect to see for each of these goals in individuals or the community?	How would we know we have succeeded in effecting this change?	What could we measure that would indicate this change?
#1. EXAMPLE: To increase caring and support in our school	• Increased student involvement • Less conflict on campus	• Greater student attendance at school and classes • Fewer discipline referrals to administration	• School attendance rates • Classroom attendance rates • Number of discipline referrals per week
#2. etc.			

Step Three: Define the Question(s)

Defining evaluation questions is one of the most important steps. This means translating general questions from Step Two into terms that can be measured. Filling out Worksheet 2, above, is a way to do some of this. "Is our program to increase protective factors in the school environment working?" is a general question. "Did our new policy and student discipline program reduce behavioral incidents within the six months since it started?" is an evaluation question that can be measured. It is important to state each question in a way that clearly defines what it is that is being measured.

Step Four: Choose the Measurement Tools

Choosing the right tool for the job will get it done quickly and properly. In general, the best measure is one that addresses the question being studied as directly as possible, or one that is already in place to gather some type of information relevant to the program evaluation now being conducted, and/or a measurement instrument that is well established. Tools have already been developed for just about anything that might need measuring in a program evaluation. The *Mental Measurement Yearbook*, published yearly and available in the reference section of most university libraries, can be a useful source for finding measurement tools. Conducting a literature review on a specific program area will yield others.

Choose established instruments carefully and consider their relevance for the program being evaluated, whether they really measure what they are supposed to (validity), and their ability to yield the same score or data on two separate occasions if no change occurred in between (reliability). Other important concerns are their comparability to other similar measures, their readability, their cultural appropriateness, and their ease of use in data collection and analysis. If it is necessary to design a measure for a specific evaluation, it is important to consult an expert so the instrument is designed correctly. Inexperience often results in a poorly designed instrument and a bad instrument can ruin an entire evaluation project.

Most variables that are measured in a program evaluation fall into one of the following categories: attitudes, knowledge, skills, behavior, or environmental factors. This data can be collected by self-reports, interviews, surveys, and from records in archival sources, observation, and/or current records. If the outcome being evaluated is actual behavior change, don't just measure attitude change. Figure out a way to actually measure behavior; better yet, measure both. Since attitudes are not always good predictors of behavior they cannot be used to provide the answer to the ultimate question: Did behaviors change as a result of this program? If a program does appear to change attitudes but not behaviors, based on looking at both, this may mean that a program is on the right track and simply needs some fine tuning for the attitude change to carry over to behavioral change. Prevention researchers have found, for example, that whereas several drug prevention curricula change knowledge and attitudes in the short-term, an adequate dosage (in terms of number of initial sessions), implementing the curriculum exactly as it is designed (referred to as "implementation fidelity"), and an adequate number of booster sessions for several years are necessary for attitude change to translate to behavior change in the long run (Botvin, 1992).

Finally, use a variety of measures whenever possible in finding the answers to the questions that are the focus of the evaluation. For example, for a program attempting to reduce school violence by teaching mediation skills to students, attitudes and knowledge about conflict resolution techniques could be measured using a student self-report instrument, mediation skills acquisition could be assessed using observers to objectively evaluate how well students picked up the skill, and mediation skill use in the real world could be determined by asking students

in personal interviews and surveys, by using observers, and by surveying family, friends, and other collaterals. Furthermore, existing data already being gathered could be analyzed to assess the frequency of violence at school before and after the program was implemented, and the student body could be surveyed about their feelings of safety before and after the program. If all of these measures yield convergent results, this is strong evidence of a successful program. If they do not, the thoroughness of looking at the program from several different perspectives provides useful information about how the program can be improved.

Step Five: Design Your Evaluation
An evaluation design is simply a set of instructions or procedures about when, how, and from whom to collect data in order to answer the questions that have been posed. The design will largely be determined by the questions that need answering. Table 1 provides guidelines that can be used in designing the evaluation. Those inexperienced with evaluation design should consult an expert in research design and statistics for a final stamp of approval.

Table 1: Evaluation Designs

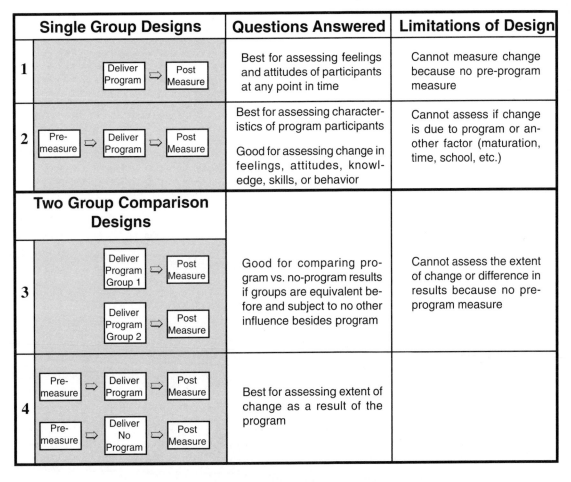

Single Group Designs	Questions Answered	Limitations of Design
1. Deliver Program → Post Measure	Best for assessing feelings and attitudes of participants at any point in time	Cannot measure change because no pre-program measure
2. Pre-measure → Deliver Program → Post Measure	Best for assessing characteristics of program participants / Good for assessing change in feelings, attitudes, knowledge, skills, or behavior	Cannot assess if change is due to program or another factor (maturation, time, school, etc.)
Two Group Comparison Designs		
3. Deliver Program Group 1 → Post Measure / Deliver Program Group 2 → Post Measure	Good for comparing program vs. no-program results if groups are equivalent before and subject to no other influence besides program	Cannot assess the extent of change or difference in results because no pre-program measure
4. Pre-measure → Deliver Program → Post Measure / Pre-measure → Deliver No Program → Post Measure	Best for assessing extent of change as a result of the program	

An important consideration in the design is the potential negative impact of the evaluation upon evaluation participants (e.g., poor performance on an outcome measure, violations of confidentiality or anonymity, membership in a no-program control group, etc.). Therefore it is also important to have the design reviewed by someone knowledgeable about this topic. Some school districts require formal approval for certain types or even all types of evaluation projects to ensure protection of those being evaluated.

Issues of anonymity and confidentiality are important concerns regarding the collection of data. Both generally result in more accurate data from individuals. Special data collection and storage steps may need to be taken to ensure anonymity and confidentiality. Also, in some school districts, confidentiality of sensitive information can be a politically sensitive issue. There may be policies against some types of confidentiality (e.g., if a student admits to regular cocaine use to school staff they may be required to report it). It is important to investigate district policies in this area to learn both the limitations to and requirements for confidentiality.

Another issue is who will be measured. Will the evaluation include every participant in the program or a smaller subset of this group? If a smaller subset of participants is selected, they must be randomly selected and representative of the larger group in order to generalize findings to this group. Random selection will usually insure a representative sample but measuring the sample on important characteristics (age, gender, culture, grade, etc.) after the sample is selected is a way to make sure the sample is close to the general population. If it is not, then results of measures on this sample cannot be generalized to the larger group. This is another area of the evaluation project that can benefit from research expertise. If in doubt, consult someone who has expertise in sampling. If this is not possible, be aware that the answers from an unrepresentative sample pertain to sample members only and *cannot* be used as representative evidence for the program as a whole.

Finally, lay out a time line for the tasks of the design, assigning responsibility for each of them, and outlining how they will be accomplished. Specifically, when will the data be collected (e.g., before, during, immediately after, and 6 months after the program)?, who will collect it?, how will they collect it?, and what will they do with it?. Include a plan for data management, organization, and analysis. Will results be tallied the "old fashioned way" or will the data be entered into a computer database? Selecting a project manager to oversee the overall process is a good idea. He or she can also deal with political and systems issues that may interfere with the project.

Step Six: Implement Your Plan
Implement the evaluation plan for a "pilot" or "trial" period of reasonable length. This may only mean pretesting all measurement tools and systems on individuals who are similar to those you will be using in your evaluation. *Do not skip this process.* Invaluable information about what has been overlooked that might cause problems or even invalidate the entire evaluation will be gained in this step of the process. Once this new information is incorporated into the evaluation design, it is time to launch the evaluation.

Step Seven: Organize and Analyze Your Data
This step should already have been anticipated in planning the evaluation design and should not pose a problem. Descriptive statistics are very straight-forward and provide a summary of characteristics of the evaluation participants and measurements. Most elementary statistics texts contain excellent chapters on how to describe data. Find the best way(s) to summarize the data for different audiences (e.g., those with different interests and knowledge levels). Make it user friendly.

Inferential statistics allows comparisons and an examination of relationships between different groups of participants. They also determine if any observed differences are meaningful or likely due to chance. They can be complicated and may only be applied to certain types of designs and data. Try a statistics text, use a statistician, or consult one for this step. There are many excellent and inexpensive statistical software packages on the market that also do most of the calculations. Again, there is most likely someone in the district who is knowledgeable about statistical processes who can be consulted for help.

Step Eight: Share the Results
This is an essential part of evaluation that is often neglected, or done poorly. It's the payoff! If results are positive, share them with everyone and anyone who has an interest. Design different reports for different audiences. Make the data live. Share what the numbers mean in terms of the difference one would see in the lives of real people. Use a variety of presentation techniques to maintain interest and an appropriate level of consciousness in the listener.

If the results are not positive, share them with those who need to know in the manner described above. Learn from the results. Some useful questions to ask include: Were the results caused by a poorly designed study, an ineffective program, or a poorly implemented program? Why isn't the program working? What is working and what is not working? The results can answer these questions and ultimately improve the program or provide the necessary information to develop a more effective one. When viewed this way, even negative results are worthwhile. If the ultimate goal is the implementation of programs and strategies that help students, "negative" results are just a stop on the road in designing approaches that make this goal a reality.

Significant results (either positive or negative) should be shared with the larger professional community. Professionals working with young people, and ultimately the young people themselves, will benefit from the creativity and the hard work that went into the evaluation. A variety of professional journals exist for just this purpose. Find one that relates to the area that has been evaluated, get a copy, and read the style and submission requirements before submitting a report.

Step Nine: Start All Over Again With New Questions

Once a first set of evaluation questions has been answered, and the results have been incorporated into an improved program, there is then something new to evaluate. New questions will almost always emerge that also need answers, and they form the basis of an ongoing evaluation process. Often, more staff are interested in helping with the new evaluation and may even want to consult on how they can do their own evaluation. Congratulations! ☯

References and Bibliography

Anderson, G. L., Herr, K., & Nihlen, A.S. (1994). *Studying your own school.* Thousand Oaks, CA: Corwin Press.

The Burows Institute of Mental Measurements. (1995). *The mental measurement yearbook.* Lincoln, NE: The University of Nebraska Press.

Henderson, N., & Milstein, M.M. (1996). *Resiliency in schools: Making it happen for students and educators.* Thousand Oaks, CA: Corwin Press.

Linney, J. A., & Wandersman, A. (1991). *Prevention plus III: Assessing alcohol and other drug prevention programs at the school and community level.* DHHS Pub. No. (ADM)91-1817. Rockville, MD: Office for Substance Abuse Prevention.

National Institute on Drug Abuse. (1993). *How good is your drug abuse treatment program: A guide to evaluation.* NIH Publication No. 95-3609. Rockville, MD: National Institutes of Health.

National Organization of Student Assistance Programs and Partners. (1991). *Evaluation tools for student assistance programs.* Boulder, CO.

National Organization of Student Assistance Programs and Partners. (1992). *Evaluation tools for student assistance programs.* Boulder, CO.

Wolfe, B. E., & Miller, W. R. (1995). *Program evaluation: A do-it-yourself manual for substance abuse programs.* Albuquerque, NM: University of New Mexico, Department of Psychology, Center on Alcoholism, Substance Abuse and Addiction (CASAA).

Craig Noonan, Ph.D., M.S.W., is a researcher and program evaluator. He is also an author, therapist, trainer, and consultant specializing in motivation for change and resiliency, and a Contributing Editor at Resiliency In Action. *He can be reached at Alternatives, 5130 La Jolla Blvd., #2K, San Diego, CA 92109, p/f (858-488-5034) or by e-mail: (wnoonan@popmail.ucsd.edu).*

Nan Henderson, M.S.W., is a national and international speaker and consultant on fostering resiliency and wellness, alcohol and other drug issues, and on organizational change. She has co-authored/edited five books about resiliency, and is the president of Resiliency In Action. *She can be reached at Nan Henderson and Associates, 5130 La Jolla Blvd., #2K, San Diego, CA 92109, p/f (858-488-5034), or by e-mail: (nanh@connectnet.com).*

Commentaries

Protective Beliefs Are a Key to Professionals' and Students' Resiliency

by Kerry Anne Ridley, L.C.D.D.

Recently I was conducting a support group for counselors from a large urban school district. The counselors were sharing concerns about their students that spanned a range of serious social problems, problems that have a tragic familiarity for educators throughout the country. They expressed concern for a boy who would soon be orphaned by the death of both parents to AIDS, a sixth grade girl who might be prostituting for family food money, and a prevalence of young people who have a parent or a sibling in the prison system.

Over the years, I've heard these counselors share stories of student abuse and neglect that are beyond the imagination of most ordinary adults. For counselors and teachers alike the face of neglect is not seen on the evening news or "made for T.V." movies, the face of neglect sits in their offices everyday. Coming in close personal contact with human situations that defy easy solutions can challenge the most buoyant person's mental health.

When a counselor becomes caught in a web of discouragement common patterns begin to emerge. The counselor may begin to doubt the potential success of the individual. *How can this young person survive or thrive with such destructive circumstances surrounding him?* In attempting to manage overwhelming numbers of young people in need, the counselor can develop mental categories which predict negative outcomes. *Here is another student staying at home alone with her siblings. With no parental supervision they are up all hours of the night. How can she possibly learn in school?* Finally, the counselor may begin to doubt his or her own abilities. *Can I really help this person? I can't even imagine the horror of what she's endured.*

These absolutely normal reactions to occupational stress can produce unintentional outcomes for the counselor and the young person. The problems presented all begin to sound the same, the young person becomes known for his or her problems rather than his or her unique humanity, and the solutions can become rote. Hope is diminished.

Yet time and time again, I have been dazzled by the ability of these counselors to manage stress. Counselors do wrestle with negative attitudes, but a tremendous degree of resiliency is the norm. I began to wonder: How were these individuals able to sustain a healthy perspective in spite of the tragic stories and consequences experienced by the students and their families? I asked the counselors attending the support group about their *protective beliefs—beliefs which protect them from the effects of adversity.* What beliefs did they have that helped them with feelings of responsibility and sometimes even inadequacy? How were they able to maintain enduring compassion and faith in the human spirit?

Four Categories of Protective Beliefs

The beliefs they expressed fall into four broad categories.

1 *Belief One: Trust that human goodness and caring surpass human destruction.* "During all the recent floods, earthquakes, and even hurricanes, for every person who looted or refused to help there were thousands who didn't commit a crime and worked tirelessly for the good of the community. Knowing this helps me when I'm preoccupied with worry about our students and all the potential dangers they face." The opinion of this counselor struck a chord of agreement with the others. Yes, violence and fear abound but human compassion is far more common and powerful.

2 *Belief Two: View oneself as a helper amongst a community of helpers.* A common theme was, "There have been many people before me who have helped this particular student and there will be many after me." Knowing the responsibility for the student's long term success does not solely depend on the current counseling relationship appeared to lighten the "psychic load" for many counselors.

3 *Belief Three: Know that most people are capable survivors who possess appropriate solutions for their challenges.* One counselor said, "I remind myself often about my students' smartness and common sense in creating solutions; their solutions are like a seed breaking through concrete." Another counselor commented, "I remember the students who come back to visit. Five years ago it seemed like sone of those students wouldn't finish high school, and others wouldn't live much longer. Somehow they've made it and want to tell us about it!"

4 The final belief was focused on the ultimate mystery of life. *Belief Four: Recognize that there are forces at work in all of our lives that are beyond human understanding.* "Who grows up healthy, and who doesn't? Who experiences one trauma after another and who doesn't?" In posing these questions a counselor spoke of her helping philosophy. "I will always try to change the world's injustice so my students may have a fair shot at a good life, but I also know I am not in control. My influence and time are limited. I have to believe there is something bigger than me guiding a person's life." Different

words were used in describing this belief–faith, collective wisdom, God, and even karma. These invisible forces were a source of comfort and reflection for many of the counselors.

The counselors who participated in this discussion had known they held a perspective or philosophy which allowed them to sustain compassion but they had never made them explicit. From this discussion they felt a new degree of clarity. They could now lead their students through a similar process.

Help Students To Identify Protective Beliefs

How can you begin an inquiry with your students about their protective beliefs? You can initiate a process of discovering with them their community of helpers, their experience with human goodness, and their own triumphs with "seed breaking through concrete" solutions. You can help make their own invisible protective beliefs more visible and potentially more useful.

In translating our own and others' protective beliefs into helping approaches we will be less likely to succumb to occupational hazards that weaken our mental health immune system. We are then better able to see possibilities and promise where before we saw predominantly limitations and despair.

On page 71 I describe the process of infusing a resiliency approach into a community-based social service program by using the *Resiliency Inventory*. ☺

Kerry Anne Ridley, L.C.D.D., is a trainer and consultant who assists schools and businesses in shifting from a predominantly "at risk" orientation to resiliency focused practices. She is the author of the Resiliency Inventory. *She lives in Austin, Texas and welcomes your experiences related to resiliency. Contact her at (512-477-1310) or by e-mail:: (karidley@aol.com).*

Integrating Resiliency Building and Educational Reform: Why Doing One Accomplishes the Other

by Nan Henderson, M.S.W.

"We just don't have time to do *one more thing*!" Those of us who have worked in prevention over the past two decades are used to hearing this lament from well-intentioned, caring, but overwhelmed classroom teachers as they are confronted with the prospect of implementing another program. Though they agree that students need prevention programming, in their frustration they often express the feeling: Why does this, too, have to be *our* job?

About five years ago, when I started a new job as a prevention program administrator with Albuquerque Public Schools (APS), I had an experience that helped me realize that the cutting edge of prevention—strategies for building resiliency in students—is not simply *one more thing* for schools to do.

Another person joined the APS prevention team when I did. She didn't have a background in prevention, per se, but had excellent training and practice in facilitating school reform—called restructuring in our district at that time—in dozens of schools throughout the district. When we began talking about our prospective backgrounds, I eagerly shared with her the emerging prevention paradigm of resiliency which was just making a splash in 1991. My new colleague listened carefully as I talked about the key concepts. Then she said, "I've never heard of this resiliency stuff, but I can tell you that everything you are talking about is the basis of school restructuring."

A wonderful collaboration was born. Together we reached the conclusion which many others familiar

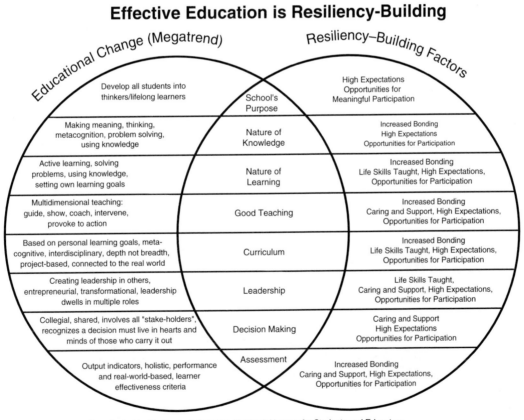

Effective Education is Resiliency-Building

Educational Change (Megatrend)

Resiliency–Building Factors

	School's Purpose	
Develop all students into thinkers/lifelong learners		High Expectations Opportunities for Meaningful Participation
Making meaning, thinking, metacognition, problem solving, using knowledge	Nature of Knowledge	Increased Bonding High Expectations Opportunities for Participation
Active learning, solving problems, using knowledge, setting own learning goals	Nature of Learning	Increased Bonding Life Skills Taught, High Expectations, Opportunities for Participation
Multidimensional teaching: guide, show, coach, intervene, provoke to action	Good Teaching	Increased Bonding Caring and Support, High Expectations, Opportunities for Participation
Based on personal learning goals, meta-cognitive, interdisciplinary, depth not breadth, project-based, connected to the real world	Curriculum	Increased Bonding Life Skills Taught, High Expectations, Opportunities for Participation
Creating leadership in others, entrepreneurial, transformational, leadership dwells in multiple roles	Leadership	Life Skills Taught, Caring and Support, High Expectations, Opportunities for Participation
Collegial, shared, involves all "stake-holders", recognizes a decision must live in hearts and minds of those who carry it out	Decision Making	Caring and Support High Expectations Opportunities for Participation
Output indicators, holistic, performance and real-world-based, learner effectiveness criteria	Assessment	Increased Bonding Caring and Support, High Expectations, Opportunities for Participation

from the book, *Resiliency in Schools: Making It Happen for Students and Educators*
by Nan Henderson and Mike Milstein, published by Corwin Press, Thousand Oaks, CA, 1996.

with the fields of prevention and school reform have also realized: Effective school restructuring produces a resiliency-building school. And resiliency building in schools is actually the foundation of effective education.

Deborah Meier, principal of Central Park East in East Harlem, New York, where 90 percent of the students graduate and 90 percent of those go on to college (in a school district where the average graduation rate is 50 percent) wrote in the July, 1995 issue of the *American School Board Journal* about her school's success: "There's a quality called 'hopefulness' that is a better predictor of success, even in college, than grade point average, class rank, or SAT score!" Reading about her school, it is clear that the all-important attitude of hope and optimism whatever the challenge, which I like to call "The Resiliency Attitude," permeates Central Park East. In addition, Meier reports the school integrates the

trends in education documented in the diagram on page 53. Report after report of schools that are successful beyond the norm, including the schools that have been mentioned by the students interviewed for the "Faces of Resiliency" feature in this journal, characterize these schools similarly: Exceptional schools are imbued with that all-important attitude and are structured around resiliency principles—whether those involved realize it or not.

Helping educators understand this connection often brings a great relief and, in my experience, increased motivation to make the changes in their school that will *both* increase student academic success and foster greater life success in the form of less involvement in risky behaviors and increased resiliency. Helping preventionists realize this connection enables them to achieve what has been for us an historically elusive goal: Weaving the recommendations from prevention into the very fabric of schools. ◉

Resiliency In Practice

Resiliency-Building Approaches to School Discipline

Clear and consistently enforced boundaries and limits in the form of family rules, school discipline policies, and community laws and norms act as a protection for students, according to risk factor research. Several schools have also woven the resiliency-building concepts of providing caring and support, recognizing and reinforcing positive behavior, providing students with opportunities for meaningful participation, and teaching the social skills necessary to "stay out of trouble" into their approaches to school discipline. The following examples of resiliency-building school discipline policies are reprinted from Resiliency in Schools: Making It Happen for Students and Educators *by Nan Henderson and Mike Milstein. The elementary school policies are primarily the result of district-sponsored resiliency training conducted over a four year period in Albuquerque Public Schools (APS). This training was funded through a School Personnel Training Grant from the U.S. Department of Education.*

Elementary School Approaches

The staff of Kit Carson Elementary School developed the following guidelines for "preventive discipline" after their participation in the APS project.

PREVENTIVE DISCIPLINE

We believe that when students are actively involved and there is frequent communication, many discipline problems can be avoided. Some of the procedures and techniques used at Kit Carson in preventive discipline are:

1. Do not consider discipline as separate or apart from the rest of the teaching process.
2. Show genuine interest in all of your students and accentuate the positive.
3. Have well defined rules (posted) as to what is expected of the children.
4. Be consistent in all things (presentation of materials, enforcement of the rules, etc.) so that the children know what is expected of them.
5. Emphasize respect for others—teachers, pupils, adults, property, etc.
6. Share the good things the children are doing with others (the parents, administration, other teachers and other children all like to hear and share in the successes of our students).
7. Cooperative school-wide [preventive] discipline program:
    a) Gold Slips are given to students who behave properly. One Gold Slip—trade for popcorn. Ten Gold Slips in nine weeks—lunch with the principal.
    b) Students who do not receive infraction notices each nine weeks will receive a prize.
    c) Use of conflict mediation.
    d) Participation in TASA [student assistance] programs.

The school also formulated an extensive "corrective discipline" policy, which clearly outlined eight key school rules and steps taken for each number of infractions. Its primary focus on "preventive discipline," however, is a resiliency-building approach—accentuate the positive to alleviate much of the need for "corrective discipline."

Another creative approach to discipline, designed to foster staff resiliency at Kit Carson, was the assignment of "buddy teachers"—individuals who could be called upon by other staff in the school in any "corrective discipline" situation. Through this approach, the staff built in caring and support for one another in what are often tense and stressful situations, and assured a greater likelihood of students being treated with caring and respect (through the intervention of a more neutral third party).

East San Jose Elementary School developed a discipline policy based on the idea that every student had certain rights, and formulated it as a list of rights for students.

EAST SAN JOSE
BILL OF RIGHTS

1. Everyone has a right to be safe and no one will be hurt.

_____ There will be no fighting, kicking, hitting, pinching, or pushing.
_____ There will be no weapons at school.
_____ Students will be at their assigned place at proper times.
_____ Students will use all equipment properly and safely.

CONSEQUENCES:

1st Offense: Time out with mediation and contract [see below]. Days in time out determined by completion of contract.
2nd Offense: Time out with mediation; parent contacted by classroom teacher.
3rd Offense: Time out with mediation; conference with parent and principal.

2. Everyone has the right to be respected.

_____ To dress appropriately.
_____ Foul language will not be tolerated.
_____ Destroying property will not be allowed.
_____ Defiance is unacceptable behavior.

CONSEQUENCES:

1st Offense: Time out with mediation and contract. Days in time out determined by completion of contract. Restitution for vandalism/graffiti.
2nd and 3rd Offense: Same as above with possible School Police involvement.

3. Everyone has the right to be drug-free.

_____ Alcohol, drugs, and tobacco will neither be used nor tolerated.

CONSEQUENCES

1st Offense: School Police and parents will be called, counselor referral, in-house suspension.
2nd Offense: School suspension.

4. Everyone has the right to be happy and treated with compassion.

_____ We will not hurt each other's feelings.

CONSEQUENCES

1st Offense: Time out with mediation. Days in time out determined by completion of contract.
2nd and 3rd Offense: Same as above.

Students violating this policy are sent to this school's "Responsibility Room" where they meet with a student mediator (a peer with training in conflict mediation) and fill out the following contract.

MY CONTRACT AND PLAN

1. Why are you here in time out?

2. What is wrong with that behavior?

3. What will you do to keep this from happening again?

_____ Student
_____ Mediator
_____ Parent
_____ Date

Resiliency-Building Intervention Strategies in Secondary Schools

How does a school intervention ("Care" or "Core") team handle students who are referred for serious or repeated violations of the school's discipline policy? Two critical approaches to supporting the resiliency building of students in these situations have been implemented by several schools. First, the intervention team focuses on the strengths of students as well as the problems. Referral forms that include equal space for identifying problems and strengths help assure that the students' strengths are looked at in equal proportion to the risks or problems. The team then poses this question in discussions about the student: "How can we use this person's strengths to facilitate solutions to the problems?"

The second approach involves making sure a student receives some help for his or her problem. Too often, schools send students out the door, assuming they will some how "be better" when they return to school days or weeks later. In reality, without increasing the web of protection diagramed by the Resiliency Wheel [shown on page 164] in all likelihood the students' problems will get worse, and the overall health of the school community as well as that of the student will suffer. A resiliency-building approach adopted by many schools is to require an assessment for alcohol, other drugs, or other significant problems, administered by an in-school or outside agency trained professional, as a stipulation for returning to school. Without this approach, the resiliency of the student and the entire school community may decline.

The following *Statement of Philosophy* attached to the substance abuse prevention and intervention policy of Pojoaque Valley Schools in Pojoaque, New Mexico demonstrates a resiliency-building approach to student assistance.

> The Pojoaque Valley School District recognizes that alcohol and other drug use/abuse is a treatable health problem. Health problems of youth are primarily the responsibility of the home and community; however, the schools share that responsibility because use, misuse, abuse, and dependency problems often interfere with school behavior, student learning, and the maximum development of each student. The schools shall intervene with students manifesting a sign of use, misuse or abuse, and make a concerted and consistent effort to educate and assist them in obtaining appropriate services.

> [The consequences of violating the substance abuse policy are a two-day suspension and] the student cannot be reinstated until a meeting is held with the principal, parent/guardian, student and others as deemed necessary by the Care Team. A no-use drug contract will be signed by the student and witnessed by the parent/guardian. As a part of the reinstatement, the parent must abide by the Care Team recommendation. This may include community service, professional drug use/abuse evaluation, counseling, etc. The parent/guardian and student will present a plan of action that is acceptable.

These are a few of the approaches schools are taking to integrate resiliency building into what has been until recently a deficit-focused arena—school policy. Further involvement of students in the discipline process, including initiation of student courts and tribunals, can be utilized to integrate even more resiliency building into schools. ☺

How We Revised Our School Policy to Foster Student Resiliency

by Georgia Stevens, L.P.C.C.

In the narrative below, school counselor Georgia Stevens details the changes in policy initiated in Rio Rancho Elementary School in Rio Rancho, New Mexico based on staff desire to increase student resiliency. She also offers some results of her initial evaluation as to how the policy revision has changed student attitudes and behaviors.

Bonding with students while making expectations clear is a challenge we've met at our school, using a revitalized discipline program that refers students with repeated problems into social skills development.

Staff training in resiliency concepts and funding through a grant (which paid for the necessary planning time) supported the revision of our entire discipline program. Teachers wanted a program that provided more immediate incentives and consequences as well as the development of intrinsic valuing of appropriate behavior. A team of primary and intermediate teachers, along with our principal and myself, met twice for several hours during the summer three years ago to create a new approach to discipline.

Responsibility was the concept we chose for focus. We wanted students to develop responsibility for themselves, their behavior, and their school. The revised rules, developed by our team, were first discussed with staff, who then discussed them with students in individual classes. They focused on disrespect toward staff and/or school property, foul language, fighting, and unsafe behavior—offenses for which discipline notices called "pink slips" are written. Pink slips can also be issued for serious harmful behavior in the classroom.

Recognition of responsible behavior is given in the revised policy to all students in classrooms where no student has received a pink slip during the previous week. The principal and myself cover playground duty at free recesses, so teachers get a break as well. Five weeks free of pink slips earn new pencils for the entire class, resulting in cheers from the students that can be heard down the school hallways! One additional incentive, carried over from our earlier policy, is also provided: A "Student of the Week" is selected by each classroom teacher, resulting in about 30 names read weekly over the intercom and awards of certificates at local fast-food restaurants presented to the students. The discipline phase of the program hinges on our "Responsibility Room," where students go during a recess soon after receiving a pink slip. We have chosen to use the long recess of 30 minutes after lunch for the "Responsibility Room." Teachers volunteer to staff this room in place of playground duty, and use the time helping students understand what led up to the infraction and what would have been more appropriate behavior. Sometimes an apology is written or a plan is developed for better behavior.

The "Skill Builders" Program

Any student who receives a third pink slip is referred to Skill Builders. Occasionally, a serious infraction will result in a referral when a student has just one or two pink slips. Five consecutive lunch recesses are spent in Skill Builders, followed by four weekly "booster sessions." Middle school students and/or a role model from the referred student's classroom sometimes participate in the skills training to provide positive models and/or inter-environmental reminders of the skills. Letters to parents, signed by the teacher, counselor, and principal, describe the reasons for a student referral to the program, the skills that will be developed, and the ways parents can support the training.

The Skill Builders training is based on cognitive behavioral approaches to behavior change, engaging the students' input, using behavioral rehearsal of covert self-statements, and "body anchors."

Step One Initially, I discuss with students what they enjoy about school and the reasons they want to avoid trouble. They generate a list of consequences they want to avoid and another list of the privileges they seek.

Step Two Next, a list of STOP words is generated—words that students can use to tell themselves to stop long enough to think a situation through. "Relax, it's not worth a pink slip" and "settle down" are covert self-commands that students have suggested for the list. A bilingual student suggested "para" which means "stop." Another suggested "no estoy bien" which in Spanish means, "I'm not well"—a phrase that told him things are not going well and he needs to think about what to do next.

Step Three The next step in the instruction is in consequential thinking, the THINK words. Students complete the sentence, "If I do that...." with short phrases.

Step Four Finally the DO list is introduced, with students generating ideas about ways to handle interpersonal problems. "Walk away," "talk it out," or "tell a teacher" are typical student suggestions. Another popular idea: "get a conflict mediator"—a validation of the credibility of our school-wide mediation program.

A practice phase follows. Students usually work in pairs to generate skits demonstrating use of the skills. The student demonstrating the skill is asked to include the following "body anchors" as he or she practices:

- hold a hand up to cue the STOP step;
- put a finger on the temple to cue the THINK step;
- give a "thumbs up" sign to cue the DO step.

On Fridays students currently in the Skill Builders group meet with students from previous groups for booster sessions. During these Friday sessions, mentors from a neighboring middle school, usually seventh graders, participate by acting in the skits, joining the discussion, giving advice, and occasionally pulling individual students aside to ask how they are doing. Fridays are the time for reflection on the question: "How have you used your STOP, THINK, and DO skills?"

Students graduate from Skill Builders after they have been in school four weeks without additional pink slips. If a Skill Builder does get into trouble, he or she continues to participate in Friday booster sessions until the achievement of four trouble-free weeks. Additional pink slips result in students going through a full Skill Builders program again, followed by four booster sessions. Some students have completed the training several times, and some of these have eventually become my assistants in training other students.

The graduation from Skill Builders consists of a simple party where student participants invite a friend for ice cream or pizza and games. Though these celebrations are uncomplicated, students love them. "This is a cool party" was written on my chalkboard by one student graduate and her friend—a sentiment often expressed by other graduates.

During the school year following graduation from Skill Builders students continue to receive recognition in increasing increments for the time they stay out of trouble. Incentives are offered at four weeks, five weeks, six weeks, etc. Last spring a local restaurant owner, whose son had completed the program, hosted a pizza party at the end of the school year only for students who had stayed out of trouble following their graduation from Skill Builders, as well as the seventh grade mentors. Parents and our school's DARE officer attended, and coupons for merchandize at local businesses were given out to the students at the party.

Results of the Program

Twenty-five students participated in the program during the first year it was implemented. Only 13 of those original program graduates attended our school the next year due to graduation to middle school and families moving out of the area. These 13 students received 25 percent of the pink slips issued in the first year of the program. The following year, this original group received only 12.5 percent of the pink slips issued during the year. Only five of the 13 repeated the program a second time during the second year. School-wide, the number of pink slips issued decreased by 14 percent during the second year of the program.

Further evaluation is needed to validate our anecdotal information and my personal observations that this program appears to increase students' help-seeking ability, use of a more appropriate repertoire of interpersonal skills, and the trust they have in the school staff.

The Faces Of Resiliency

by Nan Henderson, M.S.W.

"Most longitudinal studies of resilient children have noted that they enjoy school, whether nursery school, grade school, or high school and make it a 'home away from home,' a refuge from a dysfunctional household," writes Emmy Werner in her Foreword to Resiliency in Schools: Making It Happen for Students and Educators.

"The more successful inner-city schools tend to maintain realistically high academic standards, provide effective feedback with ample praise, and offer positions of trust and responsibility to their students," she adds. "Such structural support appears to be an especially potent protective factor for children from divorce-prone homes and minority backgrounds."

Tonya Benally, profiled below, is a living example of Emmy Werner's words. Her story demonstrates the power of a school to be "like family," and to provide—in Tonya's case—self-respect, pride, and a vision of a positive future.

Tonya Benally: "School is the Only Family I Have"

Tonya Benally says she used to take the problems she experienced at home "out on myself." She explained that she was in so much pain in a family where she felt a "lack of love and respect and support" she tried suicide three times as a way of dealing with her family problems. "Deep inside it hurt me so bad I couldn't take it anymore," she said, "because they blame me, they criticize me, and it was hard." Tonya's dad was physically abusive, drank a lot, and left when she was 13. But her family has yet to heal.

Tonya, however, has changed. Now 20 years old, she says, "Well that's their problem." And the biggest factor in Tonya's healing is her school.

"The only time I felt good about myself was when I went to school," Tonya says of the last two years of her life, during which she has attended an alternative school, Gallup Central, in Gallup, New Mexico. She described what happened to her there: "I [asked] the people at school, 'Why do you put up with me?' 'Because you're so good' [they

answered]. I was like, 'Yeah, right.' You know I tried to put myself down in front of my teachers and they'd say, 'You're not like that, Tonya.' It just blows the negative thoughts out of my mind. And I feel good for the rest of the day."

School was not always such a positive place for Tonya either. She went to a traditional high school before attending Gallup Central, and by the time she was 15 she was failing. She was using alcohol and other drugs, partially as a way to try to cope with the pain of her family situation, and was "ditching school all the time, drinking on campus, and getting suspended." Then she heard about a new alternative school opening in Gallup and she decided to enroll.

"At first it felt kind of funny," Tonya said "because the teachers were paying more attention to you. I don't usually get this attention. But the more they made it fun and exciting, the more I wanted to be there. [These things] encouraged me every day to go to school.... And I really put effort in."

Tonya had special praise for the school librarian, Ms. Hill. Tonya described her as "always nice, smiling, giving us compliments.

When I go in there, and I have a frown on my face, she says, 'What's wrong?' She just brightens your day, and you forget about all the bad things. At one point, I wasn't really doing my work. She used to tell me, 'Tonya, you go sit down over there and I won't let anybody bother you.' And she was real. She said, 'If it makes you feel better, I'll do my work, too.'" Tonya added, "She puts a different perspective on life for us, you know. The library feels like my home because she is always there."

Tonya likes the size of her school, only 150 students, and the fact that though the students are several ethnicities, including Native American, Hispanic, and Caucasian, they all get along. She also commented on all the different activities in the school, including a ropes course, numerous field trips, and parties and movies that the faculty plans.

"School is the only family I have."

"They tell us, 'We are a family.' We hear that from the principal all the time. That's why I go to school every day. Because I have people there that respect me and talk to me. I don't get that much attention at home. And there's a lot of things that I did not do in [traditional] high school that I wanted to do. Right now I am succeeding."

Tonya was just chosen as "Senior of the Month." She was asked to speak to the school board about her school. And she is graduating this spring. She said she dreads graduating, and added the fact she has to go "is making me suffer." She does intend to go to college, but is thinking of enrolling in the Job Corps first, saving money, and then attending college. When asked about what she might want to do for a career, she said, "I love the stars. I might study astronomy. I also like criminal justice. I love computers. I like music and art. I plan to go into graphic art. There's so many things I want to do."

Tonya also credits her friends for helping her turn her life around. She said she had some friends that were a negative influence but others that "told me it wasn't worth doing drugs and alcohol, to think about my future, and that the only way you can have respect from others is to do things for yourself." One friend in particular, who has already graduated from the alternative school, helped Tonya. "She was much older than I am, five years older, and she helped me get on the right track. She'd say, 'I'll pick you up at school. And I'll take you to school.' She'd like be 'mom.' And I found love and respect [from her] and my other friends at school."

Tonya's advice to adults who want to help kids bounce back is partially based on her experiences in in-patient therapy programs that she didn't find helpful. She said adults should "take it one step at a time. You know, you can't reach kids by pulling them in, you can't just throw out a rope and pull them in. You have to be steady and just take it easy. You have to wait. It's like putting a trap out for them, and you know, they'll keep coming closer and closer. And finally, you'll catch them." The bait, she added, is "love and respect." Most kids that are doing alcohol and other drugs experience a lack of respect and support, she said.

Tonya still can't quite believe the way her life has turned around. "I'm getting As and Bs and I used to have Ds and Fs all the time. It surprises me, especially when people want to interview me and take me places. I'm like, 'Are you sure it's me?' I'm surprised at myself too. But I'm so proud of myself, I just want to keep going. That pride keeps me up and doing what I like best, being in school." ❂

A Resiliency Resource Primer

Resiliency and Schools

by Bonnie Benard, M.S.W.

What follows are some of my favorites; however, this is far from an exhaustive list and many wonderful resources are not included. Also keep in mind that most of these books do not use the language of resilience but are about it nonetheless as they are focused on creating caring communities within schools that meet the developmental needs of children, youth, and adults for belonging, respect, power, and meaning.

Boyd, Julie, and Dalton, Joan (1992). ***I Teach: A Guide to Inspiring Classroom Leadership***. Portsmouth, NH: Heinemann. *This is a "walk your talk" book grounded in the assumption that the key to learning and human development for students is the teacher's commitment to his or her own learning and growth. Through stories, vignettes, diagrams, charts, and activities, this book honors all learning styles and builds in active participation and reflection around its key themes of empowerment, relationship-building, modeling, and creating a community of learners.*

Curwin, Richard (1992). ***Rediscovering Hope: Our Greatest Teaching Strategy.*** Bloomington, IN: National Educational Services. *This engaging book is premised on the belief that society's greatest risk factor is youth without hope. In compelling chapter after chapter this book offers educators the opportunity to reflect on how their school structures, policies, and practices either destroy or create hope—the key to learning and life success.*

Delpit, Lisa (1995). ***Other People's Children: Cultural Conflict in the Classroom.*** New York, NY: The New Press. *This book of essays pierces to the heart of how schools must change if we are to successfully educate teachers to become successful educators of children of all ethnicities and cultures. Caring relationships, high expectations, and opportunities to be heard and to participate underlie the many stories in this volume of teachers who successfully are educating across cultural differences.*

Diero, Judith (1996). ***Teaching With Heart: Making Healthy Connections with Students.*** Thousand Oaks, CA: Corwin Press. *This book reports the author's qualitative study of six teachers in six different high schools who are known for their positive relationships with students. Besides being rich in the voices of wonderful teachers and their students, this book identifies the nature of teacher-student relationships that make a difference, the traits, experiences, skills of these teachers; and the characteristics of schools that support nurturing.*

Fullan, Michael (1993). ***Change Forces: Probing the Depths of Educational Reform.*** New York, NY: Falmer Press. *This small-in-size bible of educational reform, drawing much on Peter Senge's theory of learning communities, clearly documents that educational change is inside-out change, beginning in the hearts and minds of individuals who share a vision and begin to build a critical mass that, indeed, can change the world.*

Gandara, Patricia (1995). ***Over the Ivy Walls: The Educational Mobility of Low-Income Chicanos.*** Albany, NY: State University of New York Press. *This qualitative study of fifty high-achieving (doctoral level) Mexican Americans from low-income families (the only one specific to this cultural group that I know of) explores how these individuals succeeded academically despite the odds and makes several recommendations for educational reforms that challenge many current assumptions—based as they are on research on middle-class European Americans students and their families. Not only is this a compelling read rich in the stories of these students, it validates the power of the school to make a difference as well as the power of a bright future—"a culture of possibility"—to motivate and sustain.*

Garbarino, James, et al. (1992). *Children in Danger: Coping with the Consequences of Community Violence.* San Francisco, CA: Jossey-Bass. *After documenting, through interviews with children and caregivers and supporting research, the realities of life for children growing up in "war zones" in the U.S., the authors document the critical importance the school plays as a safe haven, with the most important factor promoting children's mental health being a caring relationship between a teacher and his or her pupils—from pre-school through high-school.*

Gibbs, Jeanne (1995). *Tribes: A New Way of Learning Together.* Sausalito, CA: CenterSource Systems. *Tribes is the best process I know for building communities in classrooms and schools that are rich in caring relationships, opportunities for participation, and high and positive expectations. This revision of her earlier manual is grounded in resiliency and incorporates new research on cooperative learning, brain compatible learning, multiple intelligences, thematic instruction, human development, and social systems. And, for all you hands-on people, about half this book consists of activities.*

Henderson, Nan, and Milstein, Mike (1996). *Resiliency in Schools: Making It Happen for Students and Educators.* Thousand Oaks, CA: Corwin Press. *A guide, par none, for schoolwide reform that incorporates the principles of resiliency. This book is rich with examples and tools to be used in creating resiliency-building schools. As Emmy Werner states in her Foreword, this book "should be read by all administrators, teachers, and parents concerned with the future of their children."*

Hooks, Bell (1995). *Teaching to Transgress: Education as the Practice of Freedom.* New York, NY: Routledge. *Creating learning communities wherein students are not only encouraged to challenge authority but taught to "transgress" against racial, sexual, and class boundaries in order to achieve the gift of freedom is the essence of teaching and the focus of this author's account of her life as a teacher and social justice activist. This book demonstrates critical pedagogy in action and how members of oppressed groups can move beyond blame to compassion and community activism.*

Institute for Education in Transformation (1992). *Voices from the Inside: A Report on Schooling from Inside the Classroom.* Claremont, CA: Claremont Graduate School. *This short report documents a study done on a school which is actually based on the voices of teachers, students, and parents (a rarity indeed!). The issue of caring relationships is raised as the Number One concern of these groups and identified by them as the root cause of lowered achievement, high dropout rates, and burned-out teachers. Ironically, the evaluation process used in studying this school, based as it was in an empowerment process, actually began a process of school and classroom transformation.*

Journal for A Just and Caring Education (began January 1995). Thousand Oaks, CA: Corwin Press. *A wonderful new journal whose mission "is to develop the idea of schools as sanctuaries in a tumultuous world and to promote the right of all children to a just and caring education." It focuses "on what schools can do to ensure that all children are valued, have a safe and secure environment in which to learn, and have opportunities to experience kindness and cooperation."*

Kohl, Herb (1994). *I Won't Learn from You.* New York, NY: The New Press. *Titled after his powerful essay which documents the phenomenon of refusing to learn (i.e., resistance) when a student's intelligence, dignity, or integrity is compromised by a teacher, an institution, or a larger social mindset, this book of five essays takes on—in Kohl's passionate and compelling style—all the Big Ones: Hope, Excellence, Equality, Equity, Democracy in Education. Especially great are his discussions of how caring teachers must "creatively maladjust" (requires all the resiliency traits!) to work in dysfunctional systems—and his passionate discourse on the at-risk label.*

Kohn, Alfie (1993). *The Brighter Side of Human Nature: Altruism and Empathy in Everday Life.* New York, NY: Basic Books. *Kohn definitely makes the case—supported as always by tons of research —that schools that promote the development of caring offer the hope of personal and social transformation. All of Kohn's books support the resiliency perspective and provide research documentation extraordinaire (also see his books, No Contest: The Case Against Competition and Punished By Rewards: The Trouble with Gold Stars, Incentive Plans, A's, Praise, and Other Bribes.*

McCombs, Barbara, and Pope, James (1995). ***Motivating Hard to Reach Students.*** Hyattsville, MD: American Psychology Association. *Operating from the assumption that all students are motivated to learn under the right conditions, this interactive book helps the teacher to create these conditions (i.e., protective factors) in the classroom. It also explains a process for helping students understand how their own conditioned thoughts interfere with accessing their innate resilience, motivation, and desire to learn.*

Meier, Deborah (1995). ***The Power of Their Ideas: Lessons for America from a Small School in Harlem.*** Boston, MA: Beacon Press. *Meier, nationally known for "turning around" an inner-city, culturally diverse high school in Harlem (where 90% of the students now graduate and 90% of those go on to college), tells her remarkable story in this book. For any skeptics asking if resiliency-focused school reform works, give them this book. Also a critical pedagogist, Meier argues for education that is caring, built on community, based on questioning and critical thinking, grounded in high expectations for all in students, and participation by all—including parents and community.*

Moffet, James (1994). ***The Universal Schoolhouse: Spiritual Awakening through Education.*** San Francisco, CA: Jossey-Bass. *Moffet challenges the school reform movement to reach beyond bureaucratic and corporate interests and to take on a more transformative mission by creating education that centers on personal growth, including growth of the spirit—education that enables students to adapt and thrive in spite of societal challenges and technological change. The structure for this visionary education is decentralized community-learning networks which, in essence, serve to rebuild community between young and old.*

Munson, Patricia (1991). ***Winning Teachers: Teaching Winners.*** Santa Cruz, CA: ETR Associates. *I love this little book focused on teacher's self-esteem (i.e., resiliency) as the key to successful school change. Filled with vignettes, pithy statements, and lots of passion, this book is a real boost to educators' self-esteem!*

Noddings, Nel (1992). ***The Challenge to Care in Schools: An Alternative Approach to Education.*** New York, NY: Teachers College Press. *An absolutely essential book and the "classic" on what a caring school looks like. Noddings creates a vision of a school system built on the central mission of caring (which in her model incorporates the other protective factors of high expectations and opportunities for participation)and which is organized around centers of care: care for self, for intimate others, for associates and friends, for distant others, for nonhuman animals, for plants and the physical environment, for the human-made world of objects and instruments, and for ideas.*

Polakow, Valerie (1993). ***Lives on the Edge: Single Mothers and their Children in the Other America.*** Chicago, IL: University of Chicago Press. *Using the language of "at promise" (i.e., resilience), this powerful and eloquent book takes on not only the "at-risk" label but shows in classroom vignette after vignette how a teacher's high or low expectations either create possibility and hope or resignation and despair for poor children of color in inner-city schools. "An ethic of caring and a new way of seeing" the strengths of poor children and their families are the keys to successfully educating and empowering our children in these contexts and "for the unmaking of poverty and the Other America."*

Seligman, Martin, et al. (1995). ***The Optimistic Child: A Revolutionary Program that Safeguards Children Against Depression and Builds Lifelong Resilience.*** New York, NY: Houghton Mifflin. *This book by a premier psychologist provides a step-by-step process for parents and teachers to teach children the skills of that powerful resilience trait, optimism—the metacognitive skills to change conditioned thinking and the social skills that will help children be connected to others. Seligman makes the convincing case that this approach can transform helplessness into mastery and reduce the risk of depression. It can also boost school performance, improve physical health, and provide children with the sense of autonomy they need to approach their teenage years.*

Sergiovanni, Thomas (1993). ***Building Community in Schools.*** San Francisco, CA: Jossey-Bass. *The essential book for administrators on fostering resiliency in schools written by the premier authority on principalship. Sergiovanni challenges educators to change their basic metaphor for schooling to that of community-building, which means changing their basic thoughts and beliefs about students, teachers, and parents. "If we want to rewrite the script to enable good schools to flourish, we need to rebuild community." This book guides the way.*

Stewart, Darlene (1991). ***Creating the Teachable Moment: An Innovative Approach to Teaching and Learning.*** Blue Ridge Summit, PA: TAB Books. *Applying metacognitive psychology to working with students, this book helps teachers and counselors to understand the role their own thinking and moods makes in creating a positive climate for learning. Illustrated through her personal story and the stories of students she's worked with, Stewart presents an approach grounded in the principles of caring relationships, high expectations, and reciprocity—and shows how easy and fun teaching can be from this perspective.*

Swadener, Beth Blue, and Lubeck, Sally, eds. (1995). ***Children and Families "at Promise": Deconstructing the Discourse of Risk.*** Albany, NY: State University of New York Press. *The thirteen articles in this volume provide a powerful collection of both policy analysis and descriptive research studies capturing classroom"success stories" of survival, wisdom, courage, and strength in the face of apparent overwhelming odds. This book makes an eloquent plea for reframing the discourse that surrounds children and families who are poor, of color, and / or native speakers of languages other than English.*

Wang, Margaret, and Gordon, Edmund, eds. (1994). ***Educational Resilience in Inner-City America: Challenges and Prospects.*** Hillsdale, NJ: Lawrence Erlbaum Associates. *This edited volume is a must for anyone studying resilience in schools and for anyone in a position to shape public policy or deliver educational and human services, especially to urban schools. It offers numerous suggestions for furthering a research agenda focused on the study of resilience in schools.* ☉

PART THREE

Resiliency and Communities

From The Editors

The Philosophy and Mission of *Resiliency In Action*

What does the term "resiliency" really mean? Is resiliency simply bouncing back from stress and adversity or does it mean something more? What should be the long-term mission of a publishing company devoted to the topic of resiliency? These are some of the questions the editors of this journal recently grappled with during a week end meeting devoted to outlining a path for *Resiliency In Action* over the next several years.

We decided that resiliency is in fact much more than just successfully "coping with life's challenges," that inherent in the resiliency process is human transformation and transcendence. We envisioned a purpose for this journal that goes beyond just publishing research and information. Our discussions resulted in the following philosophy and mission, which we hope our readers will share:

> *The philosophy of* Resiliency In Action, Inc. *is that resiliency is an innate self-righting and transcending ability within all children, youth, adults, organizations, and communities.*
>
> *The mission of* Resiliency In Action, Inc. *is to foster resiliency by:*
> 1. *Disseminating resiliency-related information;*
> 2. *Facilitating the practical application and evaluation of the resiliency paradigm; and*
> 3. *Sustaining a national and international grass roots resiliency network.*

This issue of *Resiliency In Action* embodies both the philosophy and mission. Bonnie Benard's contribution on resiliency in communities on page 81 illustrates the philosophy of resiliency applied in community settings. The journey of one 17-year-old burdened early in his life with the "at risk" label, described in "Faces of Resiliency," page 79, illustrates how young people emerge as transcendent over both the challenges in their lives and the challenges of their labels.

Kerry Anne Ridley shows exactly how to use resiliency research in assessing and planning with clients in community agencies. A series of articles on KIDS Consortium illustrate why this organization's "community as classroom" approach has been so positively evaluated by Muskie Institute of Public Affairs and why it was awarded the 1996 National Planning Award for Public Education by the American Planning Association.

We again invite all of our readers to take part in the "networking" opportunity of this publication by sharing your comments, suggestions, and manuscripts. We also encourage and need your submissions of what is working to produce resiliency in your life and in the lives of the people you serve.

Nan Henderson, M.S.W.,

Bonnie Benard, M.S.W.,
Editors

Nancy Sharp-Light

Resiliency In Practice

Transforming Community Social Services Using Resiliency and Protective Factors Inventories

by Kerry Anne Ridley, L.C.D.D.

Imagine for a moment that you are gathered around a table with a group of caring professionals. It is your mission to define specific problems and recommend potential solutions for a troubled young person. A meal is served. The appetizer is a history of individual and family pathology. The main course is a description of the student's current academic, emotional, or social challenges complete with a comprehensive list of interventions that have either been successful or failed. If strengths are a focus, typically they are served as dessert. Full from the main meal, you must find a way to make room for the strength information.

For a variety of reasons this metaphorical meal is steeped in a history of deficiency. Habits emerge in this typical case planning process that reinforce a predominant emphasis on the client's lack of mental health and a true emphasis on resiliency is excluded.

Community agencies or schools often fall into these pessimistic habits because they lack a systematic structure to gather information regarding a client's internal character strengths and external protective factors. *The Resiliency Inventory* and the *Protective Factors Inventory* provide a structured process to document and understand the source of individual and family mental health.

A group of social workers and paraprofessionals involved in a three year demonstration grant through the Department of Justice in Austin, Texas have used *The Resiliency Inventory* alone on an experimental basis to guide their case planning process and both *The Resiliency Inventory* and the *Protective Factors Inventory* to help plan for termination of services to clients and their families.

This Department of Justice demonstration grant had been designed to provide intensive individualized in-home and in-school intervention services for youth considered "at risk" for academic failure or delinquency. These young people and their family members had experienced multiple and fragmented social services delivered by various agencies. The idea behind the grant was to keep the child's family stable and the young person out of trouble by developing a trusting relationship with a staff member who could provide "one-stop shopping" to service the families' diverse needs. The staff members developed close relationships with the families, and each of these relationships shared an essential quality similar to that of a neighbor, relative, or helping friend—they could count on them in times of need.

> *"Community agencies or schools often fall into pessimistic habits because they lack a systematic structure to gather information regarding a client's internal character strengths and external protective factors."*

My initial involvement with the grant was focused on strengthening the mental health of and relationships between the grant project staff. This was a very talented and committed group of individuals. Ultimately the training deepened an already strong "can do" spirit among the team members that was expanded into their interactions with youth and family members. Early efforts involved team building using a physical challenge course that required team members to work together to accomplish a shared goal. They also developed an understanding of states of mind which resulted in optimistic thinking and resilient reactions, and they developed conflict resolution skills. Staff members became familiar with resiliency research and *The Resiliency Inventory* (see sample questions, p. 74). Through this series of trainings I gathered a realistic understanding of day-to-day staff challenges while I established credibility with the staff.

Resiliency research outcomes reinforced staff members' personal experiences of overcoming hardship and an intuitive sense that "their kids" could make it. As they began to use *The Resiliency Inventory* and the *Protective Factors Inventory* with a few individual clients they were able to see the value of noticing the environment or person or activity that seemed to be health producing for their client.

The Resiliency Inventory is an adult-centered instrument. It reflects either the teacher, social worker, or parents' perception of the young person's resilient strengths. Learning to use *The Resiliency Inventory* was easy for this staff. They followed four steps: becoming familiar with the eleven Resiliency Factors, observing or reflecting on a student's behavior, recording this information and key insights on the inventory, and planning a beneficial course of action. Approximately two years into the project, efforts were initiated to graduate families from the program, as the funding was phased and would soon run out. The grant project had achieved impressive results. As reported in the December 30, 1994 issue of the *New York Times*, "From 1991, the year before the project began, to 1993, the project's second year, juvenile arrests in the target area rose at one third the rate of other poor sections of the city.... In the project's first year, the children who received intervention had half the involvement with the courts as the control group." These results were based upon the close and sometimes informal daily contact with grant staff. Staff members did everything from bring chicken soup to a sick child at home alone to receive phone calls from teachers when grades slipped or a class was cut. These relationships blurred traditional social work boundaries and thus made the closure or "graduation" process more complicated for project staff and clients. Weaning individuals from staff services proved more challenging than termination of clients from a more traditional social service structure.

> *"Most young people growing up in adversity will grow into healthy adulthood. Sixty-five to seventy percent of the young people they had helped would go on to live a happy and healthy life."*

As I consulted with the grant staff on the graduation process, I became aware of a pessimistic and discouraged tone that was out of character for these

> *"Staff members did everything from bring chicken soup to a sick child at home alone to receive calls from teachers when grades slipped or class was cut. These relationships blurred traditional social work boundaries...."*

individuals. They were worried. How could their clients continue to make progress without staff support when they stumbled? Who would negotiate the complex web of social services with them? How could a staff member now face a parent who thanked the heavens whenever they helped her family learn to resolve a conflict without violence to inform the family they would soon "graduate" from grant services? Why did such good social service programs always end just after they proved their effectiveness? Would the staff members find new fulfilling work? These were normal questions tinged with the loss of not being able to continue working with their clients whom they had come to care for so deeply. It was a time of intense change.

I gently challenged the staff to look at the trickle down effect if their attitude remained negative. I did this with a few of my own questions. What was the "story" inherent in their attitudes that was being communicated about each client's ability to manage his or her life? Were clients being shown both their long-standing and new found strengths to handle life challenges? Were staff members communicating a future of possibility or limitation? Then I reminded them of the resiliency research we had learned about earlier. Most young people growing up in adversity will grow into healthy adulthood. Sixty-five to seventy percent of the young people they had helped would go on to live a happy and healthy life.

There is a Sufi saying that guides much of my consultation work. "Necessity breeds new organs of perception." This saying speaks to the fact that meaningful change often does not take hold until an individual or organization "knows in their bones" current behaviors are not working and are internally motivated to change. It wasn't until the staff members were faced with their own patterned "at risk" thinking habits that they became motivated to structure a process that was firmly focused on resiliency-enhancing hope for the future.

We decided to use both *The Resiliency Inventory* and the *Protective Factors Interview* as tools to guide the staff and family members through a closure process focused on their strengths and needs. This planning process, we decided, would encompass a major portion of the graduation ritual. Though not every counselor participated in this process, those who did found it to be very helpful in shifting their attitude. In addition, the youth and their families were often surprised at how capable they really were once all their strengths and support systems were documented.

The graduation process began with the youth client and his or her family meeting with the case worker. An overview of the graduation process was shared by the counselor. A brief overview of resiliency and protective factors philosophy and research was also shared. The basic message was one of "you are capable; as a family you have long-standing strengths and skills; and together we will plan for needs outside of your current support system." In addition to long-standing abilities families were asked to describe additional skills and knowledge they had received as a result of participating in grant services. The goal was to help the family members articulate what they could do and handle after grant services ended.

Use of the *Protective Factors Interview* (see sample questions, p. 74) and the *Protective Factors Inventory* in this process centered on the perception of the young person. The interview tool explored relationships or activities that provide caring and support, high expectations, and meaningful participation and contribution to better understand the young person's perception of the people, values, and activities which buffer him or her from adversity. Experience has shown that helping professionals often value protective factors differently than do young people

> *"It wasn't until the staff members were faced with their own patterned 'at risk' thinking habits, that they became motivated to structure a process that was firmly focused on resiliency-enhancing hope for the future."*

and their families. Therefore, regardless of the helper's perception, we wanted to know who the young person perceived as an ally; whom he or she listens to; his or her areas of interest and motivation; and finally, the expectations he or she holds for himself or herself.

This interview process is instructive to the helper and the client as it not only reveals when individuals have opportunities for meaningful participation but also when those opportunities are lacking. The helper now has a comprehensive portrait of the young person, including both the internal character strengths and the external support system. From this balanced portrait strategies are developed using the relationships and existing strengths to influence a healthy future.

Infusing a resiliency perspective is a process, not an event. True transformation requires an ongoing relationship with a trusted teacher or change agent. Ideally this individual is clear on the value of focusing on mental health vs. dysfunction, is compassionate towards early resistance to a new approach, and is patiently waiting for the "teachable moment" when learning takes hold and develops a life of its own. *The Resiliency Inventory* and the *Protective Factors Inventory* can provide a structured process to gather information, increase awareness of healthy functioning, and value the young person's perception of his or her situation. I applaud those of you who are currently involved in this process. Those considering this worthy "leap of faith" will find that the benefits serve you and your clients in surprising ways. ◉

Kerry Anne Ridley, L.C.D.D., is a trainer and consultant who assists schools and businesses in shifting from a predominantly "at risk" orientation to resiliency-focused practices. She is the author of The Resiliency Inventory. *She lives in Austin, Texas and welcomes your experiences related to resiliency. Contact her at (512-477-1310) or by e-mail: (karidley@aol.com).*

The Resiliency Inventory: SAMPLE QUESTIONS

RESILIENCY FACTORS		PRIMARY BEHAVIORS	OBSERVED		
			Rarely	Sometimes	Frequently
	Chooses positive alternatives	1. Tends toward keeping out of trouble; i.e., guides self and others toward positive alternatives that may be unpopular	☐	☐	☐
		2. Sees self in positive light	☐	☐	☐
		3. Attempts different actions to approach the same problem	☐	☐	☐
		4. Exhibits independence appropriate for own culture	☐	☐	☐
	Tolerates frustration	1. Is able to show s/he does not know something	☐	☐	☐
		2. Uses varied approaches for communication of frustrations	☐	☐	☐
		3. Shows ability to prevent future frustration, e.g., through asking for help or talking a problem out	☐	☐	☐
		4. Shows respect for own and others' property and emotional boundaries	☐	☐	☐
	Sense of humor	1. Shows enjoyment of humor	☐	☐	☐
		2. Uses humor to defuse conflict or reduce tension	☐	☐	☐
		3. Helps self and/or others through humor	☐	☐	☐
		4. Creates humor	☐	☐	☐

PROTECTIVE FACTORS INTERVIEW

CARING AND SUPPORT

1. Over the years who has consistently believed in you and supported you? Give an example of HOW they have done this over the years.
2. Who in your family can you turn to for support? (Parents, grandparents, aunts, cousins, etc.)
3. What friend(s) do you turn to for support during hard times?
4. Over the years, what teacher has meant a lot to you? Give an example of WHY you liked this particular teacher so much.

CONTRIBUTION-EFFICACY

1. Have you participated in any volunteer community activities to help others? Give an example of what you did and how often you do helping activities.
2. Describe something you have done that you are proud of doing (friends, home, school, neighborhood).
3. If you could fix one problem in the world, what would it be? What skills do you have to help solve this problem?

The following profile of the KIDS Consortium ELF Woods Project is reprinted by permission from the Spring, 1995 issue of Voices of Change, *a publication of the Maine Center for Educational Services in Auburn, Maine. The journal was funded by a grant from the Pugh Charitable Trust.*

Sharing the Power: The ELF Woods Project Taps the Energy and Talents of Students as They Improve Their Community

The "snake trail" was a winding, eroded tar path, east of Edward Little High School in Auburn, Maine, neglected, littered, and notorious as a hangout for truants and troublemakers. In the fall of 1992 Brian Flynn, an English teacher, challenged his students to a simple writing assignment: "What would you do to improve the snake trail?" At first, students dreamed up impossible ideas—a water slide, castle, chair lift, flame throwing lights—and then some practical ones—a gazebo, pond, campground, trail system.... As students grew excited about the possibilities, they began to insist, "Instead of just talking about fixing up the area, why don't we actually do something?"

Since that time, over 300 students have been involved in designing and implementing a 50-page master plan to transform 40 acres of wilderness into a place that is safe, aesthetically pleasing, environmentally sound, and enjoyable for students and community residents alike. The master plan outlines the purpose, benefit, necessary modifications, term for completion, cost, and required manpower for the following six recommendations:

- 400-yard walkway resurfaced with asphalt and accented with cobblestone;
- Lights to facilitate evening commutes;
- Landscaping including picnic tables, benches, trash receptacles, and signs;
- Mountain biking trail with switchbacks and berms;
- Cross country trail for competitive athletic use;
- Obstacle course, complete with walls, tire swings, ropes, cargo net, and rocks.

The Model

The ELF (Edward Little Franklin) Woods Project is one of dozens fostered by the KIDS (Kids Involved Doing Service) Consortium, a 501(c)(3) private, nonprofit organization. KIDS as Planners is an innovative educational process [facilitated by KIDS Consortium] which engages students in working to solve real-life problems in their communities as part of math, science, English, social studies, and other subjects. In addition to land-use planning, students of all ages in over 50 towns across New England are protecting wildlife, preserving cultural artifacts, documenting local history, assessing public health, cleaning up rivers and ponds, designing parks and playgrounds, and generally "getting involved" in making a difference, not as a "nice" activity, but as an integral part of comprehensive planning and educational reform efforts.

The process directly addresses academic failure and lack of social bonding, the risk factors most common to substance abuse, juvenile delinquency, teen pregnancy, suicide, school dropout, and other destructive behaviors. In fact, research has shown that opportunities for young people to participate in the life of the community enables them to develop problem solving abilities, social competence, autonomy, and a sense of hope and future—attributes that enable them to "bounce back" from "at risk" environments.

The Town as the Classroom

Auburn sits on the Androscoggin River which, 20 years ago, provided lifeblood to dozens of shoe and textile manufacturing companies. But today, unemployment stands at 9%. The changes within the community are leading to changes in its schools. Over the past two years, a design team comprised of school and community members has been developing a strategic plan to restructure education in the Auburn school system "so that all students learn and succeed in a changing world."

The ELF Woods Project is the manifestation of this bold new approach to education. While English classes are still responsible for reading literature, building vocabulary, and writing journals and book reports, the City of Auburn has become the "test" for learning and applying these skills in a real-world context. In addition to writing, revising, and editing the master plan, students are involved in the following activities:

- Research, from conducting a site analysis to plot topography, wildlife, vegetation, water flow, and other natural features to investigating present and desired uses of the property through interviews with students and community residents and an analysis of historical records;
- Public speaking, from debate and consensus-making with fellow students to negotiation with city officials and formal presentations to the student body, school board, city council, civic organizations, and national audiences;
- Using technology to design maps, illustrations, charts, and timelines to effectively communicate the desired vision;
- Teaching, from producing television and film clips to apprenticing younger students and facilitating groups of teachers to help them plan community projects.

> *"Through the ELF Woods Project, students have been able to develop and apply a variety of talents including linguistic, logical, spatial, artistic, interpersonal, and leadership abilities."*

In order to balance the demands of content and process, teachers must establish parameters within which students can share the power and take responsibility for their own learning. Ultimately, "sharing the power" works both ways. When a teacher empowers students to make decisions about their own learning, they, in turn, must be willing to share their talents with the group. Through the ELF Woods Project, students have been able to develop and apply a variety of talents including linguistic, logical, spatial, artistic, interpersonal, and leadership abilities. Greg Lavertu, class of '94, admits that he was classified as an "at risk" student, "which means I wasn't supposed to get

this far." But the experience helped him grow, and now, as a student at Unity College and a member of the Maine Conservation Corps, he recognizes that "everybody has something to offer, and it's our duty as intellects and human beings to take what that person has to offer." Sharing the power is the process that values student abilities and demands student performance.

Apprentice Citizenship

"If we are to apprentice young people as citizens of a democratic society, educators must value the application of knowledge over the mere acquisition of knowledge," asserts Marvin Rosenblum, executive director of the KIDS Consortium. "Every kid deserves the opportunity to make a difference." Indeed, what makes KIDS as Planners different from other "project-

> *"If we are to apprentice young people as citizens of a democratic society, educators must value the application of knowledge over the mere acquisition of knowledge."*

based," "hands-on," and experiential learning methodologies is that students take action. Josh Stevens, a junior, explains, "Without approval, the master plan would have been just a 50-page plan sitting on a shelf somewhere." Instead, the students set up a referendum and brought it to the student body at Edward Little. The outcome? Over 360 students voted in favor, with only 59 opposed—a resounding six to one ratio.

From there, students presented the plan to the school board and then to the city council, finally negotiating a $15,000 Community Development Block Grant to implement the plan. To date, students have raised over $34,000 with help from 30 public and private agencies, including International Paper, Maine Community Foundation, Geiger Bros., General Electric, and Project SEED. Public officials and private citizens have also served as important resources. Lee Jay Feldman, Auburn city planner, helped students develop the master plan. John Footer, a local stone mason, helped students harvest cobblestones. Specialists from the Soil and Water Conservation District certified control measures. A professional surveyor assisted students in plotting the features of the obstacle course. Currently, students are negotiating with General Durgan of the Air Force

National Guard to provide about $80,000 worth of cable for the lights.

This kind of personal achievement is both public and permanent. "When students accept challenges and act on them, their success is what really builds self esteem," reflects Alumni Allen Campbell. There is no substitute for creating something with your own mind, writing something with your own pen, or building something with your own two hands. Ironically, students have said that it is not what other people do for them that gives them confidence and strength, but what they do for themselves and what they do for other people in their community. Most of the time you will find that they have just never been asked.

> *"Ironically, students have said that it is not what other people do for them that gives them confidence and strength, but what they do for themselves and what they do for other people in their community."*

Critical Mass

Last year, the KIDS Concortium trained over 600 people in the KIDS model. By bringing together educators, preventionists, public officials, business leaders, and community members to explore their own town as a classroom, KIDS workshops serve as catalysts to help schools break free of the "special project" design that plagues so many educational innovations. They also help create a critical mass of people willing to work together to structure and sustain learning opportunities that empower young people.

At Edward Little, for example, the ELF Woods Project has fostered interdisciplinary learning. Pam Buffington, a computer technology teacher, helped students generate professional reports and products for the project. With the help of science teacher Margaret Wilson, students created scientific extracts to document flora and fauna native to the woods. This year, as a spinoff to the ELF Woods project, students in Tina Vanasse's geometry classes are designing and building a greenhouse that will operate as a student-run business.

Students are not problems to be solved but priceless resources with talent and energy. Likewise, teachers are not repositories of information but guides and facilitators for student learning. "Mr. Flynn looked to us for answers as much, if not more, than we did to him," reflects Greg Lavertu. When, at last, schools, towns, businesses, and community-based organizations can share the power of their talents and expertise, we can create learning that empowers and education that matters. ☯

KIDS Beautify Norwich's Heritage Walkway

by the Norwich Connecticut Schools' Third Grade Classes

One day we were studying social studies. We talked about our community and what was fun in Norwich. One of the places we mentioned was Heritage Walkway. It is a 1.4 mile walkway that starts at the marina and ends at the old powerhouse on the Yantic River. We noticed that the walk was very dirty. People treated it like a trash can. We wanted to clean it up. It is important to all of us that nature is clean.

We made a plan to pick up trash, to plant flowers, and to put up some birdhouses. We listed all the things we needed to do the job. Then we listed the materials and the equipment we would need. Then we asked ourselves what steps would be needed. Then we put the steps in order. We thought of possible problems. Once we were done doing that we thought of the solutions for all of them.

We wrote a letter to Ms. Bram-Mereen, the assistant city planner, and asked if the third grade classes and Mrs. Mercier's kindergarten class could help clean it up. She sent a letter back saying we could help out on the city's Earth Day Cleanup. We invited her to come to talk to us about it. She gave us maps and told us that after the cleanup we would all have pizza and soda. She also gave our school a banner for taking part in the cleanup.

On Saturday, April 20, parents helped us to clean up. Ms. Bram-Mereen took care of the garbage cans and bags. We took care of the gloves. We worked hard for two hours. Ms. Bram-Mereen gave us little rose patches to thank us for helping.

We chose to plant flowers at a place near the power house. So far we have tested the soil for its pH level, worked the soil to remove grass and weeds, and planted some day lilies. Pretty soon we will plant more flowers. Then we will put up some bird houses that our families have made and sent in.

We Learned a Few Things, Too

Many varied and unusual things that we've learned along the way during our Heritage Walkway Project are:

- letter writing
- telephone manners
- making graphs
- writing math story problems
- testing soil for the pH level
- what perennials and annuals are
- estimating how long it takes to walk a mile
- estimating area
- estimating perimeter
- measuring area & perimeter
- measuring distances
- dividing tools among groups
- planning projects
- making decisions
- drawing murals
- working in groups
- writing summaries
- adding details to paragraphs
- using the computer to write
- drawing on the computer
- making a computer report about our project
- talking to people who can help us learn about our community
- helping our community is fun
- planting seeds and watching them grow
- learning what plants need to grow
- how birds like their own space

The Faces Of Resiliency

by Nan Henderson, M.S.W.

The drop out prevention, resiliency, and treatment literature is filled with research evidence about the detrimental impact of negatively labeling young people, adults, families, and communities. This literature is also rich with reports of how a single person or opportunity can turn around the life of a person, family, or community so labeled. L.W. Schmick's story personalizes this research. His wisdom, shared below, reiterates how labels do the opposite of helping, and how, in Bonnie Benard's words, resiliency is often the result of "one person or one opportunity or one caring family member, teacher, or friend, who encouraged a child's success and welcomed his or her participation."

L.W. Schmick: Challenging the "At Risk" Label

When L.W. Schmick was in middle school, he realized he was in a class that "was different" from other kids. By his freshman year in high school, he knew that his classes were for "at risk" students. Though he says he "wasn't ever mad at teachers for seeing that and being aware of that," he thinks the label was detrimental to himself and his peers.

"Putting an 'at risk' student in a separate class just separates them more. And I think that's what a lot of "at risk" students are trying not to do [be more separate]. I think they should be blended in more so they are not put in their own little group," L.W. explained.

> *"One of the results of being labeled, he said, is that students feel since they've already been labeled, why even try."*

One of the results of being labeled, he said, is that students feel since they've already been labeled, why even try. He used to say to himself, "It doesn't matter. I'll be 'at risk.' No big deal." He added, "It just seemed like everyone was waiting, watching for us to fail." He and his peers felt that all their behaviors were "under a magnifying glass."

L.W. was labeled "at risk" after he got into "a lot" of trouble in fifth and sixth grade. He and his mother had just moved to Maine from New York State, and for him the move "was a big deal." He had to leave his entire family behind, including his father who had

been divorced from his mother when L.W. was only six months old, but who was still an important person in his life. His reaction to the move: "I was big for my age, so I had older friends around. I got in a lot of fights. I got in trouble at school, and I didn't get along with teachers very well." L.W. got suspended from school in sixth grade.

He says that in looking back at that time, he realized one of the major reasons he got into so much trouble was "I just wanted to fit in... and it is pretty hard to fit in when you're a six foot red head. Blending into a crowd isn't the easiest thing to do." This is one reason he feels that being separated in middle school into a class for tough kids only made things worse. He was thrown off the middle school basketball team "for being mean," he received a lot of detention, and he started drinking.

L.W. credits his parents with providing him with some of what helped turn his life around. He said he always felt unconditional love and support from both of them. His mom stopped working two jobs so she could be home when he got home from school. His dad encouraged him to find a vocation in life, which meant staying in school. And L.W. himself said he never seriously considered dropping out of school because he realized that would "be quitting and I don't like to quit."

His life began to change his freshman year in high school when he was forced to find new friends (who were more connected to school) because "all my other friends dropped out." In fact, only 2 of the 15 students in his "at risk" middle school class—the class "no one really wanted to mess with, the class for 'the bad kids'"—graduated from high school. L.W. was one of the two. And he graduated with the respect of his teachers, his peers, and his community thanks to a KIDS Consortium trained teacher (see article on KIDS Consortium on p. 75) to whom L.W. gives most of the credit. L.W. said it is because of this teacher and the opportunity this teacher offered to become involved in a KIDS Consortium Project that he is headed this fall to college to become a teacher himself.

"In my sophomore year, I had an English class with Brian Flynn," who started the ELF Woods Project (see article on p. 75). "A lot of teachers when they see an 'at risk' student, they automatically distrust and they don't give them some of the responsibilities they would give other students... because they're 'at risk' supposedly," L.W. said. But Brian Flynn "showed me respect and trust. He gave me a lot of power to take responsibility. He said, 'If you want an inch, take an inch. If you want a mile, take a mile.'" And, he added, in Brian's class, "I wasn't set apart as different. I was able to mix in. He saw me as just another person, not as an 'at risk' student."

> "A lot of teachers when they see an 'at risk' student, they automatically distrust and they don't give them some of the responsibilities they would give other students... because they're 'at risk' supposedly."

When asked what else about Brian Flynn was so different than other teachers he had previously had, L.W. added: "[Most] teachers see students as students and they're above you when they're teaching you and

you listen to what they say because that's what is right. But Brian took a lot of what the students had to say, and that's how we did a lot of the things in the class. Someone would say 'it would be better like this,' so we'd try it like that. He shared his power with us."

After his experience in Brian's class, and working on the ELF Woods Project, L.W. said he became more involved with his community. And he gained more respect for community, "for all the hard work that it takes to do some things." The experience of having some of his work in the ELF Woods Project vandalized also taught L.W. "how people hurt when you destroy their things."

After his sophomore year L.W. stayed involved. He worked with the local National Guard to put lights along a trail behind his school. He worked with General Electric to get all the equipment and with the city of Auburn to get the permits.

L.W. Schmick: "Just another person: Not an 'at risk' student."

After his work with the Elf Woods Project, and his continuing service in his junior and senior years, L.W. said, "That 'at risk' label had been erased. I liked school more." Other people saw him differently, he said, and when this happened, "then I changed."

His advice to teachers dealing with difficult students: "I can see how teachers would be a little weary of an 'at risk' student. But it doesn't necessarily mean that we're dumb or that 'at risk' [students] are less able to do things, it just means that sometimes for circumstances beyond their control they're 'at risk.' Which was my case, I think. So try to treat us like you treat everyone else." ℮

Nan Henderson, M.S.W., is a national and international speaker and consultant on fostering resiliency and wellness, alcohol and other drug issues, and on organizational change. She has co-authored/edited five books about resiliency, and is the president of Resiliency In Action. *She can be reached at Nan Henderson and Associates, 5130 La Jolla Blvd., #2K, San Diego, CA 92109, p/f (858-488-5034), or by e-mail: (nanh@connectnet.com).*

Research Report

Fostering Resiliency in Communities: An Inside Out Process

by Bonnie Benard, M.S.W.

During the last decade much has been written on the breakdown of community and neighborhood life, the disintegration of natural social bonds in the face of massive economic and technological changes—linkages that create a sense of belonging and identity and, in Emmy Werner's words, "that give meaning to one's life and a reason for commitment and caring" (1982). In fact, a majority of people (and most scholars) would agree that ultimately the problem behaviors of alcohol and other drug abuse, domestic and youth violence, crime and delinquency, early pregnancy, and child abuse share as a root cause the loss of these critical social networks so vital to the healthy development of children and families. Social scientists and child and family advocates alike are sounding the clarion call for rebuilding communities to support human development. Even the White House, judging from Hillary Rodham Clinton's recent book (1996), has acknowledged the universal wisdom of the African proverb, "It takes a village to raise a child."

Furthermore, as John Gardner concludes in his powerful essay on community, "Without the continuity of the shared values that community provides, freedom cannot survive." Gardner goes on to state, "Strong and resilient communities can stand between the individual and any government that tries to impose dictatorial solutions from the right or left…. Undifferentiated masses never have and never will preserve freedom against usurping power" (1991, p. 5). Even economists and political scientists are calling the rebuilding of communities the key to survival as a nation, world, and even a species. According to Jeremy Rifkin in his seminal book, *The End of Work*, and several other scholars, the world is entering the 21st century in the throes of the third industrial revolution, which is transforming the in-

dustrial age to the post-market economy—a "new phase in world history," and "one in which fewer and fewer workers will be needed to produce the goods and services for the global population." Rifkin concludes, "Only by building strong, self-sustaining local communities will people in every country be able to withstand the forces of technological displacement and market globalization that are threatening livelihoods and survival of much of the human family" (1995, p. 250).

"Humans are Community-Forming Animals"

While the current technological, social, and economic forces are unique in human history, threats to and actual dissolution of comunity life have been common throughout human history. As Gardner writes, "Disintegration of human communities is as old as human history. Disease, natural disasters, conquest and absorption into emerging urban centers were the most common causes." However, he points out, "There were always processes of regeneration at work to counter disintegrative forces. As old social groupings broke down, new groupings tended to form. *Humans are community-forming animals*" (1991, p. 9).

Just as the resiliency paradigm focuses on the "glass half full" versus the risk paradigm of the "glass half empty," Gardner states it is the generative rather than the disintegrative function "that deserves our closest attention. The regenerative powers of human society have not weakened. The capacity of humankind to create and re-create social coherence is always there—enduring and irrepressible" (1991, p. 9).

One of the major assumptions of resiliency theory, differentiating it from other approaches to individual and social change, is that human systems are innately resilient. My favorite definition of resilience, by Robert J. Lifton, states that resilience is "the human capacity for transformation and change" (1993). At the individual level this means people are genetically wired with the capacities for social competence and caring, problem solving and

> **"It is the generative [not the] disintegrative function 'that deserves our closest attention....'"**

change, autonomy and identity, and for hope and meaning. At the community level—consisting of individuals in relationship—this translates into communities also having this inherent transformative capacity to adapt and change.

What has become apparent, however, is that, given the powerful degenerative forces at work today, the process of building or emerging community must be intentional: "Passive allegiance isn't enough today. The forces of disintegration have gained steadily and will prevail unless individuals see themselves as having a positive duty to nurture their community and

> **"People are genetically wired with the capacities for social competence and caring, problem solving and change, autonomy and identity, and for hope and meaning."**

continuously reweave the social fabric" (Gardner, 1991, p. 11). While the field of community development and discipline of community psychology are replete with examples of successful community-building efforts and processes, I want to focus on two approaches that are especially grounded in the resiliency belief of everyone's innate capacity to contribute and change themselves and their communities in positive ways. The approaches I will focus on here are John McKnight's and John Kretzmann's Asset-Based Community Development and Roger Mills' Health Realization approaches to community change.

Asset-Based Community Development

Care is the manifestation of a community. The community is the site for the relationships of citizens. And it is at this site that the primary work of a caring society must occur. If that site is invaded, co-opted, overwhelmed, and dominated by service-producing institutions, then the work of the community will fail. And that failure is manifest in families collapsing, schools failing, violence spreading, medical systems spinning out of control, justice systems becoming overwhelmed, prisons burgeoning, and human services degenerating (McKnight, 1995, p. x).

This quote from John McKnight's cutting critique of the harmful role the human service bureaucracies have played in undermining community life provides the theoretical foundation for his and John Kretzmann's excellent, accessible guidebook to community change, *Building Communities from the Inside Out* (1993). According to these community development "guides" from the Neighborhood Innovations Network at Northwestern University, the helping professions, grounded as they are in a medical model that thrives on disease and ignores the capacities of people, often do more harm than good, turning citizens into clients and communities into client neighborhoods. "As a result, many lower income urban neighborhoods are now environments of service where behaviors are affected because residents come to believe that their well-being depends upon being a client. They begin to see themselves as people with special needs that can only be met by outsiders. They become consumers of services, with no incentive to be producers" (1993, p. 2). What McKnight and Kretzmann provide in *Building Communities* is a path out of this self-fulfilling vicious cycle, a process for inviting forth the often hidden—and usually unacknowledged—gifts of marginalized groups, especially the young, the old, the disabled, the poor, and the culturally diverse.

> **"The helping professions... often do more harm than good, turning citizens into clients and communities into client neighborhoods."**

Instead of focusing on a community's problems, needs, and deficiencies, they offer an approach that builds on the community's capacities, skills, and assets—inherent in even the poorest of neighborhoods—enlisting them as the resources for and agents of change. "The key to neighborhood regeneration, then, is to locate all of the available local assets, to begin connecting them with one another in ways that multiply their power and effectiveness, and to begin harnessing those local institutions that are not yet available for local development purposes" (p. 6). Their process begins, therefore, not with the usual needs assessment of deficiencies and problems but with a *community asset map* that identifies the strengths, skills, and gifts of the community individuals, associations, and institutions (i.e., libraries, businesses, schools, parks, police, nonprofits, etc.). Besides being *asset based*, their approach is *internally focused*, concentrating on the agenda building and problem solving capacities of local residents, and lastly, it is *relationship driven*. Because of the massive social and economic changes that are severing the ties between young and old, between friends, between work and home, "one of the central challenges for asset-based community developers is to constantly build and rebuild the relationships between and among local residents, local associations, and local institutions" (1993, p. 9).

> **"Their process begins... with a community asset map *that identifies the strengths, skills, and gifts of the community individuals, associations, and institutions."***

The authors have generously provided an example of a seven-page Capacity Inventory to be used by one person interviewing another to gather the information necessary to help that person contribute to the community. This tool gathers information about the variety of skills the person has as well as his/her perceptions of strengths; the kinds of community work the person has done and would be willing to do; past enterprising interests and experience; and personal information. Once a community group has this information and identifies the talents of people, fitting the talents to neighborhood needs is fairly simple. Thus, the local group acts as a connector, according to Kretzmann and McKnight, by first identifying capacities and then connecting them to people, groups, and places that can use the capacities.

Identifying and Connecting the Gifts of All People

A major focus of their process is identifying and connecting the talents and gifts of marginalized groups: young people, old people, people on welfare, people with developmental disabilities, and people with artistic gifts. These are groups that often get labeled and then targeted for services that begin the cycle of dependency and the silencing of their voices

and gifts. Taking each of these groups in turn, Kretzmann and McKnight illustrate—both graphically and in stories—how they can be connected both in one-on-one relationships and to associations and organizations. In subsequent sections they use the same process to demonstrate how local associations, organizations, and institutions can connect with both individuals and each other.

Lastly, the authors tackle the core of the challenge to rebuild communities: revitalizing the community's economic life. "The key to building sustainable local economies is in developing a strong resource base—both human and physical—which is appropriate for that particular community." Though they don't go into the numerous community economic development approaches that exist, they do discuss three less well known approaches: the use of the voluntary sector, locally controlled lending institutions, and physical infrastructure development. Inherent in community-based economic development is the process of community mobilization and planning. Grounded in an ongoing process of mapping capacities in individuals, citizen associations, and local institutions and in building relationships, mobilizing the community's assets fully for economic development and information sharing purposes means looking for ways to create exportable goods and services and ways to exchange information. This process will "strengthen the village well [which] rebuilds the central nervous system of a community, without which the process of restoring health and wholeness becomes unimaginable" (p. 351).

It also means convening the community to develop a vision and a plan. The vision is based on asking the simple but compelling questions, "Who are we in this community? What do we value most? Where would we like our community to go in the next five, ten, twenty years?" The planning process requires three agreed upon commitments: (1) to begin with assets; (2) to expand the table; and (3) to combine more long-range planning with immediate problem solving. Lastly—and only lastly—remains leveraging outside resources to support locally driven development. It is only when local capacity is already being tapped—when citizens are already contributing time and talent and thus see themselves as resources and not consumers—that outside funding should be brought in. Help from funders and government agencies then becomes a support and not a detriment to regenerating communities.

Regenerating communities—as the title of this wonderful guide reflects—must come from "the inside out." This means citizens must reclaim "the *power, authority, and legitimacy* that have been stolen by the great institutions of our society." As helping professionals, "We must commit ourselves to reallocation of power to the people we serve so that we no longer will need to serve. Only then will we have a chance to realize the American dream: the right to be a citizen and to create, invent, produce, and care" (1995, p. 100).

Health Realization/Community Empowerment

A growing number of practitioners in the field of addictions, education, community organization, community policing, organizational development, therapy, and counseling have also been using an approach which has demonstrated its effectiveness at facilitating the development within people—youth

> **"*Regenerating communities... must come from 'the inside out.'*"**

and adults—of the positive belief that they are innately resilient, that they do have the capacity to develop caring relationships, to solve their own problems, to feel good about who they are, and to be optimistic about their future. The Health Realization/Community Empowerment model developed by Roger Mills is being applied in schools, community-based organizations, housing projects, treatment centers, hospitals, businesses, and community-wide collaborations around the country. While Health Realization evolved independently of resilience research, Mills and his colleagues (1994) use resilience research as a knowledge base for their model.

The Health Realization approach evolved from the application of the principles of a new wellness paradigm in psychology, Psychology of Mind, to the prevention, early intervention, and community development arenas. Beginning with a demonstration project in a Dade County, Florida housing project in the late 1980s, beset with the results of poverty and racism, including high rates of violence, drug dealing, domestic violence, teen pregnancy, and school failure, Health Realization is now also demonstrating its effectiveness in not only dramatically reducing the rates of all these problems but of building a sense of community pride and well-being in communities across the nation. Some of the findings from pre- and post-evaluations of the 142 families and 604 youth involved in the three-year Dade County project include significantly

improved parent-child relationships in 87% of the families, a 75% reduction in delinquency and school-related problem behaviors, a 65% decrease in drug trafficking, an 80% decrease in teen pregnancy, and a 60% decrease in substance abuse (Mills, 1993). Recent findings from the one-and-a-half year Coliseum Gardens Project in Oakland, California include a cessation of all gang warfare and ethnic clashes between the Cambodian and African-American youth, a 45% reduction in violent crime (including no homicides since the project began), a 110% increase in youth involvement in the Boys and Girls Club. A more massive effort in the South Bronx, the Comprehensive Community Revitalization Project involving six large community development corporations that jointly own and manage 8,000 units of housing, reports significant increases in collaboration among the participating organizations, significant increases in resident participation and involvement in youth leadership activities, and high levels of participation in job training or employment.

Resilience as an Innate and Directly Accessible Human Characteristic

While Mills did all the "right stuff" as a highly competent community psychologist—especially getting community ownership early on and promoting collaboration across several systems—what makes Health Realization unique and, I hypothesize, so successful is that it is not only grounded in the principle that resilience (the capacity for mental health despite exposure to severe risk) is *innate* in all human beings but that resilience is *directly accessible*. According to Mills, the capacity for mental health, wisdom, intelligence, common sense, and positive motivation—no matter what language one chooses to use—is in everyone despite his/her "risk factors." It is also potentially available at all times, and can be realized without reliving or working through the past. The goal of Health Realization is to "reconnect people to the health in themselves and then direct them in ways to bring forth the health in others. The result is a change in people and communities which builds up from within rather than is imposed from without" (Mills, 1993). Health Realization's basic change strategy for effecting this reconnection is educational, not therapeutic, and consists of teaching the basic understanding of the nature of our innate resilience, how to access it, and what gets in the way.

According to this approach, thought is the basic common denominator undergirding all human experience. Like breathing, thinking is a continuous natural life function. Even individual perceptions, feelings, and behavior are the effects of thought; what one thinks determines how one feels, acts, and believes.

> *"The capacity for mental health, wisdom, intelligence, common sense, and positive motivation—no matter what language one chooses to use— is in everyone despite his/her 'risk factors.'"*

It is through thought that individuals *construct meaning* in their lives. "Whatever we experience as 'our life' is determined by how we think," according to this principle. It is a person's thought system that creates what seems real and accounts for separate realities—differing perceptions of what seems real. As Mills explains, "This is why two people can be in the same situation and perceive it totally differently from each other. For example, someone can live in a subsidized housing development and be grateful for the opportunity to have low cost shelter, be able to stop worrying about where they will live, and get on with meeting the other needs in their lives, such as education, job training, and day care. Another person in the same situation might perceive that they are sinking downward, that they will never get out, or that they don't like the kinds of people they must live around" (1993, p. 7).

Thought is the vehicle through which people can either access innate wisdom and resilience, as in the former example, or through which they access, as in the latter example, conditioned thinking: the messages or expectations of the past that have been internalized from others, and from environments. These create personal assumptions, beliefs, memories, judgments, biases, attitudes, expectations about oneself and about other people. Oftentimes, far too much of what is learned from parents, schools, and society communicates a message of oppression—that one is not good enough (because of being female, black, young, poor, disabled, for example), that one "will never get out," that one cannot change. When people accept this conditioned thinking about themselves, when they see themselves as *victims*, they also begin to see other people through this negative filter of blame and low expectations—resulting in feelings of depression,

anger, hostility, fear, and despair that often manifest themselves in further victimizing behaviors (towards oneself and others) such as alcohol and other drug abuse and violence. The work of Health Realization is to help people learn to recognize and let go of this negative, self-defeating thinking and free their minds to access their innate well-being and resilience.

The Importance of Caring and Supportive Relationships

Health Realization does this "teaching" only after and through creating a positive context for change grounded in caring and supportive relationships. As Mills states, "As helpful as the Health Realization/ Community Empowerment Model is in bringing about positive change, it will fail if the proper steps are not taken when introducing it to individuals or communities.... Perhaps the most vital ingredient is the establishment of empowering relationships" (1993, p. 29). And foremost in relationship building is the *helpers'* ability to take care of themselves, to keep themselves in a state of well-being and mental health, and to view their clients with high expectations, to see their innate health. Mills refers to "being in a state of service" in which, "We have no personal agenda other than what is in our client's best interest"

> *"The work of Health Realization is to help people learn to recognize and let go of this negative, self-defeating thinking and free their minds to access their innate well-being and resilience."*

(1993, p. 30). In this state of mind the helper sees everyone as "doing the best they can given how things appear to them"; listens with compassion, without blame; and welcomes the active participation and ownership by the clients, being merely a guide and a coach to people's accessing their innate wisdom. "Walking your talk" is at the core of the Health Realization approach: "The teaching of the HR/CE Model requires that you grasp and live its principles in your life. The greater your understanding, the more powerful your impact on others because you will know how to nurture relationships and foster a climate for change" (Mills, 1993, p. 36). Once this foundational relationship is in place, the Health Realization approach uses good, plain old community organizing principles: enlisting a core group of people, creating a forum for them to meet regularly in small groups, and facilitating the establishment of collaborative relationships with government or private agencies as well as other service providers.

Asset-based Community Development and Health Realization both demonstrate the power of the resilience paradigm to effect successful change at both the individual and community level. The belief that one *can* change evolves from a focus on strengths, a sense of self-efficacy, and a belief in one's innate well-

> *"When people feel a sense of their own efficacy, they will transform their own families, schools, and communities."*

being and resilience, not from a focus on deficits, risks, and problems. As one participant in the Oakland Coliseum Garden's project states, "I'll tell you something that's different about this program, different from anything else you've done. In most programs you learn to identify the illness. We're not going to do that now. We're looking for the health" (Slater, 1994, p. 12). Both of these approaches give the prevention, early intervention, and treatment fields a way to move beyond the experts "fixing" people—even fixing systems— approach. When people feel a sense of their own efficacy, *they* will transform their own families, schools, and communities.

Ultimately, as models of the resilience paradigm, Asset-Based Community Development and Health Realization are processes of community building facilitated by the belief that all of us are connected at a level deeper than our respective cultures, ethnicities, genders, ages, etc. When we build community together we are breaking down the walls of fear that separate us from each other and from our collective power. As McKnight writes so well,

> We all know that community must be the center of our lives because it is only in community that we can be citizens. It is only in community that we can find care. It is only in community that we can hear people singing. And if you listen carefully, you can hear the words: "I care for you, because you are mine, and I am yours" (1995, p. 172). ℮

References

Clinton, Hillary Rodham (1996). *It takes a village: And other lessons children teach us.* New York, NY: Simon and Schuster.

Gardner, John (1991). *Building community.* Paper prepared for the Leadership Studies Program. Washington, D.C.: Independent Sector, September.

Kretzmann, John, & McKnight, John (1993). *Building communities from the inside out.* Evanston, IL: Center for Urban Affairs and Policy Research, Northwestern University.

Lifton, Robert (1993). *The protean self: Human resilience in an age of fragmentation.* New York, NY: Basic Books.

McKnight, John (1995). *The careless society: Community and its counterfeits.* New York, NY: Basic Books.

Mills, Roger (1993). *The health realization model: A community empowerment primer.* Alhambra, CA: California School of Professional Psychology.

Rifkin, Jeremy (1995). *The end of work: The decline of the global labor force and the dawn of the post-market era.* New York, NY: Jeremy Tarcher.

Slater, D. (1994). Miracle on 66th Avenue. *East Bay Express,* October 31, 1, 10-20.

Werner, Emmy, & Smith, Ruth (1982, 1989). *Vulnerable but invincible: A longitudinal study of resilient children and youth.* New York, NY: Adams, Bannister, and Cox.

Bonnie Benard, M.S.W., has authored numerous articles and papers on resiliency and provides speeches and training on resiliency throughout the country. She can be reached at Resiliency Associates, 1238 Josephine, Berkeley, CA 94703 (510-528-4344), or by e-mail: (bbenard@flash.net).

A Resiliency Resource Primer:
Resiliency and Communities

by Bonnie Benard, M.S.W.

The field of community development contains many fine theoretical books and pragmatic manuals for mobilizing communities, which I don't emphasize here. Rather, the following is a list of some of my favorite resources that speak more to building and reinventing community as we move into post-industrial society. Most of these books address the critical question of our time: Can youth and families be provided with the supports and opportunities that facilitate healthy development in light of the technological and corporate forces that have been gradually breaking the natural intergenerational bonds that have sustained the human family during its existence?

Bellah, Robert, Madsen, Richard, Sullivan, William, Swidler, Ann, and Tipton, Steven (1992). **The Good Society**. New York, NY: Vintage Books. *By the same authors as **Habits of the Heart**, this book looks critically and with historical perspective at our political, economic, educational, and religious institutions, which have grown out of control and even beyond an ability to understand them. It makes the case that a compassionate and caring society is only possible through active citizen participation.*

Bellah, Robert, Madsen, Richard, Sullivan, William, Swidler, Ann, and Tipton, Steven (1986). **Habits of the Heart: Individualism and Commitment in American Life.** New York, NY: Perennial Library. *This landmark book is based on the authors' massive five-year cultural study of hundreds of individuals and various American communities. Central to their study were the questions: "How ought we to live? How do we think about how to live? Who are we, as Americans? What is our character?" Central to their findings was the conclusion that Americans, largely confined to an identity of individualism, have lost a sense of being in community with others and, concomitantly, a sense of moral purpose and coherence in their lives.*

Blyth, Dale (1993). **Healthy Communities, Healthy Youth: How Communities Contribute to Positive Youth Development**. Minneapolis, MN: Search Institute. *Using data from 112 communities that have surveyed 9th-12th grade students with the Search Institute's student profiles, this report examines the way youth experience their community's strengths and how these factors contribute to youth development. Among other conclusions, their data, presented in the Institute's great and compelling graphs, demonstrate that while caring and supportive families make a major difference in the lives of their **own** youth, family factors do not differ very much between the healthiest and least healthy communities.*

Coontz, Stephanie (1992). **The Way We Never Were: American Families and the Nostalgia Trap**. New York, NY: Basic Books. *A brilliant examination of the history of the family which clearly makes the case—and illustrates it with lots of data— that stable communities and economies are the bedrock of stable families, not the reverse!*

Forsey, Helen, ed. (1993). **Circles of Strength: Community Alternatives to Alienation**. Philadelphia, PA: New Society Publishers. *A fine collection of essays on community-building experiences —all focused on creating ecologically sustainable communities. The various stories illustrate that there is no one right way, yet the bottom line principle must be the respect for all of life.*

Gardner, John (1991). ***Building Community***. Paper prepared for the Leadership Studies Program. Washington, D.C.: *Independent Sector*, September. *A wonderful treatise on community and its place in protecting democratic freedom along with responsibility. Gardner describes the essential characteristics and elements of effective communities and welcomes the reinvention of community—in whatever form it may manifest—in our swiftly changing world.*

Horton, Myles with Kohl, Judith, and Kohl, Herbert (1990). ***The Long Haul: An Autobiography***. New York, NY: Anchor Books. *An inspiring story—filled with stories!—of the life of Myles Horton who for more than 50 years trained leaders, including Martin Luther King, in community organizing for social justice. His empowerment philosophy, like that of Paolo Freire's in Brazil, was based on developing local, indigenous leadership.*

Ianni, Francis (1989). ***The Search for Structure: A Report on American Youth Today***. New York, NY: Free Press. *Ianni provides rich, in-depth research support (over a decade of observations and interviews with thousands of adolescents in families, schools, peer groups/gangs, youth programs, street corners, and even jails in ten diverse communities) for the roles community support, resources, and opportunities play in promoting positive youth development. His findings challenge the prevailing notion that "youth culture" is a separate social system immune from the community context.*

Kretzmann, John, and McKnight, John (1993). ***Building Communities from the Inside Out***. Evanston, IL: Center for Urban Affairs and Policy Research, Northwestern University. *A user-friendly and inexpensive guide to capacity-driven community development, complete with "Capacity Inventories" for mapping individual, organizational, institutional, and economic strengths.*

Lerner, Michael (1996). ***The Politics of Meaning: Restoring Hope and Possibility in An Age of Cynicism***. Reading, MA: Addison-Wesley. *While really a policy framework for creating a resilient society based on caring and meaningfulness rather than on the current ethos of selfishness and cynicism, the agenda and strategies Lerner lays out are commonsensical, human, and doable. If only Americans can create the political will by—you guessed it!— building community through the creation of grassroots mobilizing.*

Lofquist, William (1983). ***Discovering the Meaning of Prevention: A Practical Approach to Positive Change***. Tucson, AZ: AYD Publications. *I consider this the classic prevention text by the "guru" of prevention and positive youth development. Lofquist's concept of prevention is grounded firmly in the community development process and in building on people (including youth) as resource models. If only this developmental model had become the modus operandi of the prevention field.*

McKnight, John (1995). ***The Careless Society: Community and Its Counterfeits***. New York, NY: Basic Books. *In his compelling story-telling way McKnight takes on four community "counterfeiting" systems: human service systems, professionalism, medicine, and the criminal justice system. He shows how the institutionalization (i.e., the growth of bureaucracy) of caring roles have worked to undermine community. McKnight calls for "opposing those interests of governmental, corporate, professional, and managerial America that thrive on the dependency" of people, that have turned citizens into clients. This book should be required reading for all helping professionals.*

Mills, Roger (1993). ***The Health Realization Model: A Community Empowerment Primer.*** Alhambra, CA: California School of Professional Psychology. *This short "primer" concisely and clearly summarizes the health realization approach to planned change, an inside-out process that illustrates the systemic nature of resiliency. Based on teaching people the simple truths about their innate resilience and mental health and about how their thinking affects their feelings and behaviors, this simple but deeply systemic approach has demonstrated miraculous results at the community level.*

O'Brien, Raymond, Pittman, Karen, and Cahill, Michele (1992). ***Building Supportive Communities for Youth: Local Approaches to Enhancing Community Youth Services and Supports***. Washington, D.C.: Center for Youth Development and Policy Research. *A document commissioned by the Carnegie Council on Adolescent Development that provides an overview of community initiatives "out there," it discusses several promising initiatives, and concludes with a discussion of critical elements to success, as well as the powerful role the voluntary sector plays in not only the initial development of initiatives but in their implementation and service delivery.*

Rifkin, Jeremy (1995). ***The End of Work: The Decline of the Global Labor Force and the Dawn of the Post-Market Era***. New York, NY: Jeremy Tarcher. *Daring to discuss the unspeakable, Rifkin boldly—backed with more data than you wish he had!—documents the alarming move to a 21st century society devoid of employment opportunities for a majority of people. However, this visionary also proposes a viable solution which includes the voluntary sector and the rebuilding of local working communities.*

Schor, Juliet (1992). ***The Overworked American: The Unexpected Decline of Leisure***. New York, NY: Basic Books. *For those people with jobs, Harvard economist Schor documents the trend toward "overwork" and asks the question, "Why are we—unlike every other industrialized Western nation—repeatedly choosing money over time?" And, "What can we do to get off the treadmill?" She, like Rifkin, forces us to examine the deep, systemic questions about who Americans are, what we're doing, and why we're doing it.*

Shaffer, Carolyn, and Anundsen, Kristin (1993). ***Creating Community Anywhere: Finding Support and Connection in a Fragmented World***. New York, NY: Jeremy Tarcher. *This book focuses on exploring the wide variety of community forms in late 20th century America—from support groups, workplace teams, new forms of residence sharing, and neighborhood associations to electronic networks, intellectual salons, and spiritual communities. Besides discussing the personal stories of individuals in search of community, it profiles successful communities in the U.S. It also serves as a self-reflective guide for readers to assess what types of support and belonging they want and need in their lives as well as a practical guide for developing community-building skills, i.e., effective communication, conducting productive meetings, working through conflicts, etc.*

Whitmyer, Claude, ed. (1993). ***In the Company of Others: Making Community in the Modern World***. New York, NY: Jeremy Tarcher. *As Eric Utne says in the introduction, Whitmyer has "assembled a veritable pantheon of some of the best thinkers and visionaries of our time." This makes for a rich exploration of the concept of community and the many forms community can manifest. Like the Shaffer and Anundsen book, it also offers practical tips for building and sustaining community.* ☺

PART FOUR

Creating Connections: Mentoring, Support, and Peer Programs

Research Report

Mentoring: New Study Shows the Power of Relationship to Make a Difference

by Bonnie Benard, M.S.W.

The assumption of the resiliency approach in working with youth is that by meeting youth's developmental needs for safety, belonging, respect, accomplishment, power, and meaning, adults are promoting positive youth development *and*, thereby, preventing problems like alcohol and other drug abuse, teen pregnancy, violence, delinquency, and school failure. This perspective is supported not only by the strongest possible research base—longitudinal prospective studies on human development—but also by research on healthy families, effective schools, competent communities, successful change, learning organizations, and positive program evaluations. What these distinct bodies of research have documented is that successful development in *any* human system is dependent on these needs being met through the relationships, beliefs, and opportunities within the respective system. Caring relationships that convey high expectations—including a deep belief in a youth's innate resilience—and that provide opportunities for ongoing participation and contribution have been found *in natural settings* to be the key to successful development in any human system, and for positive youth development. However, what the resiliency approach to prevention has not had until now is an *evaluated planned preventive intervention* focused on creating this protective relationship.

Last fall Public/Private Ventures (P/PV), a national not-for-profit research corporation based in Philadelphia, published the fourth and final volume of its three-year, $2 million evaluation of Big Brothers/Big Sisters of America (BB/BS)—an *impact study* of the oldest and most carefully structured mentoring effort in the U.S. According to the authors of the study, titled *Making A Difference*, "Our research presents clear and

encouraging evidence that caring relationships between adults and youth can be created and supported by programs, and can yield a wide range of tangible benefits" (p. iv). Furthermore, *"The most notable results are the deterrent effect on initiation of drug and alcohol use, and the overall positive effects on academic performance that the mentoring experience produced"* (p. iv). In essence, the resiliency/youth development approach to healthy development and successful learning are validated in this scientifically reliable impact evaluation.

> *"The most notable results are the deterrent effect on initiation of drug and alcohol use, and the overall positive effects on academic performance that the mentoring experience produced."*

Study Overview

Briefly, P/PV, using a classical experimental research methodology with random assignment, conducted a comparative study of 959 10- to 16-year-olds who applied to BB/BS programs in eight geographically diverse cities in 1992 and 1993. Half of these youth were randomly assigned to a treatment group for which BB/BS matches were made or attempted; the other half were assigned to waiting lists. After 18 months the two groups were compared. Participants in a BB/BS program were less likely to start using drugs and alcohol: 46% less likely to start using illegal drugs; 27% less likely to start drinking. However, the effect was even stronger for minority Little Brothers and Sisters who were 70% less likely to initiate drug use than other similar minority youth! Little Brothers and Sisters were about one third less likely than controls to hit someone. They skipped half as many days of school as did control youth, felt more competent about doing schoolwork, skipped fewer classes, and showed "modest gains in their grade point averages"—with the strongest gains among minority Little Sisters (p. iii). Lastly, they improved their relationships with both their parents and their peers relative to their control counterparts.

Of particular note is that probably all of these youth—both treatment and control groups—would be considered "high risk" youth:

- 90% lived with only one of their parents;
- over 80% came from impoverished homes;
- over 40% received either food stamps and/or cash public assistance;
- 40% came from homes with a history of alcohol and drug abuse;
- nearly 30% came from families with a record of domestic violence; and
- nearly 30% were victims of emotional, physical, or sexual abuse.

Conversely, the Big Brothers/Big Sisters were generally well-educated young professionals. About 60% were college graduates; nearly two-thirds had a total household income over $25,000 (with 40% over $40,000). Also of note, about three fourths of the volunteers were white. In essence, despite this enormous social distance between the youth and the volunteers, they were able to establish successful relationships—across their class and race differences. To what, then, does P/PV credit this accomplishment?

The three earlier studies in P/PV's four-part evaluation of BB/BS answer this question. These earlier studies looked respectively at (1) program practices (implementation of the program model), (2) volunteer recruitment and screening, and (3) the nature of the relationships between volunteers and youth (how they form, are sustained, and end). From these earlier examinations the researchers attribute the successful outcomes to two overall characteristics: the *one-to-one relationship and the program's supportive infrastructure.*

Characteristics of Effective One-to-One Relationships

First of all, the relationship was of sufficient *intensity*. From my 15 years of reviewing prevention evaluation research, the *lack* of intensity is continually identified as a barrier to positive results. However, in the 400

matches studied here, more than 70% of the matches met three times a month for an average of 3-4 hours per meeting and 50% met one time a week. This comes to around 144 hours of direct contact a year, not counting telephone interaction.

> **"Sustained relationships were those in which the mentor saw him/herself as a friend, not as a teacher or preacher."**

Secondly, even though this outcome study did not examine the nature of the relationship between the adult and youth, the third companion study (*Building Relationships With Youth in Program Settings*, 1995, May) illuminated the nature of the relationships that were of sufficient intensity and duration to produce these effects. Certainly coming as no surprise, but presenting powerful validation of the resiliency perspective, is the finding of this third study that sustained relationships were those in which the mentor saw him/herself *as a friend, not as a teacher or preacher* (IV, p. 51). These "developmental" relationships were grounded in the mentor's belief that he or she was there to meet the developmental needs of youth—to provide supports and opportunities the youth did not currently have.

> While most developmental volunteers ultimately hoped to help their youth improve in school and be more responsible, they centered their involvement and expectations on developing a reliable, trusting relationship, and expanded the scope of their efforts only as the relationship strengthened (III, p.ii).

These volunteers placed top priority on having the relationship enjoyable and fun to both partners. Furthermore, they were "there" for the young person, listened nonjudgmentally, looked for the youth's interests and strengths, and incorporated the youth into the decision-making process (gave them "voice and choice") around their activities. From a resiliency perspective, they provided the three protective factors of a *caring relationship* that conveys *positive expectations and respect*, and that provides *ongoing opportunities for participation and contribution*—and saw risks existing in the *environment*, not in the youth.

In contrast to these developmental relationships (fortunately, two thirds of the 82 relationships examined were developmental!), were the "prescriptive" relationships in which the adult volunteers believed their primary purpose was guiding the youth toward the values, attitudes, and behaviors *the adult* deemed positive. "Adults in these relationships set the goals, the pace, and/or the ground rules for the relationship. These volunteers were reluctant to adjust their expectations of the youth or their expectation of how quickly the youth's behavior could change" (III, p. iii). A majority of these prescriptive volunteers were basically there to *fix kids*—typically to improve school performance—and most of their shared time was spent in conversation—not fun activities—around grades and classroom behavior. For these volunteers, risk lay within the youth:

> What seemed to stand out for these prescriptive volunteers was less the deficiencies present in the youth's environment, and more, particularly in terms of morals and values, those present in the youth themselves—deficiencies prescriptive volunteers frequently sought to rectify (III, p. 40).

Not surprisingly, the adults and youths in these matches found the relationship frustrating and nonsupportive. Of these prescriptive relationships, only 29% met consistently (compared to 93% of the developmental) and at the 18-month follow-up, only 32% were ongoing (compared to 91% of the developmental) (III, p. 18). What is particularly frightening in reading some of the interviews with the youth and the prescriptive volunteers is the fact that these relationships are probably doing more harm than good—are becoming themselves another risk factor in an already stressed young life as illustrated by the following poignant statements:

Youth: When I went out with my Big Brother he... said okay, let's go get the library card and let's go to the library and check out a book. But I stayed at the library all day and he kept coming back, and telling me I didn't have the right information. So I studied there until closing time in the library. I was sitting there doing a report on toads and frogs, and when he came back, I had my report done, but I didn't have a rough draft. So like I wrote word for word out of the book; he said that's cheatin'.

Interviewer: He said that's cheating?
Youth: I just sat there and dropped in tears.
Interviewer: You started crying?
Youth: I mean it's something that I just can't hold them in...
Interviewer: What upset you about that?
Youth: I don't know. I didn't wanna stay there, I felt like I was supposed to write the report in my own words. Like some of it I got out of the book and some of it came out of my own head... I had to do it over.
Interviewer: You had to do it over?
Youth: Yeah, and he picked me up from the library and it was raining. (III, p. 63)

In contrast, this is the voice of a developmental volunteer:

> [When he told me about a bad grade] I kind of focused on his other grades first; he said that he had done a good job with the other ones. And then I asked him if he wanted to do better in it, and then I kind of asked him how he could do better. And it was a pretty simple thing because he just didn't do a couple reports. So we decided that, you know, the next ones he got I would help him with them if he wanted. And we did that twice. You know, *so it's like what can we do together to do this...* When I came home with even a B or even an A-, sometimes it would be well, why did you get a minus here. It wasn't like, oh you did great. So I was sensitive to that (III, p. 59).

The youth-centered approach—asking the youth what he needed and wanted—and then offering help as a shared activity, as well as the strengths-focus, sensitivity, and empathy displayed by this volunteer stands in sharp contrast to the earlier volunteer who didn't ask what the youth wanted, who left the youth alone and on his own with no assistance, who clearly had decided the youth *should* spend time at the library, and who displayed only insensitivity and lack of empathy. According to the researchers,

> That participation in BB/BS was able to achieve transformative goals [outcomes like reduced alcohol use] while taking a general developmental approach lends strong support to the emerging consensus that [ironically!] youth programs are most effective in achieving their goals when they take a more

supportive, holistic approach to youth" (III, p. 51). Certainly, this study proves the deep truth of Nel Noddings' (1988) statement: "It is obvious that children will work harder and do things—even odd things like adding fractions—for people they love and trust."

Program Infrastructure: "Prerequisites for an Effective Mentoring Program"

From the studies of BB/BS' program practices and recruitment and screening as well as earlier Public/Private Ventures' research on mentoring, the researchers conclude that "the following program irreducibles are prerequisites for an effective mentoring program:"

- Thorough volunteer *screening* that weeds out adults who are unlikely to keep their time commitment or might pose a safety risk to the youth;

- Mentor training that includes *communication and limit-setting* skills, tips on *relationship-building* and recommendations on the *best way to interact with a young person*;

- Matching procedures that take into account the preferences of the youth, their family and the volunteer, and that use a professional case manager to analyze which volunteer would work best with which youth; and

- *intensive supervision and support of each match by a case manager* who has frequent contact with the parent/guardian, volunteer and youth, and provides assistance when requested or as difficulties arise (IV, p. 52).

> **"Serving the needs of mentors is as important as serving the needs of youth."**

Supervision is a hallmark of the BB/BS approach to mentoring... [and] the program practice most associated with positive match outcomes" (I, p. 61). The earlier study found that those sites following the BB/BS procedures for regular supervision had matches that met at the highest rates; those agencies that reduced this function had problems. As several studies of mentoring have discovered, serving the needs of mentors is as important as serving the needs of youth; you can't have one without the other! According to Ron Ferguson's (1990) earlier study,

> Most programs expect to use volunteer mentors to supplement the love and attention that their paid staffs provide to children, but those that have tried have experienced only limited success at finding mentors and keeping them active. *They have discovered that fulfilling mentors' needs is as important for sustaining their involvement as fulfilling youths' needs is to sustaining theirs* (p. 15).

This is a finding directly paralleling what educational researchers have found about meeting the needs of *teachers* as a fundamental prerequisite to engaging students!

Another critical benefit of having paid staff is the stability and continuity they provide. Case managers ensure that youth are not left on their own if their mentor leaves. In fact, several investigators have found that even in programs that employ volunteer mentors, it is the case managers/youth workers that are often the real mentors to youth (Freedman, 1993; Higgins et al., 1991; Ferguson, 1990).

Implications for Prevention, Education, and Youth Development

1   *The youth development/resiliency approach is key to successful learning and social development.*

Perhaps the finding with the greatest implication for prevention and education is the power of a *non*-problem-focused intervention to produce positive—and superior—results compared to the targeted problem-focused interventions that dominate the prevention field, from substance abuse to dropout, to teen pregnancy, to violence prevention.

> Participation in a BB/BS program reduced illegal drug and alcohol use, began to improve academic performance, behavior and attitudes, and improved peer and family relationships. *Yet the BB/BS approach does not target those aspects of life, nor directly address them.* It simply provides a caring, adult friend. Thus, the findings in this report speak to the effectiveness of an approach to youth policy that is very different from the

problem-oriented approach that is prevalent in youth programming. This more developmental approach does not target specific problems, but rather interacts flexibly with youth in a supportive manner (IV, p. 1).

I would extend this conclusion to the whole youth-serving arena, including families and schools. The development of a caring, trusting, respectful, reciprocal relationship is the key to reducing risks, enhancing protection, and promoting positive youth development in *any* system.

> **"The development of a caring, trusting, respectful, reciprocal relationship is the key to reducing risks, enhancing protection, and promoting positive youth development in any system."**

2   *Creating "mentor-rich" environments must be a major focus.*

As I stated in an earlier work on mentoring, an approach to mentoring especially compelling to me is the concept of infusing mentoring—as a way of being with youth—into social institutions: families, schools, and communities. Creating what Marc Freedman (1993) [see related interview on p.101] refers to as "mentor-rich environments"—environments that create lots of opportunities for young people to interact with an array of caring adults must be the focus.

> Creating mentor-rich settings—schools, social programs, youth organizations—is one way of moving beyond the chimera of *super-mentoring*, in which a single charismatic adult is called on to be a dramatic influence, providing all the young person's needs in one relationship. In reality, young people need more than one relationship to develop into healthy adults (p. 111).

He states,

> Our aspiration should be to create planned environments conducive to the kind of informal interaction that leads to mentoring. Indeed, such an approach is rooted in the historic strength and traditional practice of extended and fictive kin structures in many low-income communities—particularly African-American neighborhoods (p. 112).

What this means is expansion of the world of adult contacts for all youth in their natural environments. This means supporting families in their efforts to parent via family-centered social policies that promote flexible work policies, parental leave, time off to work in schools, decent wages, family healthcare benefits, and quality child care. Communities must also create opportunities for youth to be directly involved with more adults through community service, work apprenticeships, more involvement in local government, and so on. Young people need more opportunities to interact and form relationships with the older generation—the generation that currently is abdicating its responsibilities to the young.

3   *Creating mentor-rich environments means relationships must be the central focus of reform efforts.*

Creating mentor-rich environments in schools, community-based organizations, and communities as a whole means relationships must be the top priority in any prevention effort or educational reform. As this study so eloquently proves, a focus on outcomes alone inevitably leads to youth-fixing, control strategies in our institutions—and often deleterious ones. For example, an outcome of reduced alcohol and drug use often leads schools to zero tolerance strategies which expel youth from school and push them onto the streets. At its extreme, this prescriptive approach leads to the imprisoning of more and more young people.

> **"[To] expand the world of adult contacts for all youth in their natural environments... means supporting families in their efforts to parent via family-centered social policies that promote flexible work policies, parental leave, time off to work in schools, decent wages, family healthcare benefits, and quality childcare."**

The BB/BS study, along with all the research on resiliency and positive youth development, shows clearly the path for youth policy and educational reform. Unless there is a focus on the mediating variables of relationships, beliefs, and opportunities for participation, the desired outcomes of reduced alcohol and other drug abuse, school success, and compassionate and responsible citizens will never be achieved. This is the key message of resiliency research and the BB/BS evaluation; this is *the* message to sell to preventionists, educators, youth and educational policy makers, *and* adult society. All these constituencies must see that (1) What works is known!, (2) It's never too late to transform young lives, (3) Caring is not a "touchy-feely" add-on luxury but a critical necessity to educational and social change and perhaps the most important, and (4) Adult society has a civic and moral responsibility to the next generation—to "other people's children."

Other People's Children

The last point remains the ultimate challenge. While mentoring programs, as the BB/BS evaluation shows, have demonstrated their power to promote healthy development and prevent problem behaviors, they ultimately serve only a few of the millions of children who could benefit and have a hefty price tag of $1,000 a match. Moreover, they are a limited intervention in the realm of systemic social change. Just as disadvantaged children have been and continue to be socially created by policies that systematically deny them opportunities to succeed in society, to change this situation requires new social policies. These policies must address the most powerful risk factor a growing number of children and youth, and their families, face: poverty. Many policy experts agree with Stanley Eitzen's (1992) vision of just what these changes must look like:

> Since the problems of today's young people are largely structural, solving them requires structural changes. The government [and the government is all of us, folks!] must create jobs and supply job training... as well as exert more control over the private sector. In particular, corporations must pay decent wages and provide adequate benefits to their employees.... There must be an adequate system for delivering health care, rather than our current system that rations care according to ability to pay. There must be massive expenditures on education to equalize opportunities from state to state and from community to community. There must be equity in pay scales for women. And finally, there must be an unwavering commitment to eradicating institutional sexism and racism (p. 590).

That these systemic changes will be costly there is no disputing; however, far more costly will be society's refusal to pay what it costs to provide the developmental opportunities and supports all young people need. As Mike Males (1996) states in *The Scapegoat Generation*, his compelling investigation of America's War on Adolescence, "The deterioration in public support for families with children [is] a direct result of declining tax revenue and school funding [and] reverberates across generations" (p. 285). He claims, "America's level of adult selfishness is found in no other Western country," citing a 1995 National Science Foundation-funded study that found the U.S. ranking first in per-person affluence, "producing a higher gross domestic product with 250 million people than the other 17 nations, population 400 million, combined!" Furthermore, "The U.S., by an even larger margin, also ranks first in child poverty" (p. 7).

> **"Relationships must be the top priority in any prevention effort or educational reform."**

While mentoring is a limited intervention, what it offers besides a transformational experience to the young people involved, is the opportunity to reconnect the young and old, to reweave the intergenerational threads that are essential to a healthy society. While

> **"What [mentoring] offers besides a transformational experience to the young people involved, is the opportunity to reconnect the young and old, to reweave the intergenerational threads that are essential to a healthy society."**

Males acknowledges that "the path to intergenerational cooperation [is] difficult at this advanced state of deterioration..., it lies in *inviting* adolescents into adult society." Furthermore,

> What is needed is not a revolution of fiscal policy or remedial plan, but one of *fundamental attitude*. Nothing good will happen until elder America gazes down from our hillside and condominium perch and identifies the young—darker in shade as a rule; feisty; lustful as we were; violent, as we raised them to be; no different from us in any major respect—as our children," (pp. 291-292).

According to Freedman (1996), mentoring offers just this opportunity to *identify* and realize our shared humanity.

> Mentoring amounts to the "elementary school of caring" for other people's children, the children of the poor. It is a specific context in which to initiate the process of reconstructing empathy.... Mentoring brings us together—across generation, class, and often race—in a manner that forces us to acknowledge our inter-dependence, to appreciate, in Martin Luther King, Jr.'s words, that "we are caught in an inescapable network of mutuality, tied to a single garmet of destiny" (pp. 134, 141). ☻

References

Note: The Big Brother/Big Sisters evaluation was published in four volumes available through Public/Private Ventures, 2005 Market Street, Suite 900, Philadelphia, PA 19103; 215/557-4400:

I. *Big Brothers/Big Sisters: A study of program practices* (1993, Winter).
II. *Big Brothers/Big Sisters: A study of volunteer recruitment and screening* (1994, Fall).
III. *Building relationships with youth in program settings* (1995, May).
IV. *Making a difference: An impact study of Big Brothers/Big Sisters* (1995, November).

•••

Benard, Bonnie (1992). *Mentoring programs for urban youth: Handle with care.* San Francisco, CA: WestEd. (June).

Eitzen, D. Stanley (1988). Problem students: The sociocultural roots. *Phi Delta Kappan*, December, 296-298.

Ferguson, Ronald (1990). *The case for community-based programs that inform and motivate black male youth.* Washington, DC: The Urban Institute.

Freedman, Marc (1993). *The kindness of strangers: Adult mentors, urban youth, and the new voluntarism..* San Francisco, CA: Jossey-Bass.

Higgins, Catherine, et al. (1991). *I have a dream in Washington, D.C.: Initial report*, Winter. Philadelphia, PA: Public/Private Venture.

Males, Mike (1996). *The scapegoat generation: America's war on adolescents.* Monroe, ME: Common Courage Press.

Noddings, Nel (1988). Schools face crisis in caring. *Education Week*, December 7, 32.

Bonnie Benard, M.S.W., has authored numerous articles and papers on resiliency and provides speeches and training on resiliency throughout the country. She can be reached at Resiliency Associates, 1238 Josephine, Berkeley, CA 94703 (510-528-4344), or by e-mail: (bbenard@flash.net).

Mentoring as the Most Promising Prevention:
An Interview with Marc Freedman

by Bonnie Benard, M.S.W.

In 1992 when I was researching the topic of mentoring, [see the related article on the Big Brothers / Big Sisters evaluation on page 93], I discovered a Public / Private Ventures' document by Marc Freedman, The Kindness of Strangers: Reflections on the Mentoring Movement *(1991). It was far and away the most comprehensive, insightful, and critical look at mentoring that had been written. In 1993 the document was expanded into the book,* The Kindness of Strangers: Adult Mentors, Urban Youth, and the New Voluntarism *(Jossey-Bass) which still remains the seminal work in the field. Freedman's understanding of the promise mentoring holds to create the caring relationships "between young and old" that Emmy Werner states are the key to effective prevention as well as the limitations of one intervention to rebuild the sense of belonging and community youth—and adults— are hungry for makes him, and his work, a valuable ally in spreading the resiliency message.*

BB: Marc, you played a seminal role in getting the Big Brothers/Big Sisters evaluation [see the related article on p. 93], which validates the power of relationship to promote positive youth development, to happen. What got you personally interested in the concept of mentoring?

MF: It came through two different sources. One was doing research on youth service projects around the country. These urban youth service corps were organized in teams and each team had an adult supervisor or team leader. When I went out and did field work on those projects—especially interviewing young people—I was struck by how prominent the relationships with the team leader were in prescribing what they were getting out of the corps. It wasn't a one-on-one relationship, but it just seemed that in this program the critical ingredient for the young person's success was this relationship. I was struck at the same time by how rarely this *affective* aspect of programs is discussed in the program evaluation literature. I think [this is] primarily because evaluators of programs—and part of the reason for program evaluation—tend to come from economics and quantitative sociology. It has been very difficult to figure out how you could take account of those relationships.

So what I wanted to do with the book in part was to put what I was seeing in these programs [the importance of relationships] into the broader context and understand what kind of importance it could hold. It was really to try to bridge this gap between what young people were saying was important to them in the program and what was showing up on these evaluations which tended to focus much more on more impersonal aspects—especially the curricula.

BB: I think this is still the major challenge. I've been in the substance abuse prevention field, where they've spent lots of money on program evaluations—and they never look at relationships, only program content. I just read an *Education Week* article yesterday that was discussing the rise in illicit drug use of 12-17-year-olds and when they get around to discussing what to do, it's the same old list of curricula and canned programs. And then there's a book like your book and a study like this BB/BS evaluation as well as the many qualitative studies capturing the voices of youth—and they tell you what is important.

> *"The only real way to reach teenagers is through real people. They need to hear the message from adults. They don't need slogans from politicians or supposed role models or from the media."*

MF: Right. In fact within the context of those drug reports, we know that beginning in 1992, drug use increased by 105%. And the two major responses seem to be that Dole has argued that what we need to do is greatly increase the military in the war on drugs and, basically, to get out the troops and batten down the border. And the Clinton response has been, as Barry McCaffree has been talking about, how we need a new propaganda push—more subway posters and celebrities telling them to say no. While I'm sure the Clinton approach is sounder, neither one of them take into account that *the only real way to reach teenagers is through real people.* They need to hear the message from adults. They don't need slogans from politicians or supposed role models or from the media. They need real relationships. I guess the greatest argument on behalf of that approach would be the Big Brothers/Big Sisters study because that occurred at exactly the same period that this drug use increased. It started in 1992, and we found by looking at a control group of kids who were on the waiting list with kids assigned Big Brothers and Big Sisters, there was a 40% decrease in those young people with Big Brothers and Big Sisters in starting to use drugs. And 40% were from families that had a history of substance abuse; all were from single parent families; and they were predominately minority—African American—kids.

> **"At the exact same period when drug use is doubling, we find that by providing consistent adult relationship, you get the exact opposite trend: Drug use is essentially cut in half as opposed to doubling."**

BB: All the ones labeled "high risk."

MF: Exactly. At the exact same period when drug use is doubling, we find that by providing consistent adult relationship, you get the exact opposite trend: Drug use is essentially cut in half as opposed to doubling. What's so striking about that is that we found in a separate in-depth study of relationships within the context of Big Brothers and Big Sisters, that the mentors who were most successful were not the ones who tried to promote the drug avoidance curriculum or tried to basically tell young people what to do, but the ones who just concentrated on becoming friends with the young people.

BB: This P/PV companion study on relationship is so powerful and totally validates all of the beliefs that I've been trying to put out there along with a bunch of other people, certainly starting with Emmy Werner— that *how* you are with the person makes the difference; that you need to develop that caring relationship and play to the strengths of young people and find their gift and give them opportunities to be involved and contribute and be reciprocal.

Now this is a question I have: Is it going to be difficult, given that the outcome study in Volume IV didn't look at the nature of relationships, to tease this very critical connection out? If that last outcome study could say, "OK. This is the *type* of relationship that gives us these really positive outcomes." It's that one little connecting piece that I want!

MF: I agree with you—it would be ideal if we had that kind of information in the last study because now it's really looking at the confluence of the different studies and trying to draw some conclusions.

BB: Frankly, it scares me that since this study is obviously already beginning to have impacts on federal and state policy (I think the California Department of Alcohol and Drug Programs is initiating something, as well as the Governor!)—people will go for the *program*, and they won't look at *how* the program is done as an important part. When I read those voices of the kids in the study on relationship, it scared me that some of those very prescriptive mentors—their attitudes in the way they work with the kids—would actually harm the youth! [And the kids were so loving and still accepting of somebody that was really giving them negative messages...]

MF: Absolutely. I think that there are three lessons we need to emphasize from this study. One is that the sustained kind of relationships that Big Brothers/ Big Sisters produces can have some real effect. Two is that you can only produce these relationships if you have programs that provide adequate screening and follow-up support. It takes a lot to produce a sustained relationship, and it costs a lot too. It costs about $1000

> **"You can produce these relationships only if you have mentors who focus on building a real relationship and not try to storm in and prescribe to young people how they should lead their lives."**

a match. But we know from looking at Big Brothers/ Big Sisters along with other kinds of mentoring that there is a dramatic difference in terms of the kind of care and attention that goes into a program like Big Brothers/Big Sisters. And the difference is that Big Brothers/Big Sisters produces a lot more substantial relationships, a lot more frequent relationships. Three, you can produce these relationships only if you have mentors who focus on building a real relationship and not try to storm in and prescribe to young people how they should lead their lives.

BB: Do you see as a result of this evaluation that Big Brothers/Big Sisters will put more emphasis on screening and training people about relationship development?

MF: I think Big Brothers/Big Sisters has always emphasized that, and I think they'll get more money to do that—to screen and support more relationships than they were beforehand. Now they can go to funders with stronger evidence that the extra care they take is worth it. One of the reasons they were interested in having this study done is that a lot of other less careful mentoring programs are going to the same funders and claiming to be able to produce results with a lot less staffing.

But on the other side, there were some other lessons that came out of our research which suggests change within Big Brother/Big Sisters. A number of applicants who never make it to the Big Brothers/Sisters matching—about three-quarters of the people who approach the program with an interest in helping young people—one way or another are either discouraged or weeded out before they get to being matched. In part, that is good. But in a lot of cases people get discouraged because it's so long from the time you apply until the time you're matched that a lot of people out there who probably would be good Big Brothers or Big Sisters are being discouraged. While a lot of these people might not be appropriate as a Big Brother/Big Sister, they could help kids in other ways.

> **"Mentoring can be a social program for adults under the guise of being one for kids."**

BB: That's a lot of people who have the interest to even approach an organization like Big Brothers/Big Sisters. There are so many things that come out of your work that parallel Jeremy Rifkin's conclusions in his book, *The End of Work.* He states that in spite of the U.S. having perhaps the worst public policy support for children and families, the U.S. has the highest rate of voluntarism in the industrialized world. And something you pointed out in your book, the importance of mentoring as a way to get middle-class people—the ones that are isolating themselves in the suburbs—in touch with especially poorer young people and in some way build a movement—through voluntarism—that would support public policy changes around children and family issues.

MF: I agree with that although I have several responses. One of the striking discoveries for me in interviewing mentors is the extent to which mentoring can be a *social program for adults* under the guise of being one for kids. You suggested that maybe the adults who come forward to mentor, even though they're sympathetic to kids to start, have no idea

what these young people are facing. In many cases, they end up learning as much as the young people, and in some cases they can become advocates on behalf of kids. The theme of Big Brothers/Big Sisters' conference this year was advocacy for positive youth development. They're trying to move more aggressively into having that potential within their movement. Part of what these mentors can do is work directly with kids, but in concert they might be able to help the wider community understand why it's important to fund better schools and youth programs and more youth programs.

On the other hand, there are some limits as to what volunteers can do. Voluntarism, even though it's a big part of American life, is declining. The last Gallop poll of 1993 showed over five years a decline of 54-48% in terms of the percentage of Americans who were volunteering. There was a decline in the number of hours that they're putting in and a decline of about ten million volunteers during that period. I think that the main reason we're seeing that is just that people are working so hard.

BB: Exactly. That brings up Juliet Shor's book, *The Over-Worked American,* which relates directly to this issue.

MF: Shor's book says the average American works 164 more hours a year since l971. That's almost an extra month a year. One of the ways that has impacted communities is that it's particularly women who are hard hit by the increase in working hours because the tremendous movement of women into the work force has reduced the amount of time available for women to volunteer. And for the last 100 years, women have been the mainstay of the volunteering movement. For example, PTA memberships have dropped from 12 million to 7 million over the last 30 years. As Arlie Hochild's work at UC Berkeley has shown, since women still continue to do most of the child rearing and domestic duties besides working outside the home, the average working woman works fifteen hours a week more than the man. Over a year that's an extra month of 24-hour days.

You can see why it's a lot harder to also add on that extra shift of being a Big Brother or Big Sister. So I think what Big Brothers/Big Sisters and the other mentoring programs try to do is to concentrate more on younger people before they've had kids and before they've gotten married. They have a lot of mentors in their 20s and early 30s and a lot of college students. The untapped resource, I think, is older adults, which you talked about earlier. At the same time there is a decrease in volunteer time for people in the middle generation, you have people retiring earlier, living longer, and remaining healthier who could make a huge difference in communities.

BB: And who are at a point in their lives—the stage of generativity—where they decide they've made their living and are looking for meaning and maybe what they can do to give back.

MF: Exactly. We lack the institution to engage that segment of the population. Partly our institutions have ignored the potential there. In groups like Big Brothers and Big Sisters, there are very few older adults. But then our culture has also degraded the idea of generativity; we have replaced it with the leisure village of recreation.

> *"The untapped resource...is older adults....At the same time there is a decrease in volunteer time for people in the middle generation, you have people retiring earlier, living longer, and remaining healthier who could make a huge difference in communities."*

BB: And I don't know if children are even allowed in many of them! That seems to get to be a very scary dilemma, where you have so many older adults isolated from children and young people. I just read a new book by Mike Males called *The Scapegoat Generation: America's War on Adolescents*. He shows how most of the policies, and you can certainly see it in Clinton too, start blaming kids for problems like substance abuse, violence, etc.—that we blame them for their natural response to this society that we adults have created.

He concludes from his carefully documented research that unless we can engage older adults to care for the next generation, our country is going to continue to decline in all indicators of health and especially in the sense of community belonging. For example, if you look at Florida, which I don't think any Democrat has won since Jimmy Carter, there's a state filled with retirees—many of whom are even afraid of young people. The walls have been erected so well. And he said that our ultimate challenge is to make the connection—to "rebuild the village."

You started to talk about Big Brothers/Big Sisters maybe moving more into an advocacy position. Do you know if the Federal Government is interested in this study and would be interested in putting more money into this in any way?

MF: There's tremendous interest within the Clinton Administration to try to support mentoring programs, and there was money in the Clinton Crime bill. There was money in the original welfare reform proposals, that all would have gone for mentoring and relating these activities, and that was all cut out by the Republican Congress. But through National Service there's enormous mentoring going on in a variety of different ways. Americorps has funded programs like Friends of the Children in Portland, Oregon, where Americorps serves as full time mentors for young people in the second grade and they actually spend time in the classroom with them. They provide a bridge between home, and they'll work with between four and eight kids.

There is also interest on the part of the National Service Corporation and Harris Walford, the president, in trying to use Americorps volunteers to help groups like Big Brothers/Big Sisters doing mentoring to recruit and screen and increase the number of those mentors who can be placed and supported. So that's a great opportunity there. In addition, the Corporation runs Foster Grandparents. There are 25,000 foster grandparents that work one-on-one each year with 90,000 kids, making them actually bigger than Big Brothers/Big Sisters. In fact, it's the biggest one-on-one program for kids in the country. It's also a program that Emmy Werner is a huge fan of, and I am as well. It's a program for low-income older adults, almost entirely women over the age of sixty-five. And since its beginning as a War on Poverty program, it's mandated that the foster grandparent volunteers have to work one-on-one with disadvantaged or disabled young people.

But you know on the bipartisan side, there are a number of Republicans who are really interested in mentoring as well. To give you an idea of the national bipartison appeal, two Senators who are former Big Brothers are Christopher Dodd on the one hand, who is one of the leading liberals in the Senate, and Dan Coates from Indiana, who is one of the most high-profile conservatives. In fact, Coates has proposed a bill which would pour substantial amounts of Federal dollars into Big Brothers. So there is some potential bipartisan interest.

BB: You know in some way the whole idea of relationships and what mentoring stands for is so deeply human that no matter who you are or your political values, it strikes at your heart and your deep sense of what it is to be a human being and what's important in life. Any of us alive and any of us functioning know that we have to thank our relationships for being here. However, you coined the term "the overselling of mentoring"—that mentoring can divert attention from needed policy reforms that would address restructuring our youth-serving institutions.

MF: The great fear I have is that some Republicans will use mentoring as a smoke screen to cover-up cutbacks to really basic youth services in schools and things of that sort. And that is something that we have to be—and I'm always—wary of.

BB: One point I just loved in your document and book and that totally strikes home with me since I'm concerned with restructuring systems like schools, communities, and organizations is that the real issue is how we create *mentor-rich environments* where there are lots of opportunities for young people to interact with lots of adults, where that kind of chemistry can happen in a natural sort of way. This is what Emmy [Werner] refers to when she talks about the key to successful prevention is to create the natural social networks where things aren't so much programs but that you are really supporting the natural connections between friends, family, neighbors, young and old, etc.—by having enough people in kids lives in the institutions they are in.

MF: There are two arguments for that. One is the number of children that we can reach. I mean there are profound limits on the young people that can be reached in the way that Big Brothers and Big Sisters goes about it. After one hundred years, there are 75,000 people in Big Brothers/Big Sisters and half as many people on the waiting list. Dagmar McGill, the Associate National Director of Big Brothers/Big Sisters, estimates that between 5 and 15 million kids could benefit from what they provide. Well there's a big gulf between seventy-five thousand and 5 to 15 million.

So then the question is, how could we reach more of those kids? One way is through Americorps and Foster Grandparents or National Service participants who have the spirit of volunteerism but are working half-to- full-time so they can reach multiple kids. And another route is to try to figure out where young people are spending their time, and to try to see how those institutions, namely schools and community youth programs, could be changed so they become opportunities for more relationships to form with both volunteers and staff.

The project I'm working on now is the Experience Corps, which is in many ways an attempt to build mentor-rich environments in urban elementary schools and inner city neighborhoods (in the South Bronx, Philadelphia, Minneapolis, Portland, Oregon, and Port Arthur, Texas). One of the things that I learned from studying mentoring, and is confirmed by the Big Brother/ Big Sister study, is that while it's incredibly important for kids to have mentors, the big issue is to have mentors who can put in a sufficient amount of time to form real relationships. We know that the segment in society who has the most time at this juncture are retirees. So this project is an attempt to not only create mentor-rich environments in the schools but to mobilize essentially the group in society which has the time to provide this kind of relation.

> *"What we're trying to do is to put a sufficient number of older volunteers in schools so that they could actually change the environment of the institution so that they became essentially mentor-rich environments. And, in the process, to try to rebuild the constituency for public schools among neighborhood elders who are a greater and greater share of the population."*

In the past, older adults have been involved in working in schools in a variety of ways, but they tend to be peripheral roles. What we're trying to do is to put a sufficient number of older volunteers in schools so that they could actually change the environment of the institution so that they became essentially mentor-rich environments. And, in the process, to try to rebuild the constituency for public schools among neighborhood elders who are a greater and greater share of the population.

BB: Something you've pointed out, as well as others like Ron Ferguson's research at the JFK School of Public Policy at Harvard, is that it's often the *case manager or youth worker* that actually is playing the real mentoring role. I think that the "I Have a Dream" mentoring study also found something like that. This seems to have some real profound implications: If we can support more community-based youth-serving programs—and the youth worker staff—or support teachers in schools by reducing class size or making sure all schools have counselors or bringing in volunteers into these institutions, we can make a real difference. It seems like this type of restructuring—supporting youth workers, teachers, counselors, etc. that are natural mentors—is just not as "sexy" as volunteer mentoring programs.

MF: I think that people have a hard time realizing that mentoring is not the exclusive province of volunteers. Groups like Big Brothers/Big Sisters which have been around for so long and are so widely known have defined the mentoring movement so much that people assume it has to be something that is a voluntary activity. But what we know from real life is that *most*

> *"I think that people have a hard time realizing that mentoring is not the exclusive province of volunteers. But what we know from real life is that most mentoring relationships form in the context of work or school—a teacher and a student, a coach and an athlete, an employer and employee."*

mentoring relationships form in the context of work or school—a teacher and a student, a coach and an athlete, an employer and employee. Most real mentoring does occur between people who are in paid positions working on something.

The main problem is just that we have identified mentoring so exclusively with Big Brothers/Big Sisters that we don't realize that there are a lot of others already spending an enormous amount of time with young people and who are naturally in a strong position to form those kinds of relationships—these are people like teachers and coaches and youth workers. In many ways they are in a better position to reach a wide number of young people.

BB: Somehow we can't seem to muster the political will to get us interested in promoting youth development. People ask me when we talk about youth development, do you think we should just get rid of the term "prevention"? People like Karen Pittman think that we probably should. My concern is, would we have *any* dollars spent for youth programming if people weren't afraid of the problems—like substance abuse, violence, etc.—that youth can present?

MF: We've gotten to the point where fear is the principle motivator—and it's not a very good motivator. It's a lot easier for people to retreat than it is for them to act. So, there's much more of the trend towards disengagement than there is toward reengaging in programs like BB/BS. It's easier to move to the suburbs or some walled community. The number one growing occupation in the U.S. is security guards.

BB: And the number one growth industry in California is prisons. And the ironic and sad thing about it all is that people go into those walled communities and kind of numb themselves on TV, work, or drugs, when reengaging with especially young people could give them a sense that their life had meaning. What advice would you offer the prevention field?

MF: I would go back to the subject that we talked about earlier. At the same time that substance abuse among teenagers is doubling, we've shown pretty systematically that these kinds of relationships can produce exactly the opposite trend. What is so striking is that these were not professional substance abuse counselors. These were not people who were focusing on the problems of youth. All they were were people who just wanted to be friends with young people—the ones who were most effective. *I think it just highlights how much we need to get back to the basics of what kids need, and that will not only improve their immediate quality of life by providing caring relationships with adults, but probably prove to be a more effective vehicle for preventing problem behaviors.* ☉

Marc Freedman is Vice-President of Public/Private Ventures, a national program development and research organization focused on helping young people in poverty. He can be reached through P/PV's main office at One Commerce Square, 2005 Market Street, Suite 900, Philadelphia, PA 19103 (215) 557-4469.

The Faces Of Resiliency

Juanita Corriz: A Relationship with a Big Sister Taught Her to "Want Everything There is Good For Me in Life"

by Nan Henderson, M.S.W.

Too often, programs fostering resiliency and positive youth development have only case example data or, sometimes, only quantified data to show their effectiveness. Big Brothers / Big Sisters of America offers both, providing the only large-scale study to-date quantifying the effectiveness of their structured approach to mentoring, as well as countless examples of the resiliency-fostering effects of this program in the lives of individual youth. Juanita Corriz is one such example. In a recent interview, she added a wildly enthusiastic face of resiliency to the quantitative data also included in this issue of Resiliency In Action, *as she talked about her Big Sister, Sharyn Obsatz, and about what their relationship has done for her.*

Juanita Corriz is a 15-year-old in Santa Fe, New Mexico with a focus: "I want to graduate, to get my education done, to think for myself, and to stay out of trouble." She also sees herself as a role model for her three younger brothers and sisters. "I want people to look up to me in my family. Like my brothers and sisters... that's what I'm trying to do, I'm the oldest and I have three young ones looking up to me, you know. And if I can do it, hopefully, they'll want to do it, too."

Juanita has made a decision to have a different life than her mother, who dropped out of high school at 17 "with only two credits left" to have a baby. Juanita's father had left; he "was promised to marry another woman," she explained. "My mom was disappointed but she knew she could make it, just me and her, on her own. I also have two brothers and one sister," she added. Her mother relied on welfare and food stamps to support her four children until Juanita was ten. Then she went to work as a night custodian at the State Capitol. Juanita has seen her father only twice in her entire life, and credits her mom for doing "her best to raise us... she's always been there for us, and she's been our strength to carry into life."

Juanita reported that her mom set an example for her by getting off welfare, going to work, "trying to make it." And her mother also helped her by encouraging her to stay in school and learn from her mistakes, to try to

"become something better for myself." One of the best things Juanita's mother did was to initiate contact with Big Brothers/Big Sisters of Santa Fe when Juanita was 12.

Juanita eagerly reported that she had a 3.0 in school last year and is working to get at least one 4.0 this year. "I'm going to try to do good because I know I can do good," she said. When asked how she developed that understanding, Juanita said that she learned it, "Pretty much from my Big Sister, Sharyn." After being on the Big Brothers/Big Sisters waiting list for two years, Juanita was matched with Sharyn Obsatz, a Minnesota native who became the county reporter for the Santa Fe newspaper, *The New Mexican*, in 1994.

Juanita explained the process: A caseworker from the program "came up to my house and interviewed me by myself, asked me questions like what I like to do and what are my favorite things...to match me and another person for what we like to do. And they compared my paper and Sharyn's paper, and they saw that we had a lot of similarities, so that's how they make the match." She added, "Me and Sharyn met, and we hit it off!"

Juanita said that she and Sharyn do all kinds of fun activities together. "The first time we hung out together, we went hiking and just talked. And since then we've taken dance lessons...we go out to eat...sometimes we have sleepovers. We do our nails and watch T.V. and pig out. Then we've had times where we just go and sit under a tree and read for awhile."

Their bond has grown far beyond just having fun together. "She made such a big difference for me because my mom sometimes…with four of us hardly has time to spend with all of us individually. But I have Sharyn as a best friend… to become very close to me. I've grown to love her, and we understand each other. Like, if anything happened, she was there for me. She's just been there for me in hard times and good times. She's just very understanding. I hope we stay paired until I graduate."

**Juanita Corriz and her Big
Sister, Sharyn Obsatz**

Sharyn, Juanita said, has been a role model and a mentor for going on to college. Sharyn asks her about school every weekend and is available to call for help on homework during the week. And she gives Juanita this message: "She knows I can do it, that I'm very smart, to get a good education, and to try the best I can. And she's trying to get me to read more; she likes to read," Juanita added.

But on Fridays, it is the fun they will have together Juanita anticipates. "Without Sharyn, the weekends would be more boring. I wouldn't really look forward to the weekends. [Now], I get happy, you know, on Fridays, when I'm going to hang out with my Big Sister and see her and talk to her… [tell] her what happened at school, and stuff. I feel if I hadn't met her, school would probably be harder for me because Sharyn is somebody I look up to, you know. If I hadn't had Sharyn, I would have had nobody to really look up to, or to care about my grades—other than my mom—to really push me to doing the best I can do knowing I can do it."

She adds that having Sharyn in her life helps her stay out of trouble. "If it wasn't for my Big Sister, I would probably have an attitude like my cousins, you know, who say that nobody else is doing it, so just drop out, and who cares about school. But I'm doing good, and kids my age aren't usually doing good these days. I want to get everything there is good for me in life."

Juanita said she thinks about being an interpreter after attending college. "I know how to speak Spanish real good and English. And I'll be taking French. So, I'll know three languages, and then I [want to] get in two more languages."

And she has a vision of herself in three years as the second of "about 20 cousins" to graduate from high school. "I want people to look at me and say, 'Wow! Juanita did it. Good for her! She deserves a lot in life because she tried her hardest to make something of herself.'" Her vision of her future includes becoming a Big Sister herself one day. "I would like to come back to Santa Fe after college and be a Big Sister here because I've seen the way it helped me. Hopefully, I can help somebody else." ☯

Nan Henderson, M.S.W., is a national and international speaker and consultant on fostering resiliency and wellness, alcohol and other drug issues, and on organizational change. She has co-authored/edited five books about resiliency, and is the president of Resiliency In Action. *She can be reached at Nan Henderson and Associates, 5130 La Jolla Blvd., #2K, San Diego, CA 92109, p/f (858-488-5034), or by e-mail: (nanh@connectnet.com).*

Resiliency In Practice

Building Resilience Through Student Assistance Programming

by Tim Duffey, M.Ed.

The Maine Department of Education Student Assistance Team Unit has trained over 320 building-based student assistance teams in the past five years. The Unit has received national recognition for the strength of its programming and high quality support materials. The program has been highlighted at the National Student Assistance Conference and the National Conference for Coordinators of Homeless Children and Youth. Denver, Colorado schools recently received training in the Maine Model as a prototype of service delivery for their system. The 250-page training manual utilized to train teams is regularly mailed to all state Safe and Drug-Free Schools and Communities Coordinators. This dissemination has resulted in frequent citation of the manual's quality and comprehensive nature by student assistance professionals around the country.

The process utilized by the teams trained in the Maine model is outlined below.

1. **An Identification Process:**
   School personnel or other concerned persons initiate referral to student assistance team. Student self-referral also is possible. Referrals are based on *observable behavior.*

2. **An Intervention Process:**
   Trained student assistance team members discuss referral information and develop short term action plan outlining steps to be taken, timelines, and accountability for completion.

3. **A Referral Process:**
   Action plans indicate appropriate referrals for assistance to resources within and outside the school setting.

4. **An Implementation Process:**
   Individual team members or designated referral sources carry out recommendations. Designated team member serves as "case manager" to monitor plan implementation.

5. **A Follow-up Process:**
   Team evaluates success of intervention strategies on a regular basis. Adjustments are made as necessary.

Though the membership of Maine student assistance teams is determined by individual schools, emphasis is placed on team composition reflecting the diverse training, experience, and professional expertise available within Maine schools. Administrators, classroom teachers, nurses, school counselors, special educators, Chapter One and/or migrant educators, chemical health coordinators, and school social workers are all roles likely to be represented on local student assistance teams (SATs). In many instances, cooperative agreements (emphasizing confidentiality) with local law enforcement and social service providers allow community professionals to add their unique backgrounds to the teams.

This multi-disciplinary approach, built upon effective team development, provides a means of operation rarely found within existing school structures. The process builds a sense of "our students" rather than "your students." This approach differs from the prevalant paradigm of student assistance, where students are identified by who is seen to have primary responsibility for them and their behavior (classroom teacher, special education, school counselor, etc.) and as a result, school staff feel isolated and overwhelmed with the nature of issues they are left to deal with... seemingly on their own.

In addition to emphasizing a multi-disciplinary approach, the Maine project's focus has evolved over time from one targeting the "at risk" population to one that emphasizes the strength and power of addressing resiliency and asset development for ALL children and youth. This change in focus reflects recent shifts in the field of prevention recognizing the potential for increased harm by labeling a child "at risk" (Benard, 1993, 1995) and the tendency to describe children "by the problems they face rather than by the strengths they possess" (Benard, 1989). The result has been a stronger alignment with resiliency and asset development research.

History of the Maine
Student Assistance Project

The student assistance effort in Maine grew from a variety of sources during the 1980s. A grassroots demand by school staff to address increasing needs for alcohol and other drug services within schools led to high level dialogue by Department of Education staff. This discussion led to a statewide *Task Force Report on Affected Children* (Department of Education, 1988). Among the findings of this report was the fact that many children affected by the alcohol or other drug use, abuse, or dependency of another person in their lives were being referred to special education. Behavioral patterns of these affected children often mimicked those of learning disabled students. Such patterns often led teachers to refer these youngsters for a special education screening.

The report stated that when these students did not qualify for special education services, they often fell in the proverbial "crack" between programs. They were not succeeding in the regular education setting as currently constructed, yet they did not meet special education criteria enabling them to receive assistance from learning specialists. The Task Force recommended that a better system be developed to ensure all Maine school children receive appropriate assistance to achieve success. It was also clear that alcohol and other drug issues were not the only concern facing Maine students, families, and educators. From its earliest stages, this project was designed to be flexible enough to address the wide range of concerns facing Maine youth. To meet the needs evident within schools, this process would have to provide staff a more effective intake and referral mechanism for students *regardless of the underlying issues*.

Sharon Rice, Special Education Director in Auburn, Maine, served as a member of the development and implementation team that brought the program to reality. "In addition to the physiological and neurological difficulties many children face, we must also recognize that our youth are mirrors of societal trends," she says. "They reflect the fragmentation of our culture. Our challenge is to move beyond the fragmentation into more wholeness within our entire society, of which our schools are but a single part." The program was designed to bring together key players in the educational system to meet this student need.

Department staff began to explore the potential for student assistance programs in use by other states as a means to address the varied needs of Maine students. In addition, the efforts of business and industry to improve problem solving and product delivery through the use of interdisciplinary teams was explored as a means of improved service delivery. A model began to take shape incorporating these two fields of education intervention and industrial teaming. In the process, a wide range of constituents were consulted to formulate these supportive services for Maine's children and youth. School counselors, nurses, social workers, teachers, and administrators were among those contacted for input into the model.

A hallmark of the Maine model is an emphasis on essential team skills. Skills critical for the successful formation and operation of any team-based program over an extended period of time were seen as critical tools. Meeting skills also received attention, ensuring teams access to the skills and resources needed to conduct efficient meetings. Such attention to honoring the time investment various professionals provide such an effort was a unique feature of the Maine approach to student assistance.

The resulting model was submitted to the US Department of Education (USDE) "Personnel Training Grant" process for funding consideration. In 1990, the Maine Department of Education received its first allocation of funds from the USDE to begin disseminating the model to Maine schools. The formation of the "Student Assistance Team Unit" within the Department ensured that consistency in training, technical assistance, and follow-up services were in place for schools adopting the student assistance philosophy and Maine's model for delivery.

Measures of Success

The program has utilized a variety of evaluation methods to measure the success of the project. One indicator of success is the finding that nearly 80% of trained teams continue to function beyond the first year following initial training. With the multitude of demands facing educators today, longevity of a project often reflects an investment of time and resources that provide a measure of reasonable "return on investment." In follow-up contacts, student assistance team members frequently cited a sense of accomplishment in working in these teams that they said they feel lacking in much of their work. They said they know their time will be well spent in the meetings attended and they will be among peers of a common mind working to improve conditions for all students. Also, members reported they appreciate the team focus on developing action plans that address specific, observable behaviors which enhance student performance, as well as identifying systemic issues impacting all students and staff.

The annual SAT project evaluations have uncovered other interesting results. Over half the schools surveyed indicated that referrals to special education are "more appropriate" as a result of utilizing this process. Comparison of student assistance team sites and non-SAT sites indicate that those schools having teams are more likely to have an effective referral process in place for alcohol and other drug issues. The SAT process was described as "beneficial" by 100% of those surveyed in trained sites, and "effective" by 73%. In addition, 68% of respondents indicated that a written follow-up procedure was used in the team's strategy planning (Medical Care Development, 1995). Such consistent follow-up is often lacking in student referral and intervention processes.

Resiliency Integration

Over the past three years, the Student Assistance Team Unit staff have made a concerted effort to provide local teams with a foundation in resiliency principles. This information has been viewed as essential to keep the work of this project at the forefront of effective prevention and intervention programming. Initial team training now contains a segment outlining the research on resiliency and positive youth development. References utilized focus on the work of Bonnie Benard, Peter Benson, Emmy Werner and Ruth Smith, Steve and Sybil Wolin, and Nan Henderson and Mike Milstein,

among others. Regional Networking meetings of existing teams have highlighted resiliency research and philosophy as well.

Unit staff are frequently called upon for resiliency-based presentations in conferences and training sessions conducted by other Department of Education staff. Their involvement has led to inclusion of resiliency principles as central tenets within several Department publications. *Fostering Hope: A Prevention Process*, developed by the Department's Prevention Team (Maine Department of Education, 1996) and the state's Improving America's Schools Act (IASA) application are two examples of documents now reflecting the resiliency paradigm. Such inclusion is reflective of Department staff members' belief that school reform and resiliency building are simultaneously achieved.

In November 1994, an historical event resulted from the resiliency foundation being built by Department of Education personnel. A day-long resiliency training was held with representatives from ALL departments of state government impacting families and youth. The memo announcing the event was a piece of history in itself. This document was the first to invite staff from these departments with signatures from each of the departments' Commissioners. The workshop facilitated development of common language for all in attendance, regardless of their work unit. While bureaucracies are notoriously slow to change, the initial effort of this event is still having ripple effects. Various departments continue to converse intra-departmentally regarding the implications of resiliency research on their activities.

Sample forms provided to local teams have also undergone change to reflect the resilience-building paradigm. Student referral forms have been drastically altered from the deficit-focused forms used in the 1980s to forms balancing statements of concern (based on observable behaviors) with statements of student strengths and assets.

The sample form on the following page is one example. Developed by SAT Unit staff, it is designed to assist local SATs in building student intervention plans that align with resiliency principles. Such additions ensure that asset and resiliency development are considered in balance with behavioral concerns and are consistent with current thinking on this topic (Henderson and Milstein, 1996; Henderson, 1996). The SAT unit is currently considering a further re-

---

SAMPLE
Resiliency-Based Action Planning Form

Student: _____   Grade: _____
Referred by: _____

Statement of presenting problem(s):

To enhance the quality of interventions, identify how each of the six elements of building resiliency will be addressed for this student.

Pro-Social Bonds
Identify positive connections this student currently has with people (peers & adults), programs, or activities, clubs and organizations.

Positive bonds will be fostered for this student as follows, based upon identified interests and strengths:

Social Skills
Describe strengths observed in this student's social skill development. Identify life skills training they have received/are receiving.

The social skill development of this student will be enhanced in these ways:

Clear and Consistent Boundaries
The following efforts are in place to provide clear and consistent boundaries for this student school-wide:

Clarity and consistency of boundaries school-wide will be enhanced for this student in the following ways:

Care and Support
This student is provided clear messages of care and support in the following ways:

Messages of care and support for this student will be strengthened in the following ways:

High Expectations for Success
Clear messages of high expectations for behavior and performance are provided this student in the following ways:

High expectations will be strengthened for this student by:

Meaningful Participation
This student is currently involved in the following ways that provide meaningful participation within and outside the school setting:

Meaningful participation for this student will be enhanced by:

---

vision of assessment forms based on two that recently appeared in the *Student Assistance Journal* (Henderson, 1996). [These are included on page 114.]

Student assistance team members are being encouraged to consider how they can effectively inform students of resiliency characteristics and assist them with identifying and describing those present in their lives. This emphasis on identification of strengths and assets versus a problem focus will impact ways of thinking for both students and staff. Protective factors identified by Hawkins and Catalano (1992), resiliency factors described by Benard (1993), [both reflected in sample action planning form], and the resiliency elements of insight, independence, relationships, initiative, humor, creativity, and morality described by the Wolins (1993) are outlined for team integration to existing efforts.

Future Trends

The Maine legislature recently approved six guiding principles recommended by the Task Force on Learning results. This structure will shape the future education for all Maine students. The student assistance process provides a critical mechanism to ensure students have the environment and structure needed to realize a readiness to learn and thereby achieve designated content standards as outlined in these principles.

A May 1996 *Report of the Governor's Task Force on Adolescent Suicide & Self-Destructive Behaviors* contained the following recommendation: "*All schools are encouraged to have student assistance teams.*" This indication of support reflects the positive impact these teams have had within Maine schools. According to Roger Richards, coordinator of the Student

Assistance Team Unit, "The data supporting the effectiveness of this program is resulting in an expanding role for these teams. Inclusion within the recent *Governor's Task Force Report* is a clear example." He adds, "Increasing needs of Maine students creates a growing demand for an effective response mechanism. We are seeing an ever widening professional need to work in this way for the benefit of all youth in our schools." ℮

References

Benard, B. (1993). *Turning the corner from risk to resiliency.* Portland, OR: Western Regional Center for Drug-Free Schools and Communities, Northwest Educational Laboratory.

Benard, B. (1995). How schools can foster resiliency in children. In *Western Center News.* September. Portland, OR: Western Regional Center for Drug-Free Schools and Communities, Northwest Educational Laboratory.

Hawkins, J.D., Catalano, R.F., Jr., et al. (1992). *Communities that care.* San Francisco, CA: Jossey-Bass.

Henderson, N. (1996). SAPs that build student resiliency. In *Student Assistance Journal.* March/April. Troy, MI: Performance Resource Press.

Henderson, N., & Milstein, M. (1996). *Resiliency in schools: Making it happen for students and educators.* Thousand Oaks, CA: Corwin Press.

Maine Department of Education (1988). *Task force report on affected children.* Augusta, ME.

Maine Department of Education (1994). *Student assistance team training manual.* Augusta, ME.

Maine Department of Education (1996). *Fostering hope: A prevention process.* Augusta, ME.

Medical Care Development (1995). *Maine student assistance team process evaluation, 1994.* Augusta, ME.

Office of Substance Abuse (1996). *Report of the Governor's Task Force on adolescent suicide & self-destructive behaviors.* Augusta, ME.

Wolin, S. J., & S. (1993). *The resilient self: How survivors of troubled families rise above adversity.* New York, NY: Villard Books.

Tim Duffey, M.Ed., is Past President of the National Association of Leadership for Student Assistance Programs, co-founder of the New England consulting group, Common Ground In Prevention, and a former Feature Editor of Resiliency In Action. *He can be reached at Common Ground In Prevention (207-839-6319) or by e-mail: (tduffey47@aol.com).*

The following forms, adapted from "SAPs that Build Student Resiliency" by Nan Henderson, which appeared in the March, 1996 Student Assistance Journal, *provide additional examples of student assistance paperwork reflecting the process of integration of resiliency principles into student assistance programs.*

Assessment of Environmental Resiliency-Builders

NAME OF STUDENT _____

1. **Positive bond's in this student's life:**
   People
   Interests/Activities
   Describe your connection to this student:

2. **Situations where the student experiences structure/clear boundaries:**

3. **The student has learned these life skills (as evidenced by their use):**

   The student is currently receiving life skills training (describe):

4. **Individuals/organizations/settings that provide this student with caring and support:**

5. **Individuals/environmental situations that communicate high expectations for success to this student:**

6. **This student is involved in helping others/making positive contributions in the following ways:**

   How can these environmental resiliency-builders be used in intervening with this student?

Assessment of Internal Characteristics of Resiliency

NAME OF STUDENT _____

Check the following personal resiliency-builders you have observed in this student (in addition to problems). (Source: *Resiliency in Schools: Making It Happen for Students and Educators* by Nan Henderson and Mike Milstein, published in 1996 by Corwin Press). These are ways that individuals cope with stress and adversity in their lives, and research indicates one or more of these can be identified in every student (and in every adult).

❏ Relationships - Sociability/ability to be a friend/ability to form positive relationships
❏ Service - Gives of self in service to others and/or a cause
❏ Life Skills - Uses life skills, including good decision-making, assertiveness, and impulse control
❏ Humor - Has a good sense of humor
❏ Inner Direction - Bases choices/decisions on internal evaluation (internal locus of control)
❏ Perceptiveness - Insightful understanding of people and situations
❏ Independence - "Adaptive" distancing from unhealthy people and situations/autonomy
❏ Positive View of Personal Future - Expects a positive future
❏ Flexibility - Can adjust to change; can bend as necessary to positively cope with situations
❏ Love of Learning - Capacity for and connection to learning
❏ Self-motivation - Internal initiative and positive motivation from within
❏ Competence - Is "good at something"/personal competence
❏ Self-Worth - Feelings of self-worth and self-confidence
❏ Spirituality - Personal faith in something greater
❏ Perseverance - Keeps on despite difficulty; doesn't give up
❏ Creativity - Expresses self through artistic endeavor
    (From research by Richardson, et al., 1990; Werner and Smith, 1992; Hawkins, et al., 1992; and Wolin and Wolin, 1993)

How can we further nurture/build upon these resiliency builders in this student's life?

How can they be used in intervening with this student?

PART FIVE

Resiliency and Youth Development

Connecting Resiliency, Youth Development, and Asset Development in a Positive-Focused Framework for Youth

by Peter Benson, Ph.D.

In efforts to increase the health, well-being, and life chances of America's youth, two paradigms coexist. Both are important, but they have different implications for policy and practice. The historically dominant paradigm focuses on naming, counting, and reducing the negative. The "negative" includes developmental risks (e.g., poverty, family dysfunction, unsafe schools and neighborhoods, negative peer pressure) and problem behaviors (e.g., teen pregnancy, substance use, school dropout, antisocial behavior, the violent resolution of conflict). For lack of a better descriptive term for this approach, let's call it a problem-focused paradigm. This approach—this way of thinking and conceptualizing—often dominates the way communities plan, organize, and implement youth-serving policy, program, and practice.

> *"Problem-free is not the same as health, a concept which demands the pursuit of the positive as much or more than reduction of the negative."*

The problem-focused paradigm is fueled by several cultural dynamics. Funding programs, particularly at the federal level, often create categorical initiatives attacking particular problem behaviors. These programs are housed in bureaucracies with problem-focused names. The Center for Substance Abuse Prevention and the Center for Disease Control come to mind. The language of problem and the language of risk are reinforced by a litany of research studies organized to track and monitor high-risk behaviors and by a media (television, radio, print) which, according to recent journalism studies, accents human mayhem. As much as two-thirds of all news rotates around conflict, destruction, violence, and disaster. Lesser emphasis is given to stories of connection, integration, harmony, unity, compassion, and justice.

> *"The two sides of the coin, reducing the negative and promoting the positive, are not opposites. There is a synergy, an interaction between these."*

The problem-focused approach is deeply entrenched. It both reflects and shapes a predilection to think, plan, and evaluate in terms of problems. It is dedicated to reducing or controlling negative developmental experiences or acts, through prevention, early intervention, social services, and/or treatment when problems escalate. It is an important and useful approach to healing what ails us as a culture. Indeed, health-compromising, future-jeopardizing, safety-threatening environments and actions must be tackled head on. But by itself, this approach is limited and incomplete. As one wise sage of youth development, Karen Pittman, puts it, problem-free is not the same as health, a concept which demands the pursuit of the positive as much or more than reduction of the negative.

Promoting the Positive: The Other Side of the Coin

In raising healthy and whole children and adolescents, like attention needs to be given to naming, counting, understanding, and promoting the positive. It is the other side of the coin. The two sides of the coin, reducing the negative and promoting the positive, are not opposites. There is a synergy, an interaction between these. For example, the strategy of promoting the positive (e.g., belonging, connection, engagement, empowerment) can reduce the negative. And reducing family dysfunction or economic inequality, for example, clears the way for belonging, connection, and empowerment to occur.

Three approaches to naming and promoting positive psychosocial development have emerged in the 1990s. They travel under the names of "resiliency," "youth development," and "asset development." Each of these three is both a conceptual model naming core elements of positive human development and an area of practice seeking to alter policy, environments, and individual-level characteristics.

Of the three, resiliency has the deepest research tradition (see Benard on p. 121). Its scientific grounding is in studies of children and adults who overcome or transcend adversity. In essence, it discovers and names the strengths, experiences, and environmental conditions which bolster, inoculate, and protect. This new and significant journal, *Resiliency in Action*, provides the best, ongoing synthesis of this field's research and practice.

> **"It has become normative for most youth in all communities to lack many of the developmental assets."**

Youth development is an emerging and somewhat eclectic conceptual framework seeking to define the skills and competencies youth need to be successful in a rapidly changing world. It is more a philosophy than an area of direct, integrated scientific inquiry. Youth development practitioners advocate paying attention to needs, skills, and competencies during the second decade of life, with an accent on organizing youth programs, schools, and community policy to be particularly responsive to engagement, belonging, connection, and empowerment.

Perhaps the strongest articulator of this model/philosophy/way-of-thinking is Karen Pittman, now Vice President for the International Youth Foundation. In 1991, Pittman and Michelle Cahill produced a seminal paper titled *A New Vision: Promoting Youth Development*. It provided a first attempt to name the critical components of youth development needed to promote "fully-prepared" adults. The model included both needs (safety, belonging, self-worth, independence, closeness, competence, self-awareness) and competencies (health, sociability, vocational competence, citizenship, knowledge, reasoning, and creativity).

> **"Not surprisingly, the three models both share intellectual space and at the same time possess unique accents."**

Asset development is a relatively new conceptualization of healthy child and adolescent development, rooted in an ongoing national research and community change initiative at Search Institute in Minneapolis. The recent configuration of developmental assets synthesizes research on 30 initially identified environmental and individual dynamics (recently expanded to 40, see chart on p. 134), which serve as protective factors inhibiting health-compromising behavior and/or as enhancement factors which promote academic achievement and parallel forms of success.

The 40 assets are grouped into eight categories: support, empowerment, boundaries and expectations, the constructive use of time, commitment to learning, values, social competencies, and positive identity. The national research, based on assessments of public school students—both middle school and high school—in 600 school districts, documents both that it has become normative for most youth in all communities to lack many of the developmental assets and that as the number of assets rises, multiple forms of "high risk" behavior decrease and multiple forms of thriving (school success, affirmation of diversity) increase (Benson, Galbraith, & Espeland, 1994, and Benson, in press).

Resiliency, Youth Development, Asset Development: Unique, Yet Similar

These three approaches, each naming essential elements of psychosocial development, emanate from somewhat different sources. *Resiliency* researchers tend to identify developmental factors which distinguish individuals who cope successfully with adversity—versus those for whom adaptation is less effective. *Youth development* and its advocates and practitioners tend to focus on the competencies needed to help youth transition from adolescence into successful adulthood. Implied in this approach is a deep critique of how this society relates to adolescents, particularly those in urban or other settings in which systems and policy are too inattentive, unresponsive, or counterproductive. *Asset development* is a framework which articulates basic developmental necessities during the first two decades of life. Asset development theory extends the cultural critique, arguing that many of the core processes of healthy development, rooted ideally in norms and relationships within community, are ruptured or incomplete for most American youth.

Not surprisingly, the three models both share intellectual space and at the same time possess unique accents. The content similarities are pronounced. Each model highlights the importance of caring relationships, meaningful participation in decision-making, organizational life and community, problem-solving skills, social competencies, adult advocacy, and personal efficacy. The implication of this heavy overlap is that some of the "good stuff" plays multiple human development roles.

Each of the three approaches to naming the characteristics of healthy human development have high face validity. And each has devotees developing strategies and tactics to build and promote the elements of healthy development. This is creative and exciting work, with evaluations underway or emerging to help refine models and understand best practices. The Kellogg Youth Initiative Partnerships initiative, designed to unleash youth development energies in Michigan communities, is grounded in an ongoing learning and reflection process. Project Competence at the University of Minnesota is an ongoing program development and research effort to "understand the development of competence and resilience in the presence of risk." And Search Institute's efforts to mobilize communities will be

Again, the distinctions named above are about tendencies and instincts, not absolutes. Over time, it appears that the distinctions are becoming blurred. Resiliency is increasingly discussed as a general human competence that should be nurtured in all youth and adults; developmental assets are being appropriated by program developers in designing short-term interventions.

Integrating and Synthesizing the Models

It is difficult—at this moment in history—to articulate which approach (resiliency, youth development, asset development) is the best for addressing a particular need. This ambiguity is fed by conceptual overlap and the infancy of evaluation studies. Until the science of promoting positive healthy development catches up to its practice, practitioners have to make difficult choices about how to proceed. If one must choose just one approach, then I would suggest tilting to the

	Resiliency	Youth Development	Asset Development
Key Strategies	Development of hands-on-programs and interventions	Transformation of youth-serving systems via training, planning, and policy	Uniting all sectors of community; unclashing and sustaining long-term movements of residents and systems
Target Populations	Vulnerable children and adolescents	Ages 12-21	All children and adolescents

informed by a new five-and-a-half year Colorado initiative to unite communities, systems, and citizens around the asset development model. About twenty percent of a $10 million grant from The Colorado Trust will be devoted to evaluation, including longitudinal studies of the impact of community mobilization on developmental assets.

In promoting the characteristics of positive human development, multiple strategies are needed as shown in the chart above. Though all three "schools of thought" speak of all three strategies, resiliency has particular strength in shaping hands-on strategies, with particular applicability to vulnerable youth. Youth development practitioners have particular strength in awakening youth-serving programs and systems to systemic commitment to positive development. The asset-development model has its strength in unleashing community-wide efforts.

resiliency paradigm for shaping interventions and approaches needed *now* for vulnerable or troubled or "at risk" youth and to the asset-development paradigm for reclaiming the power and energy of intact, whole, and effective communities.

But this is not the kind of choice I'd advocate. Because the three models are highly complementary, and because all youth need greater systems of support in both the short-term and long-term, the integration and synthesis of the three models will take us further.

None of us—researchers, model developers, or practitioners—yet knows enough of the truth about promoting positive development in a child-unfriendly world to claim we know the way. Hence, this essay is, more than anything, an invitation to build bridges of dialogue across the three "schools of thought," to unleash the kind of research dollars needed to refine and integrate and encourage practitioners to experiment with synthesizing the approaches and then sharing their wisdom with all kindred spirits and soul mates. Ultimately, if this is to become a child-friendly culture, we will need the strength of cooperation, shared inquiry, friendly debate, and an openness to change.

> **"Resiliency, youth development, and asset development are variations on a theme."**

Resiliency, youth development, and asset development are variations on a theme. And the theme is more important than the players. ☉

References

Benson, P.L., Galbraith, J., & Espeland, P. (1994). *What kids need to succeed*. Minneapolis, MN: Free Spirit Publishing, Inc.

Benson, P. (in press). *From peril to possibility: The urgency of creating healthy communities for children and adolescents*. San Francisco, CA: Jossey-Bass.

Masten, A.S., et al. (1995). The structure and coherence of competence from childhood through adolescence. *Child Development, 66*, 1535-1659.

Pittman, K.J., & Cahill, M. (1991). *A new vision: Promoting youth development*. Washington, DC: The Center for Youth Development and Policy Research.

Dr. Peter Benson is President of Search Institute, an organization of more than 20 social scientists and educators dedicated to "practice research benefiting children and youth" and creators of the "Healthy Communities • Healthy Youth™" initiative. He has authored several publications, including What Kids Need to Succeed.

Resiliency Interview

Changing the Condition, Place, and View of Young People in Society: An Interview with Bill Lofquist

by Bonnie Benard, M.S.W.

BB: You've been a visionary in this whole field of youth development. A couple of issues ago *Resiliency In Action* featured Jeanne Gibbs, whom I think was a real visionary in trying to put a human development perspective into education. Your work has been trying to put that whole human development/youth development perspective into all of youth services and youth-serving systems.

Would you define what "youth development" means to you?

BL: Youth development refers to the overall condition and place of young people in the community, how they are viewed and valued, opportunities of development available to them, resources available to them when they have problems, opportunities they have to contribute policies that effect them, the quality of their relationships with peers and adults.

My definition really takes a fairly broad look at the circumstance and life experience of young persons—both internally as they develop as individuals and their external relationships as they interact with the people around them and the basic institutions of our society.

BB: It shouldn't be considered a radical perspective to have the kind of child-centered or youth-centered service system that you advocate and yet somehow it still seems to be the case. Would you share how you came to this perspective, just a little bit about who you are and what you've done?

BL: I guess it would go back to my own early experience. I was born in Mississippi and grew up in the South during the time of segregation. I became aware fairly early on

that the culture of my family and the values that I got from my family were far and away stronger for me than the culture of the community in which I lived.

> *"Youth development refers to the overall condition and place of young people in the community, how they are viewed and valued, opportunities of development available to them, resources available to them when they have problems, opportunities they have to contribute policies that effect them, the quality of their relationships with peers and adults."*

I moved from Mississippi to Virginia when I was nine years old for a few months and then to North Carolina, which I consider home. The strength of my family culture personally overpowered that strong southern segregationist culture. And that was a real issue just by virtue of where I lived.

It became a very personal thing both in regard to race as well as many, many other issues. I think the same values that inform our attitude about race inform other attitudes. My dad was a Presbyterian minister who worked for social agencies in a variety of things in Asheville, North Carolina. He would frequently bring home people that he was working with and sort of used our house as an informal foster home. That was a routine experience at our house in my later elementary years and junior high and senior high years. I think that had a lot of influence on me.

I went to seminary for three years and during that time became convinced that I wanted to work in child welfare. I attended the University of North Carolina School of Social Work after seminary. Another influence that

I found important was volunteer work in the summers that was organized by the American Friends Service Committee, the Quakers. I worked in a "Native American Community" in Maine and one that was in Europe, and one that was in the Illinois State Training School for Boys, outside Chicago. After graduation, I went to work in a church-related children's home. So from the beginning, I was involved in youth-focused kinds of things.

I then went to work for the University of North Carolina School of Social Work as a faculty field instructor at a juvenile court and worked there for about six years. Then I got involved in the late '60s in the youth service movement. That's when I really got into prevention work.

I had a community or sociological bent probably more strongly than a psychological bent. I was an undergraduate major in sociology, and I was interested in institutions. By institutions, I mean the basic institutions of family and school, religious institutions, the economy, and government, and the impact those have on people, and the interaction we have with the institutions that we participate in.

Also, I've come over the years to have a stronger and stronger feeling that the way a community or society views and treats its young people, that's basically the way it views and treats all of its citizens. Young people serve as a metaphor for people of all ages. And the general belief we have about youth development can generally be applied to people of all ages.

> *"The way a community or society views and treats its young people [is] basically the way it views and treats all of its citizens. Young people serve as a metaphor for people of all ages."*

BB: That's certainly what Margaret Mead said, too. You're in good company. I think Meister Eckhardt, a mystic in the Middle Ages, said something like, "God is like a river and is accessed by many different wells." No matter what language we use, we're talking about the same good stuff.

BL: People all around the world are essentially looking at the same phenomenon, though we come at it from different angles. But there's an inherent consistency frequently found as people look at different philosophies, different theologies, different ways of politics—that we're all dealing with the same phenomenon wherever we are in the world.

BB: It seems that you're getting at that deep humanity that we all share. Obviously, your family and the loving and caring of your father in taking in other young people allowed you to see the humanity of marginalized groups.

BL: Yes, and especially being in the South at that time. The civil rights movement to me was a very exciting time. It represented a breaking out of that confining culture that really did violence to many, many people, both black and white.

BB: We need another one! Now, you've had this perspective for over 20 years. You started the wonderful publication, *New Designs for Youth Development* in 1980. It's interesting to me that people are starting to rediscover youth development. I go a lot of places and hear people talking about Karen Pittman and the work that she did while she was at the Center for Youth Development and Policy Research in Washington, D.C. I think this organization brought a lot of new attention to youth development through Karen's leadership in getting a strong funding base and her focus on trying to develop a policy perspective that's very different from where we seem to have arrived in prevention.

This brings me to another issue of looking at the whole question of prevention and its relation to youth development. When you wrote *Discovering the Meaning of Prevention* (1983), which is still one of the best books in the whole field, you very diplomatically discussed how prevention has typically been defined from a public health perspective in terms of primary, secondary, and tertiary, but that the whole medical model approach has kind of moved us towards approaches of fixing deficits—in kids especially—and fixing them with programs. It seems to me that this has been the federal policy approach channeling the moneys that have flowed to the prevention field.

Finally, my question: Do you think that this risk-focused approach, the idea that we can fix individuals and kids with programs, has maybe had a negative effect—what John McKnight calls an "iatrogenic" effect—that may be hurting youth development efforts?

BL: I've labeled it the "diagnose problem" model. One of the problems with it is that it's determined from the point of view of the person doing the diagnosis, who is usually a professional. While that's an important perspective, it's a very limited and limiting perspective. It's linear. It's from the perspective of the way the diagnoser is looking at it. And the shortcoming of the model is that when we ask, "Where does success lie?", that model really doesn't give a way back towards success.

I think that what's happened as a result is that we have terribly, terribly fragmented human service work by seeing some programs (which really are sets of activities) as being prevention and some as being treatment. And the context of intervention is a real muddy context anyway, so that any effort to change anything is really an intervention process. We need an alternative model to this "diagnose problem" perspective.

I've tried to develop and use for the past 18 to 20 years now an alternative model that I called the "Arenas of Human Service Activity." I now call it the "Arenas of Action" because I think it's much broader than just human service work. My approach makes a distinction between *development* and *problem solving*. I define development as an active process of creating conditions and fostering personal attributes that promote the well-being of people; problem solving is a reactive, corrective effort to bring about change where there is a recognized problem. Both of these are obviously very important. I think most of what we do falls pretty clearly and cleanly into one or the other.

> *"What the 'diagnose problem' model doesn't do is show the dynamic interplay between development and problem-solving work—and that success lies on the development side."*

What the "diagnose problem" model doesn't do is show the dynamic interplay between development and problem-solving work—and that success lies on the development side. Effective treatment is going to lead people towards a positive development mode or way of viewing life and relating to life. What we need is a model which might start with problems but points back in the other direction towards development.

BB: Towards developing people so that they can feel a sense of their own power and begin to solve their own problem—which is the only way they'll ever be

solved to begin with! I've been reading a book called *No Enemy Within* by Dawna Markova, a Jungian psychologist, and she states that in our culture we have become experts at diagnosing problems and at putting all the problems inside ourselves and all the solutions outside ourselves—where only experts can solve them. They can do this with programs! I thought this was a good way to say it.

> *"Radical is not a dirty word. I think it's an important word— basic, fundamental questioning of the status quo."*

BL: On the other hand, in the alternative model, the nature of a specific action is determined by the purpose of the activity and not by a diagnosis. In this more dynamic model, human service planning can move clearly and easily between development and problem solving depending upon the purpose. In this way success and problem solving can be described as moving toward development work, and development work can be seen as an alternative to problem-solving work. Treatment professionals can more clearly become involved in development work, thus enriching the concept of treatment in opening new opportunities for the professional and the beneficiary of the work. People in treatment can be participants in development work, both as resource people and as beneficiaries. And partnerships can be shaped that bring people together in new ways. I'm finding people's response to this alternative way of looking at things is one of excitement and hope.

BB: Oh, yes. Why, then, do you think this perspective is always—I called it radical earlier—a kind of "counter-cultural" perspective?

BL: It's radical in the best sense of that word in that it gets more deeply into the root of what we might be concerning ourselves with. Radical is not a dirty word. I think it's an important word—basic, fundamental questioning of the status quo. I think that some of the methods we use don't lead to change at all. They're more related to the status quo. A lot of the methods we're using in human service work now— and I think that increasing numbers of people agree with this—is just not getting the work done. They're not effective. They're not getting the results that we need to be getting through the work that we do. So many of our resources in human service work are used carrying out human service activities and not getting very significant results. We need to look more deeply and fundamentally at what we're doing and question that deeply; this is the beginning of fundamental or transformational change. That's what we need to be more attentive to—and the word radical relates to this.

BB: It certainly says something about having human service work really be work in the community and not just carrying out bureaucratic mandates and federal policies. It's going to take some really deep commitment to community development.

BL: I think that community development is essentially a local responsibility and a local transaction that takes place where people work and live and learn and spend their time and spend their leisure. This gets into some really important policy considerations. The localness of the work that we do needs to be supported by policies and practices and understandings that occur at those levels in government that are removed from the local situation. People that work even at the county level or the state level or the national level need to be helped to become more attuned to what local realities are.

BB: In the book *The End of Work*, Jeremy Rifkin says our essential question is, how do we achieve our sense of social identity in a world devoid of work? When he discusses solutions he says we aren't looking at the incredible power of the third sector, which is the volunteer sector, and small community-based organizations. If we can support those community-based organizations through giving our tax dollars back to these local community organizations, we would really see systems where communities truly would take care of their own.

BL: I think that what we value needs to be seen as legitimate work and there are all kinds of quality of life issues that the economy needs to be responsive to. We do need to reshape the economy. I think it's in as much need of radical transition as the other institutions. And the way those five basic institutions [family, school, church, economy, and government] interact with one another is so important to the quality of a society.

So we need to redefine the work to be done. The way I've tried to go about doing this and engaging other people in thinking about it is to think about the whole concept of a compassionate society. It seems to me that when we think about that, the alternative is an antagonistic society. A mirror that we can hold up to what we do and how we do it has to do with whether what we're doing is compassionate or whether it's antagonistic. Some of what we do even within human service work—that has the best of intentions—can become quite antagonistic, especially when the methods we use tend to view and treat people as objects or recipients rather than respect and engage them as resource people.

> *"Some of what we do even within human service work—that has the best of intentions—can become quite antagonistic, especially when the methods we use tend to view and treat people as objects or recipients rather than respect and engage them as resource people."*

BB: It's really that ultimate challenge of whether we develop compassion or whether we keep promoting a greed-based society based on consumerism. It's clearly a major challenge for the whole next century. It's kind of mind-boggling.

How do you see the concept of resiliency, and resiliency research, supporting community development in the work that you do?

BL: Resiliency research has certainly been deepening my belief that there's a powerful, powerful connection between looking at the way an individual grows and develops and the way that the community impacts us. The interaction between the person and the situation in which they find themselves is not an either/or situation at all. It's always a both/and. I think if we lean too much toward either the psychological or sociological, we get ourselves in trouble. In whatever we do, we must take both the person and the situation into consideration.

A number of years ago my wife and I went to one of Sid Simon's personal growth workshops. We went to two week-long ones. Those were both marvelous experiences. Because while Sid Simon works in the personal growth area, from the first minute of his workshop he begins to create a community context in the workshop for doing that, and everything he talks about has implications for the individual's relationship to the larger community through the relationships that they have and the quality of those relationships. The whole process of resiliency is so integral to both personal development and to community development. And there is both a personal and a community side to the concept of resiliency. I'm finding that exploring this concept in new ways is adding a whole new dimension, even to the community development side of things. What we've been trying to do in these workshops is to relate the concept of resiliency not only to what comes from the inside out from the individual but also to look at those realities that impact us and to look at the way we relate to those realities and the inner strength that we need just to live.

> *"I think if we lean too much toward either the psychological or sociological, we get ourselves in trouble. In whatever we do, we must take both the person and the situation into consideration."*

BB: One thing so compelling to me about Emmy Werner's work is that she is one of the resiliency researchers that really understands that transactional process of the person and the environment—and that both of these are human systems. It's also fascinating that no matter whether you look at an individual or a small group or a classroom or a community—these are all human systems. It's the power of the relationships that we create and the beliefs that we have about people and their opportunities to contribute and participate that are the factors that promote success in any of those systems.

BL: Exactly. I remember back in college in a zoology course, "Ontogeny recapitulates phylogeny." What I understand that to mean is that the growth and development of the individual replicates what has happened over time in the growth of the whole

> *"There is both a personal and a community side to the concept of resiliency. I'm finding that exploring this concept in new ways is adding a whole new dimension, even to the community development side of things."*

species. It can even be seen in the development of the embryo. This is getting into evolution. However, the relationship of the individual is so incredibly phenomenal. Physiologically, there is a replication or a recapitulation of what the scientists believe may have happened over time. We have within each of us, individually, that relationship to the larger picture.

I think it's so astounding and mind boggling. It's awe-inspiring when we think about it. Then when we

begin to look at the world around us and within us from a larger development perspective, we see the connectedness of things. It's not accidental that so many wonderful serendipitous kinds of things are constantly happening.

BB: I think the word "connectedness" is one of the key words in youth development. It is critical to our work that we help people see those connections. Connections to other people and to ideas and probably connections to a deeper spiritual essence is absolutely the critical essence of a developmental approach.

One last question: What is your hope for the future of the youth development movement in human services?

BL: That's a very good question. For me it's focused in one of our models that I call the "Spectrum of Attitudes." It really has to do with the nature and quality of relationships between and among people. It says, quite simply, that there are basically three ways that people view and treat other people...as *objects*, as *recipients*, and as *resources*. There are qualitative differences between and among those three things. One of the things that I've tried to do in my workshops and my writing is a consciousness-raising approach toward encouraging people to consider the qualitative differences towards those three attitudes and kinds of behavior.

What people tend to come to over and over again is that much of youth work in the past and present (because of cultural and other kinds of things) has tended to view and treat young people as either objects—of our good intentions at best, or we've actually been abusive of young people at worst—or we've seen them as recipients of our well-intended approaches to things, rather than respecting and engaging them as resources.

What I would like to see in the future of youth work is attention to what I see as a civil rights issue in our society: age discrimination, which is not unlike race discrimination and gender discrimination. We need a new kind of consciousness about young people as individuals and as people in their own right. Adults don't always know what's good for young people. We need—from the earliest ages—to begin engaging children and youth in making decisions that affect them. This starts best at very, very early ages—from birth really—in the family.

When we begin to show respect for young people as resources and our consciousness is raised in that direction, we're going to find increasingly that this is directly related to the kinds of symptomatic behaviors we see young people express. We continually find ourselves reacting to substance abuse, teen pregnancy, gang violence, delinquency, under achievement, you know all the rest. We can make a long list of them. Those symptoms are essentially related to the nature and quality of experience in relationships that young people have from the time that they're born.

> *"We need a new kind of consciousness about young people as individuals and as people in their own right. Adults don't always know what's good for young people. We need—from the earliest ages—to begin engaging children and youth in making decisions that affect them. This starts best at very, very early ages—from birth really—in the family."*

I would like to see us reconceptualize youth work from a community development perspective that doesn't so much see young people as the objects of good intentions of adults, but sees young people as key actors and participants and partners with adults. Some of the best and most exciting breakthroughs I see happening in youth work is built around that idea. It's creating new partnerships between young people and adults as very respectful relationships.

BB: I think you've said it all right there: it is that whole idea of respect and somehow making those

intergenerational linkages. While in the past, societies have seen young people as resources because their work was needed, we must reclaim that perspective once again. The work of young people is desperately needed now; it's just that adult society doesn't realize it! We need their energy, their enthusiasm, their creativity, their morality, their caring for the earth, and their work to repair all the damage adult society has done.

I think your work is putting this message out there—a message we probably need now more than ever. There is certainly a lot of youth bashing going on, unfortunately, by a lot of federal agencies that a lot of us have worked for.

BL: We need to practice that in the localness of the things that we're doing. Yet it's so related to the larger issues we see in the world of human dignity, of human rights, of democracy.

BB: It's thinking globally and acting locally. You are certainly an inspiration to all of us in doing just this. ℮

Bill Lofquist is President of Development Publications, a recent publication effort. To get a list of his publications, to be placed on the mailing list, or to inquire about his trainings, contact him at Development Publications, P.O. Box 36748, Tucson, Arizona 85740; telephone (520-575-7047). To order any of his published materials, call (800-711-3988).

Resiliency and Asset Development:
A Continuum for Youth Success

by Nan Henderson, M.S.W.

A New England school district I worked with recently has been struggling with some important questions: How does the resiliency approach to working with young people connect to the asset-development approach promoted by the Search Institute (see related articles on pp. 117 & 133)? When should one approach be used and when another? Do they overlap? Do they involve doing different things for kids? How can we sort this out for all those in our school community who are interested in both fostering resiliency and asset development for students? Finally, given the reality of limited time and resources,

> **"Fostering resiliency and asset development are complimentary approaches to working with youth."**

which approach should our district concentrate on? When I was in the district last fall, these questions were addressed to me. I am asked similar questions in communities around the country. Many of my colleagues (including the editors of this journal) report that they, too, have been asked for a clarification of the similarities and differences between the resiliency and asset-building approach to youth development.

As Benson suggests in his article on the same subject (see p.117), fostering resiliency and asset development are complimentary approaches to working with youth. It is clear to me that the choice must be to do both, rather than one or the other, because each approach provides important contributions to the positive development of young people.

Why All Kids Need Both Resiliency and Asset Development

Fostering resiliency and increasing the developmental assets of young people comprise the continuum of a comprehensive approach to improving the lives of *all* kids.

Resiliency, as Benson points out, was initially aimed primarily at youth identified as "at risk," but it is increasingly recognized as a need of all children and youth. The evolution of the definition of resiliency to *an ability to spring back, rebound, and/or successfully adapt in the face of adversity* (Henderson & Milstein, 1996), including all the environmental risks, personal traumas and tragedies, or individual challenges such as physical, mental, or emotional disabilities, clarifies why every young person alive (indeed, every person of any age!) needs to develop this capacity. It is of course more critical, and often more difficult, for those faced with greater adversity and tragedy to be resilient than for those whose lives are "easier." But some resiliency researchers and theorists argue (persuasively, in my opinion) that the process of encountering and successfully meeting challenges, and becoming wiser and stronger in the process, is, in fact, the overall purpose of life for all (Richardson, et al., 1990). No one can deny the "high risk" and uncertain nature of the world children and youth encounter today (documented by the Search Institute research finding that only a small fraction of youth experience the optimum number of assets for adolescent development) that contributes to the requirement of resiliency for all kids.

> **"The crucial foundation of a resiliency-building relationship, however, is what I have labeled the resiliency attitude."**

Developing resiliency is first and foremost a person-to-person process. Resiliency is forged in the crucible of caring human relationships, as documented by the numerous studies and personal reports (see Seita on p.139) that explore just how people do succeed in the face of often seemingly overwhelming obstacles. The crucial foundation of a resiliency-building relationship, however, is what I have labeled *the resiliency attitude*, which is characterized by the messages "I see what is right with you," "Your strengths are more powerful than your problems," "No matter what your past, you can be successful in the future," and "We will work together to find a way for your success."

While resiliency is built in relationships characterized by the resiliency attitude and unconditional caring and empowering interactions, asset development is more focused on rebuilding "the societal infrastructure" (Search, 1996) of support for children and youth, with an emphasis on organizational and community mobilization (see article on p. 133 for a detailed explanation of the asset-development approach). Examples of this approach include increasing opportunities in the community for intergenerational interaction, engaging children and teenagers in community service, and the establishment by businesses of "family-friendly" policies. In the very broad sense, asset development also focuses on local, state, and national politics and policies that relate to youth. In a narrower sense, it gives much organizational and programmatic direction to the spheres that surround each child: families, neighborhoods, schools, churches, and other community groups.

This, then, is the resiliency/youth development/asset development continuum (diagrammed above):

(1) Resiliency is at the heart, developed in caring and empowering daily interactions, which provide *right now* most of the environmental protective factors that mitigate the impact of stress in a young person's life.

(2) Youth development (as Benson explains on page117) approaches and asset development approaches are inherent in programs and organizational structures and strategies, which *may take time* to redesign.

(3 Asset development is the *long-term* guiding force of communities—improving the environmental infrastructure in significant ways, a complex and often political process that can take years.

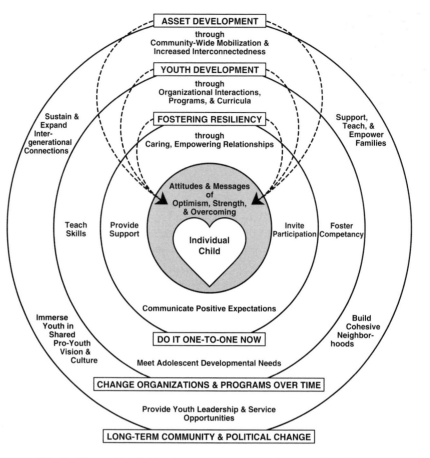

The Resiliency/Youth Development/Asset Development Continuum Needed By All Youth

Infusing the "Resiliency Attitude" Across the Continuum

The *resiliency attitude*, which can be summarized as a strength-based philosophy, must be infused across this resiliency/youth development/asset development continuum. To create intergenerational interaction

> *"The resiliency attitude, which can be summarized as a strength-based philosophy, must be infused across this resiliency/youth development/ asset development continuum."*

opportunities or service learning programs, for example, that are characterized by typical adult attitudes and behaviors towards "youth at risk"—labeling, condemning, lecturing, disempowering, and distancing (see the "Faces of Resiliency," p. 137)—will doom this potential asset building to failure.

This critical issue of attitude is, in fact, one danger of the entire asset assessment approach that forms the basis of the Search Institute research. While resiliency research is primarily a body of *life span* studies, which show how individuals *over the long run* succeed in the face of great adversity (that certainly includes "too few developmental assets"), asset research (using the "Profiles of Student Life" developed by the Search Institute) is similar to most risk research that measures only "a snap shot" of a young person's life at

> "Working with asset-building intention without 'the resiliency attitude,' results in turning a strength-based approach into a deficit-focused one, and in the process, hurting kids."

any given time. Both risk research and asset assessment document that at a given moment in time (when the research is conducted) the absence of important environmental supports is *correlated* with the presence of "at risk" behaviors, including alcohol and other drug abuse, early/unsafe sexual activity, violence and gang involvement, and problems in school. Both of these types of research fail to document, however, what many resiliency researchers (and the editors of this journal) refer to as the innate human capacity to successfully overcome the environmental risks, i.e. asset deficits—the ability *in the long run*, with the help of both internal capacities and external environmental protective factors that mitigate the impact of risks, to become successful adults that "love well, work well, play well, and expect well."

> "Every child, no matter how few his or her assets, must get the message 'you can succeed' rather than the still-prevalent attitude of doom and gloom."

In my work as a consultant and trainer in dozens of communities and school districts around the country, I have heard about disturbing distortions of the asset assessment approach that fly in the face of the resiliency research documenting the need of young people to encounter "the resiliency attitude" in their en-vironments. These include reports of school counselors and teachers using informal asset checklists (not even the scientifically validated instrument) to scare both parents and kids; classrooms

of children filling out these informal checklists and comparing scores (and sometimes taunting peers who checked only a few of the assets on their questionnaire); and children who are "devastated" when their score on the checklist is only eight or 12. These examples of working with asset-building intention without "the resiliency attitude," result in turning a strength-based approach into a deficit-focused one, and in the process, hurting kids.

Though I hope these are rare occurrences, such reports emphasize how critical it is for all who are engaged in youth development and asset de-velopment—even as we are painfully aware of the significant gaps in the "asset infrastructure" for children—to adopt the resiliency-based strength-affirming philosophy described above. Every child, no matter how few his or her assets, must get the message "you can succeed" rather than the still-prevalent attitude of doom and gloom.

I Had Only 16 Assets

One reason I believe this is true is because I had only 16 assets (out of the initial 30 identified by Search) when I was in junior high and high school, nine short

> "What would my long-term reaction have been to a check-list that showed me I had only half of the 'assets' deemed important to youth success?"

of the 25 Search recommends as optimum for youth success. And yet, like Seita (see article on p. 139), I, too, have emerged as a resilient adult. Like many other resilient adults now involved in promoting resiliency, I question how my own resilient recovery from childhood adversity would have been impacted by an early label as an "at risk" child or an "asset-poor" one. What would my *long-term* reaction have been to a checklist that showed me I had only half of the "assets" deemed important to youth success (16 assets are described as "a start, but not enough" by Benson, Galbraith, & Espeland, 1994, p.6)? Fortunately, these labels (and such unscientific use of "checklists") were not being liberally applied to kids when I was in school in the 1960s. I did have along the way several adults who knew some of my struggles and yet conveyed to me that resiliency attitude of optimistic caring and empowerment, and numerous others—never having been exposed to the current stereotypes about "youth at risk"—who conveyed success-promoting messages to all kids.

> *"Youth and asset development must happen on the foundation of resiliency research: with 'the resiliency attitude' and with the certainty that most 'asset-poor' kids will eventually succeed."*

On the other hand, I would have benefited enormously—and would have no doubt rebounded with less pain and less potential for lifelong scars—from living in a community and/or attending schools *consciously* working to create asset-rich environments (without negatively stigmatizing or stereotyping anyone). Improving the developmental infrastructure for youth is a crucial goal for families, schools, churches, community organizations, and entire communities. But youth and asset development must happen on the foundation of resiliency research: with the "resiliency attitude" and with the certainty that most "asset-poor" kids will eventually succeed. Increasing the prevalence of assets in young people's lives in the long run will no doubt make this route easier, less painful, and less fraught with danger, than it is today.

A Message for All Youth: "You Are Resilient"

I recently heard a group of students share their incredible stories of overcoming sexual abuse, addicted and homeless parents and parents who kicked them out of their homes, being regularly beaten, and

> *"Those of us who work with and parent youth need to tell them that they have within them innate resilience, and help them to identify the internal and external characteristics of their lives that they can draw upon in time of adversity."*

involvement with gangs and violence. Each of these young people had rebounded from great adversity and were now experiencing life success. True to the resiliency research, they each pointed out pivotal adults, most often outside of their immediate families, who had provided them with the caring, optimistic, role-modeling relationships that helped them to do so. They were selected by a school counselor to tell their

stories at a resiliency conference because of their resiliency. Yet, when I spoke to them about it, each of them dismissed the idea. "I'm not resilient; I just survived as best I could," was a typical comment. They all admitted they had never heard the term, but when they did hear it and learned its definition, they all insisted the word resiliency didn't apply to them. How many times have they heard they were "at risk?" I wondered. I was sure that term was one that had been communicated to them frequently.

Those of us who work with and parent youth need to tell them that they have within them innate resilience, and help them to identify the internal and external characteristics of their lives that they can draw upon in times of adversity. With this realization, I have begun talking to groups of students about their resilience, using the list of questions shown below. Often, I meet with peer mentors, natural helpers, and other groups of youth leaders. After I explain the concept of resiliency to them, I ask them what kinds of circumstances they have had to overcome, i.e. what in their lives has necessitated them drawing upon their resilience. Typical responses to this question include: parents divorced, friend died, pet died, worry about friends who are drinking, worry about friends using drugs, worry about friends engaging in unsafe sex,

---

for students...
QUESTIONS FOR DISCUSSION ABOUT YOUR RESILIENCY

1. If resiliency is defined as "the ability to bounce back from, and successfully overcome risks and adversity," why are you a "resilient" person?
   A. What are some of the struggles, challenges, difficulties you have faced in the past or currently face (go into only as much detail as you feel like sharing!) ?
   B. Share how you overcame these difficulties....
      • What did you do?
      • What beliefs about yourself and others guided you?
      • WHO helped you?
      • How did they help?
      • What else helped you?
2. How can you use these same things in the future when you are dealing with problems? What can you do that has worked in the past? Who can you go to that will give you support? Is there a way to maintain greater access to these individuals?
3. What advice do you have for other kids going through problems, risks, and difficulty?
4. What advice do you have for adults trying to help kids be resilient?
5. What barriers do you think stand in the way of kids being resilient? What ideas do you have about how we can change these barriers?

didn't make team or wasn't accepted to some other type of organization, just moved, parents are fighting, a parent has been layed off from work, struggling in school, illness or death of a family member. I then share with them characteristics of resiliency, and help them to identify the characteristics within themselves and the people and organizations within their environments that do—and can in times of stress—help them be resilient. I believe these problems are typical for all youth (and many face even greater difficulties) and that learning about resiliency can help make it a reality.

Recently, after an afternoon of such interaction with a group of students, a mother of one of the girls present approached me that evening at a community meeting. "What did you say to my daughter today?" she asked. She reported that the girl had come home with a completely changed attitude about a difficult problem she was dealing with in her life. "I know now I can get past this," the girl told her mother. "And I have some ideas about how to do it."

Messages of resiliency can be given anytime. They can have an immediate impact. They can be integrated into almost any curriculum by utilizing stories that show human resiliency and then discussing the inherent lessons. They can become a part of all of interactions with youth, by actions (as Seita so poignantly shares in examples from his own life on page 139), and in conversation. ("You are a wise girl," I tell my eight-year-old niece. Listen to that wisdom

in your heart. It will tell you what is right.") They are a crucial foundation of an integrated, comprehensive positive approach for children and youth, which starts with that message of strength and optimism in caring relationships, and includes all the programmatic and community change recommendations from the fields of youth and asset development. ℮

References

Benson, P., Galbraith, J., & Espeland, P. (1994). *What kids need to succeed.* Minneapolis, MN: Free Spirit Publishing, Inc.

Henderson, N., & Milstein, M. (1996). *Resiliency in schools: Making it happen for students and educators.* Thousand Oaks, CA: Corwin Press.

Richardson, G., Neiger, B., Jenson, S., & Kumpfer, K. (1990). The resiliency model. *Health Education, 21* (6), 33-39.

Search Institute. (1996). *Healthy communities, healthy youth: A national initiative of Search Institute to unite communities for children and adolescents.* Minneapolis, MN: Search Institute.

Nan Henderson, M.S.W., is a national and international speaker and consultant on fostering resiliency and wellness, alcohol and other drug issues, and on organizational change. She has co-authored / edited five books about resiliency, and is the president of Resiliency In Action. *She can be reached at Nan Henderson and Associates, 5130 La Jolla Blvd., #2K, San Diego, CA 92109, p/f (858-488-5034), or by e-mail: nanh@connectnet.com*

Research Report

Developmental Assets:
A Framework for All Youth

The following is reprinted with permission from the booklet "Healthy Communities, Healthy Youth: A National Initiative of Search Institute to Unite Communities for Children and Adolescents," published by the Search Institute, 700 South Third, Suite 210, Minneapolis, MN 55415, 1-800-888-7828.

Beneath the headlines about youth violence, crime, pregnancy, and other problems is an even more important and urgent story: In all towns and cities across America, the developmental infrastructure is crumbling.

Too few young people grow up experiencing key ingredients for their healthy development. They do not experience support from adults, build relationships across generations, or hear consistent messages about boundaries and values. Most have too little to do that is positive and constructive. The result is that communities and the nation are overwhelmed with problems and needs in the lives of youth.

Thus the real challenge facing America is not to attack one problem at a time in a desperate attempt to stop the hemorrhaging. The real challenge is to shift our thinking to a new approach—one that addresses deeper causes and needs. The real challenge is to rebuild the developmental infrastructure for our children and adolescents.

Though professionals and the public sector have a role to play, much of the responsibility and capacity for the healthy development of youth is in the hands of the people.

Search Institute has created a model for understanding the developmental needs of children and adolescents. Rooted in research on more than 250,000 American youth in grades six to 12, the framework identifies 40 building blocks, or "developmental assets," that all children and adolescents need to grow up healthy, competent, and caring (see next page). These assets provide a powerful paradigm for mobilizing communities, organizations, and individuals to take action for youth—action that can make a real difference.

The Power of Assets

When drawn together, these assets are powerful shapers of young people's behavior. The more assets young people experience, the more they engage in positive behaviors, such as volunteering and succeeding in school. The fewer they have, the more likely they are to engage in risk-taking behaviors, such as alcohol and other drug abuse, antisocial behavior, violence, and others (see graphs on p.135). Thus, while each asset must be understood and is important, the most powerful message of developmental assets comes in seeing them as a whole. These assets are cumulative or additive; the more the better.

In short, young people who experience more of these assets are more likely to grow up caring, competent, and responsible. This important relationship between developmental assets and choices made has been documented for all types of youth, regardless of age, gender, geographical region, town size, or race/ethnicity.

40 Developmental Assets

	ASSET TYPE	ASSET NAME	DEFINITION
EXTERNAL ASSETS	**SUPPORT**	1. Family Support 2. Positive family communication 3. Other adult relationships 4. Caring Neighborhood 5. Caring School Climate 6. Parent involvement in schooling	Family Life provides high levels of love and support Parents and child communicate positively; child is willing to seek parents' advice and counsel Child receives support from three or more non-parent adults Child experiences caring neighbors School provides a caring, encouraging environment Parents are actively involved in helping child succeed in school
	EMPOWERMENT	7. Community values youth 8. Youth given useful roles 9. Community service 10. Safety	Child perceives that community adults value youth Youth are given useful roles in community life Child gives one hour or more per week to serving in one's community Child feels safe in home, school, and neighborhood
	BOUNDARIES AND EXPECTATIONS	11. Family boundaries 12. School boundaries 13. Neighborhood boundaries 14. Adult role models 15. Positive peer influence 16. High expectations	Family has clear rules and consequences; and monitors whereabouts School provides clear rules and consequences Neighbors would report undesirable behavior to family Parent(s) and other adults model prosocial behavior Child's best friends model responsible behavior Both parents and teachers press child to achieve
	TIME	17. Creative activities 18. Youth programs 19. Religious community 20. Time at home	Involved three or more hours per week in lessons or practice in music, theater, or other arts Involved three hours or more per seek in sports, clubs, or organizations at school and/or community organizations Involved one or more hours per week Out with friends "with nothing special to do" two or fewer nights per week
INTERNAL ASSETS	**EDUCATIONAL COMMITMENT**	21. Achievement motivation 22. School performance 23. Homework 24. Bonding to school 25. Reading for pleasure	Child is motivated to do well in school Child has B average or better Child reports one or more hours of homework per day Child cares about her/his school Child reads for pleasure three or more hours per week
	VALUES	26. Caring 27. Equality and social justice 28. Integrity 29. Honesty 30. Responsibility 31. Restraint	Child places high value on helping other people Child places high value on promoting equality and reducing hunger and poverty Child acts on convictions, stands up for her/his beliefs Child "tells the truth even when it is not easy" Child accepts and takes personal responsibility Child believes it is important not to be sexually active or to use alcohol and/or other drugs
	SOCIAL COMPETENCIES	32. Planning and decision-making 33. Interpersonal competence 34. Cultural competence 35. Resistance skills 36. Peaceful conflict resolution	Child has skill to plan ahead and make choices Child has empathy, sensitivity, and friendship skills Child has knowledge of and comfort with people of different racial backgrounds Child can resist negative peer pressure Child seeks to resolve conflict nonviolently
	POSITIVE IDENTITY	37. Personal control 38. Self-esteem 39. Sense of purpose 40. Positive view of personal future	Child feels she/he has control over "things that happen to me" Child reports high self-esteem Child reports "my life has a purpose" Child is optimistic about her/his personal future

The Crumbling Infrastructure

Most people recognize that influences such as caring families, discipline, educational commitments, social skills, and other assets are important for healthy development. Yet society seems to have forgotten how to make sure young people experience and develop these things. Out of 250,000 sixth to twelfth graders who have been surveyed, the average young person experiences only about 16 of the initial 30 assets first studied by Search (see graphs on p.135). Furthermore, 76% of young people experience 20 or fewer assets.

The "asset gap" exists in all types and sizes of communities. In fact, youth in 95% of the communities studied to date report an average of 15 to 17 assets. Thus, in virtually every town, suburb, and city in America, far too many young people are struggling to construct their lives without an adequate foundation upon which to build.

What has happened? Many of the ways society has provided these assets are no longer in place because of major societal changes, including the following:

- Most adults no longer consider it their responsibility to play a role in the lives of children outside their nuclear family.
- Parents are less available for their children because of demands outside the home and cultural norms that undervalue parenting.
- Adults and institutions have become uncomfortable articulating values or enforcing appropriate boundaries for behavior.
- Society has become more and more age-segregated, providing fewer opportunities for meaningful intergenerational relationships.
- Socializing systems (families, schools, congregations, etc.) have become more isolated, competitive, and suspicious of each other.
- The mass media have become influential shapers of young people's attitudes, norms, and values.
- As problems—and solutions—have become more complex, more of the responsibility for young people has been turned over to professionals.

For several decades, Americans have invested tremendous time, energy, and resources in trying to combat the symptoms of these changes. It hasn't worked. It's time for a new approach—an approach that focuses energy, creativity, and resources into rebuilding the developmental foundation for all youth.

As we begin shifting our thinking, we can anticipate creating communities where all young people are valued and valuable, problems are more manageable, and an attitude of vision, hope, and celebration pervades community life. ℮

15 Characteristics of Asset-Building Communities

What are some of the core features of a town or city that seeks to reclaim developmental assets for all of its children and adolescents? Proposed here are 15 benchmarks.

1. All residents take personal responsibility for building assets in children and adolescents.
2. The community thinks and acts intergenerationally.
3. The community builds a consensus on values and boundaries, which it seeks to articulate and model.
4. All children and teenagers frequently engage in service to others.
5. Families are supported, educated, and equipped to elevate asset building to top priority.
6. All children and teenagers receive frequent expressions of support in both informal settings and in places where youth gather.
7. Neighborhoods are places of caring, support, and safety.
8. Schools—both elementary and secondary—mobilize to promote caring, clear boundaries, and sustained relationships with adults.
9. Businesses establish family-friendly policies and embrace asset-building principles for young employees.
10. Virtually all 10-to 18-year olds are involved in one or more clubs, teams, or other youth-servicing organizations that see building assets as central to their mission.
11. The media (print, radio, television) repeatedly communicate the community's vision, support, local mobilization efforts, and provide forums for sharing innovative actions taken by individuals and organizations.
12. All professionals and volunteers who work with youth receive training in asset building.
13. Youth have opportunities to serve, lead, and make decisions.
14. Religious institutions mobilize their resources to build assets both within their own programs and in the community.
15. The community-wide commitment to asset building is long-term and sustained.

The Impact of Developmental Assets

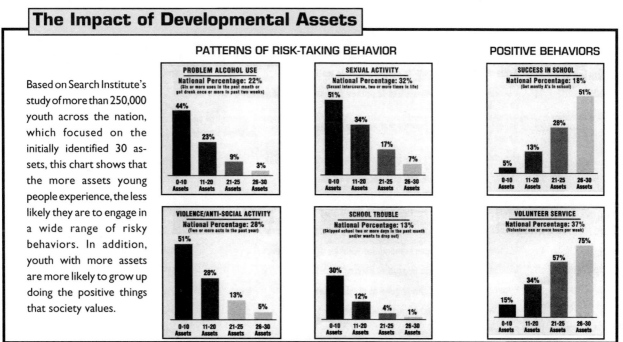

Based on Search Institute's study of more than 250,000 youth across the nation, which focused on the initially identified 30 assets, this chart shows that the more assets young people experience, the less likely they are to engage in a wide range of risky behaviors. In addition, youth with more assets are more likely to grow up doing the positive things that society values.

The Faces Of Resiliency

Students Challenge Their Community to "Flip The Page" from Negative Youth Stereotyping to Messages of Strength and Support

by Nan Henderson, M.S.W.

The Orleans Southwest Supervisory Union is comprised of two high schools, two middle schools, and five elementary schools within and around the community of Hardwick, Vermont. Located about 60 miles northeast of Burlington, Hardwick is a small community that appears as peaceful, connected, and concerned for its youth as any that could be found in the United States. Residents rarely lock their doors, crime is virtually nonexistent, and a meeting of community leaders about positive youth development that I recently facilitated packed a large conference room in a local restaurant. Indeed, the feeling of "community" and "caring for one another" in Hardwick is actually palatable just walking down the street.

This description of Hardwick underscores my amazement at the following report. Last fall, Dr. Helen Beattie, a school psychologist for the supervisory union, asked principals of the secondary schools to select a "representative" group of students to work with her in a supervisory union-wide initiative to integrate resiliency building and asset development into schools. Dr. Beattie wrote the following description of her experience talking with these students.

On November 7, 1996, sixth through twelfth grade students from throughout the Orleans Southwest Supervisory Union met to review Search Institute survey data. One introductory activity was a brainstorming session in which I asked the students this question: "How do you feel you are perceived by adults and the community 'at-large'?" The students brainstormed this list of responses:

Partiers	Troublemakers	Punks
Crunchies	Druggies	Slackers
Lazy	Unsafe Drivers	Hormonal
Ditzy Blond	Know-It-Alls	Hyper
Reckless	Inexperienced	Unreliable
Rebellious	Irresponsible	Moody
Sulky	Unmotivated	Emotional
Worthless	Poorly Educated	Mouthy

Dr. Beattie said that about halfway through this activity one of the students stopped the group process and commented, "These are all negative." Other students agreed, but the brainstorming continued in the same vein. Dr. Beattie then conducted the next part of the activity:

Next, I directed the students, "List how you would like to be perceived by adults and the community 'at-large'—how you know yourselves to be." The students then brainstormed this list:

Responsible	Confident	Explorers
Seekers	Intelligent	Trustworthy
Creative	Smart	Resourceful
Independent	Dedicated	Active
Alive	Well-rounded	Equal
Individuals	Logical	People
Normal	Hard-working	
Grown-ups of the future		

Dr. Beattie and her students laminated the results of this activity in a display that is now being shared throughout the community in an invitation to "Flip The Page" for youth in Hardwick. She recently asked the students to share their thoughts about how the community can make that shift so students receive the messages of strength and support that comprise their second list. Dr. Beattie reported on their ideas:

I asked the students this question: "How can students, adults, and the community 'at-large' help 'flip the page'?" These were their responses:

- Bring everyone in the community together to improve the community (e.g., through activities like planting trees or flowers).
- Increase interactions between youth and elders through music, drama, and community dinners.
- Engage students in community service on a regular basis.
- Bring community mentors into the school on a regular basis.
- Publicize the good things about youth.
- Let youth share their vision of an ideal community.
- Organize student-led forums or dialogue nights.
- Develop a community center as a place for people of all ages to gather.

- Engage parents and community members in the organization and staffing of extra-curricular activities.
- Encourage teens and adults to be positive role models.
- Provide opportunities for teens to tell adults how they feel they are being perceived—adults might not realize how they are stereotyping teens.

The challenge to "Flip the Page" is being brought to students, school staff, and community members throughout the district with the goal of defining a common vision and identifying the means to achieve it.

This report from the students of Hardwick suggests that all communities need to explore these questions with their youth. It is shared with the hope it will be the catalyst for similar discussions and goal-setting in families, classrooms, community agencies, churches, and all youth-serving organizations. It also illustrates again the resilient nature of youth—that they can self-identify their own strengths in the midst of many messages of deficit—and their inherent wisdom about how communities can change to benefit all citizens. ☉

Hardwick students share an illustration of an "ideal vision for our community." They are, from left to right (back row), Ginger Scott, Hazen Union junior; Dan Mercier, Hazen Union eighth grader; Kory Keene, Hazen Union freshman; (front row) Leona Stein, Lakeview Union sixth grader; Joshua Shepard, Hardwick Elementary sixth grader; Travis Reynolds, Craftsbury Academy junior; Micah Mutrux, Craftsbury Academy junior; and Anthony Wiley, Hazen Union senior.

Commentary

CCDO: Lessons from My Life to Guide All Youth Development

by John Seita, Ed.D.

John is totally unable to accept the close relationships of a foster home placement. As we discussed this, John told of his continuing wish to return to his mother. He strongly implied that he would continue to act out and get into trouble until he was returned to her. Although he recognized that his mother had some undesirable characteristics, he was quick to make excuses for her and seemed to be saying, "She's all the family I have" (Seita, Mitchell, & Tobin, 1996, p. 30).

I was moved roughly 15 times in a few years following removal from my mother's home. It is no wonder, then, that I rejected every attempted placement. No one should be surprised that I was angry and aggressive and alternately passive, quiet, and withdrawn. Perhaps I was simply responding to a harsh, rejecting, insensitive world filled with what seemed to be calculating professionals bent on identifying what was wrong with me and not much focused on what was right with me.

I have thrived despite these early tragedies, and I am here to tell my story. More important than the personal tragedies are the lessons learned about what facilitated my evolution from an angry, hurting, and institutionalized youth to an adult who, as Werner & Smith (1977) suggest, loves well, lives well, and expects well.

The intent of this article is to describe these lessons and in doing so, to propose a set of guiding principles that evolved from my own experiences, which are similar to the results of recent studies on resiliency and protective factors. These principles of

"Connectedness, Continuity, Dignity, and Opportunity" (CCDO) could serve as the national standard that undergirds all action and practice on behalf of children, adolescents, and youth.

These lessons constitute what some call strength-based approaches (Brendtro & Ness, 1995; Benard, 1994; Burger, 1994; Seita & Brendtro, 1995) and are linked to protective factors and resiliency (Werner & Smith, 1977; Benard, 1997; Williams, 1997). In my own case, CCDO occurred more by chance, rather than by intention. My sad and grim sojourn has been documented in the book *In Whose Best Interest?* (Seita, Mitchell, & Tobin, 1996) and will not be reprised here.

My sojourn, however, is illustrative and adds to the growing body of literature about protective factors and resiliency. I have labeled my journey as one of "pluck and luck." Most youth need more than pluck and luck. They need to experience purposeful efforts at creating CCDO.

A Shifting Perspective on Youth

Historically the approach in working with youth has been to label them, and to identify and attack what were thought to be deficits and so-called pathologies. In this collective, but misguided, wisdom kids are viewed as dysfunctional, deviant, disruptive, disordered, disturbed, delinquent, debased, and depraved (Brendtro, Brokenleg, & Van Brockern, 1990). Rarely was the strength in many of these societal outcasts acknowledged. The choice was made to see what was thought to be wrong with troubled youth, rather than to seek and understand what was right.

Today this approach is changing with the recognition that what has been viewed as a pathology is often a healthy response by a hurting youth to an unhealthy life ecology, which might more accurately be described as oppositional strength.

Legitimate and understandable responses to an unhealthy life ecology, however, are often not healthy for youth or for society in general. Yet, this society has been feckless at best and immoral and criminal at worst in exercising its collective responsibility for youth. "No one is certain what solutions, if any will work," writes Gleick (1996, p. 31) regarding the collective unfocused inaction on behalf of youth. Efforts need to be focused, channeled, and guided. CCDO is one way to channel and guide the policies and practices that affect youth, our communities, and our organizations.

CCDO—Not Just Another Model

Not surprisingly, because of my background, I am often asked about particular methods of intervention, so-called model programs, and the latest school curriculum. In reality, the search for model youth programs is not unlike looking for the mythical unicorn—it is a search that is bound to be disappointing. Models are simply temporary and contextual mechanisms for understanding and working with youth and are often categorical, reactive, and problem oriented. CCDO, on the other hand, is proactive, holistic, and transcends time, context, and personality because it is an unchanging set of core principles that guides our actions.

Definitions of each aspect of CCDO are provided below and expanded upon with personal illustrations.

Connectedness: Strong, positive relationships with others, especially with one person.

> Mr. Lambert was a child care worker. I didn't know where he came from or really much about him except that he seemed sincere and reached out to me. He shared genuinely his beliefs about character, values, respect, and honesty and love in relationships. I took all of it in like a sponge and pestered him with questions. He shared many of the subtleties of life that one only learns at the elbow of a caring and experienced mentor. In essence, this strong bond of connectedness formed the solid personal infrastructure for my life as a successful adult (Seita, Mitchell, & Tobin, 1996, p. 42).

Adults who work with children have long been aware of the awesome power of relationships. This was a dominate theme in the early writings in education, counseling, and youth work. However, as professional literature became more scientifically oriented, relationships were increasingly ignored. Now there are signs of a renewal of interest in the synergistic power of human relationships (Brendtro, Brokenleg, & Van Brockern, 1990, p. 58).

Connectedness is the degree to which people touch one another, that someone is there for each of us and we for them.

Continuity: A sense of continuous belonging to a group, family, or spiritual entity.

> Old friends, they mean much more to me than the new friends because they see where you are and they know where you've been. (The late Harry Chapin, songwriter and anti-hunger activist.)

Continuity represents a sense of roots, of personal history. Moreover, continuity considers a person's legacy, family, and future. Continuity can also be enhanced by a bond to a higher power or something greater than oneself.

For example, my first night away from home when I was first placed in an institution as an 8-year-old, when no one else was awake, I kneeled beside my bed weeping and in a near state of shock and started to pray. I prayed for hours, perhaps half the night. Hundreds of "Hail Marys" poured out of me. I had learned how to pray and believed that the Virgin Mother would somehow deliver me from this undeserved fate. Of course it didn't happen that night, but praying did stabilize me in my moment of crisis. Youth can be encouraged to explore their spiritual selves and connect with a higher spiritual power without promoting a specific dogma or doctrine.

Dignity: Respect and courtesy.

Dignity is revealed in explicit and implicit attitudes and behaviors on behalf of children, and more importantly, through interactions with children. Valuing children as equals deserving of honesty, appreciation, and respect not only sends messages important to how children view themselves today, but shapes the outlooks and behavior of these children as adults. The following story reflects the small messages that are sent to children that suggest their diminished status.

> Larry Brendtro, former president of Starr Commonwealth for Boys (Starr Commonwealth, at the time, was a residential program similar to Boys Town), came up to me while I sat in the Emily Jewel Clark building on Starr's campus awaiting an appointment with a counselor. I sat there with pants too short, and wearing what we in the cottages called "ankle busters" (short, cheap, and thin sox that barely reached the ankles on my size 13 feet). Larry thoughtfully remarked that perhaps staff should also wear such threadbare and short sox and as if to join me in some sort of secret solidarity society lowered his sox to ankle mast also. Larry's actions were humorous, but also pointed and well understood by me at the time (Seita, Mitchell, & Tobin, 1996, p. 90).

> Human service professionals have a long history of patronizing, infantilizing, and dehumanizing the very persons they are pledged to serve. While they may be unaware of their basic disrespect, young persons are not (Brendtro, Broken Leg, & Van Bockern, 1990, p. 67).

Small messages and signals that adults send youth are powerful, impactful, and long remembered. What adults tell children through action, inactions, structure, and verbiage all contribute to how children process the world now and in the future. Subtle messages of disempowerment often abound.

Being directed to hand out clothes with nothing on or wearing "ankle busters" for sox certainly does not rank with having no food in the house, being abused by a caretaker, or living in a drug-infested environment. This does, however, represent an insidious pattern of marginalizing children and diminishing their value and potential growth. Moreover, if the goal is to foster the development of healthy, independent, and contributing children, then examples such as this are not to be ignored or dismissed out of hand.

Opportunity: The chance to capitalize on one's strengths.

Opportunities need to be provided for youth that are consistent with their interests and talents but that also fill a role for society. Almost all youth have something that they do well. Adults should strive to identify what those sometimes hidden abilities are and seek to foster and promote them. As an adolescent, my hidden ability was basketball. Mr. Wilson, a child care worker at a residential treatment facility, nurtured my talent for basketball even before I knew it existed.

> Mr. Wilson really expected the best of me and constantly encouraged my basketball efforts. He would never let me give up, no matter what the odds seemed to be. We were playing on the outdoor cement court one late afternoon when I was about 16. One exchange saw me playing what he called "tenacious defense" as he was forced further and further from the basket. I hounded him far out of shooting range. I can still see in my mind's eye a vision of him falling out of bounds, his back turned to the court, and 25 feet from the basket. Just as he was about to land on the grass beyond the out-of-bounds line, he turned, spun in midair and launched the ball toward the basket. The high arching shot seemed to float in the air for an eternity. I was astonished when it softly nestled through the net and went in. He then turned to me, and with a smile in his face and in his eyes, said, "See, never give up" (Seita, Mitchell, & Tobin, 1996, p. 46).

I eventually excelled at basketball and found basketball as a way to start my college education. Certainly there are other dimensions of opportunity: the opportunity to be afforded a quality education, to be trained in the skills of one's choice, to have economic opportunities. The range of opportunities are endless except for those who most often need them. Happily for me, opportunities were near and abundant. Sadly, for many youth today, that is not often the case.

CCDO In Action

In closing, the following suggestions are excerpted from Seita, Mitchell, & Tobin (1996) and may be used to implement CCDO on the individual/family level and the organization/school level.

Families:

Families have a primary role for caring for and nurturing our children. Indeed, families remain the most likely place to offer and receive CCDO. The following suggestions are intended to guide families in their attempts to create a family environment that is protective.

- Create and maintain family traditions.
- Support spirituality, in whatever form it manifests itself.
- Provide all family members with opportunities to build upon his/her strengths.
- Celebrate the accomplishments of family members.
- Value each individual family member for his/her unique attributes.

School / Organization / Community:

A clear understanding of the principles of CCDO can help all of us relate to children. What follows are some simple suggestions on issues that may improve educational, organizational, and other community settings:

- Design curriculum to meet the needs of the total child in his/her life ecology rather than only within the walls of the school and its traditional domain.
- Create an ethos that meets the needs of all consumers of services including nontraditional families.
- Develop, practice, and evaluate policies that support teachers and other staff to view their roles as extending beyond the classroom/school.
- Create an organizational culture that practices a value system which respects the dignity of all students.
- Encourage and reward staff who reach out to families in their homes, work, and in other nontraditional settings.
- Respect, nurture, and understand cultural differences, backgrounds, and spiritual beliefs.

Connectedness, Continuity, Dignity, and Opportunity is not just another model. It is a better way, based upon principles to engage children and youth, for organizations and communities that serve children than simply asking, "What is the best program?" ℮

References

Benard, B. (1997). Fostering resiliency in urban schools. In Williams, B., *Closing the achievement gap*. Alexandria, VA: the Association For Supervision and Curriculum Development.

Brendtro, L., Brokenleg, M., & Van Bockern, S. (1990). *Reclaiming youth at risk*. Bloomington, IN: National Educational Service.

Brendtro, L., & Ness, A. (1995). Fixing flaws or building strengths? *Reclaiming Children and Youth: Journal of Emotional and Behavioral Problems, 4*(2).

Glieck, E. (1996). The children's crusade. *Time, 147*(23).

Burger, J. (1994). Keys to survival: highlights in resilience research. *Journal of Emotional and Behavioral Problems, 3*(2).

Seita, J., & Brendtro, L. (1995). Reclaiming the unreclaimable. *Journal of Emotional and Behavioral Problems, 3*(2).

Seita, J. (1994). Resilience from the other side of the desk. *Journal of Emotional and Behavioral Problems, 3*(2).

Seita, J., Mitchell, M., & Tobin, C. (1996). *In whose best interest: One child's odyssey, a nation's responsibility*. Elizabethtown, PA: Continental Press.

Werner, E., & Smith, R. (1977). *Kauai's children come of age*. Honolulu, HI: University Press.

John Seita, Ed.D., is a Program Director for the W.K. Kellogg Foundation in Battle Creek, Michigan, and the author of numerous articles on resiliency in youth, program evaluation, and working with youth who are resistant to relationships. He is also a frequent speaker and can be reached at the W.K. Kellogg Foundation, One Michigan Ave. East, Battle Creek, MI 49017, (616-968-4058).

PART SIX

Resiliency and Families

Resiliency Interview

Focusing Therapy on "What Families Do Right": An Interview with Steven Wolin, M.D.

by Bonnie Benard, M.S.W.

Steve Wolin, M.D., is clinical professor of psychiatry at the George Washington University Medical School, a longtime researcher in the department's Center for Family Research, and Director of Family Therapy Training. In addition to a private practice in psychiatry, Steve also directs Project Resilience, a private organization through which he and his wife, Sybil, provide training and consultation nationally and internationally (5410 Connecticut Ave. N.W., Washington, D.C. 20015, 202-966-7540).

The Wolins are the authors of The Resilient Self: How Survivors of Troubled Families Rise Above Adversity *(1993, New York, NY: Villard Books). I found this a compelling and beautiful book that documents the innate human capacity for transformation and change. Besides creating a vocabulary of strengths to counter the predominance of our deficit language in the helping professions, this book challenges all helping professionals to shift their paradigms from the "damage" to the "challenge" model. We can all look forward to their upcoming book,* Resilience in Children of Hardship, *with well-deserved anticipation.—B.B.*

BB: When I first discovered you, you were doing research with Linda Bennett. What was really interesting to me and very different than a lot of the research studying children in alcoholic families, was that you actually identified some of the positive things, even in very troubled families, that supported the kids. Could you speak to what these were?

SW: The research that you're referring to was very significant in my life. It was occurring in the mid-1980s, and was published in that time period, also. I started out being interested in transmission of alcoholism across generations; basically I was looking at the damage of alcoholism being continued over generations. The control group that I needed was a group of families that have the same alcoholism in the parent generation but no transmission. So I made a comparison of transmitter families to nontransmitter families.

I wasn't very interested in the beginning in that control group because I wanted to know what factors had gone wrong in the families where transmission occurred. I had to ask the nontransmitter families the same questions to be accurate in the study and for the people who were going to be doing the evaluation of the answers—they were blinded as to whether transmission occurred.

So we had to ask everybody: How did life go in this family? How did you handle the alcoholism of your parents? I was interested in what broke down in family life, especially family rituals, dinner time, holidays. (I was going to find that these important characteristics of family life broke down when transmission occurred more often than in those cases where no transmission occurred.) But what was more important, was I was stunned by the information I was getting from the nontransmitter families, the control group. They had really interesting stories to tell about what they had done to prevent transmission from occurring. That's what changed my life.

But more important than their answers, actually, was my asking that question for the first time in my clinical life and being so overwhelmed with the amount of information. This has changed me forever.

Now, I'm always asking people, "What have you done that worked out well?" "What have you done that was good for this family, especially during difficult times?" These questions, ten years later, are not very unusual questions for family therapists to be asking. Now lots of family therapists are interested in solutions and what has gone right. But for me as a researcher it was really a marker, a crucial experience that I had.

> "People are saying to me, 'Oh, this is exactly what I do, but I didn't know there was a name for it, [or that] it was legit to do.'"

BB: This seems to be a phenomenon of resiliency researchers: They start out doing research that's much more into studying the problem, risk, or damage and are transformed through the stories of the people they're studying. I'm thinking of a video I saw of Robert Coles who had a very similar experience through listening to children.

SW: Yes. His famous story about what happened when he interviewed Ruby Bridges. Of course he's very much interested in the children under stress and keeps asking them how are they managing with the struggle of their lives. He's always finding interesting strength-oriented things that they're saying.

Again, my work with Linda Bennett was the critical experiment in my life. It changed my perspective so that I could start to ask the question, "What does the family do right in the face of pretty adverse circumstances, in this case parental alcoholism?"

There were four very specific findings:

> "We need to…push this vocabulary of strength so that people believe it's as valid, deep, and substantive as the other stuff."

The first one was this phenomenon of *deliberateness*. [Many] studies show that deliberateness is a very important quality inside families and in children. Deliberateness is a two-part characteristic: planfullness—making a plan—and carrying the plan out. It is an ability to take initiative, have a notion of what they're doing, and conceptualizing a positive future for themselves. These [nontransmitter] families were highly deliberate. They had at least one parent and several children who were extremely careful about how family life went because they sensed what the trouble was and knew they had to protect these zones of family life. So being deliberate was crucial. In fact, there is a book that's about to come out by Bill

Doherty, a colleague of mine and a family therapist, called, *The Intentional Family: How to Build Family Ties* [ed. note: Scheduled for release May 1, 1998; to be published by Addison/Wesley]. It's all about deliberateness. He's using our research as a background to show that [families who make plans and carry them out, do much better than the families who don't]. The same thing goes with kids we talked to in that study who reported, for example, planning their future as early as age eight. They were visualizing a positive future for themselves, then taking steps to put their pennies under their pillow cases, etc.

The second characteristic of these nontransmitters was *distance*. We were measuring the frequency of visits by children who were already out of the home and the distance that they lived away from their still-drinking parents. You've got to remember that to be in this study the alcoholic still was drinking. [The nontransmitters] were having either two or fewer visits a year with their still-drinking parents, and lived more than two hundred miles away. These families had figured out that since drinking was going on, they had to take active steps to protect themselves using distance. That's where independence comes in as one of the protective factors. Being able to obtain both physical and emotional distance has been shown in many, many studies as a resiliency component.

The third finding was *spouse selection*. Since in the families that I'm talking about, the kids were now young adults, a whole bunch of them were already in serious relationships or married. So we were looking at these children of still-drinking alcoholics, and saw how important spouse selection was to them. Many described the care with which they were selecting the families that they were marrying into. They were clearly looking around for a surrogate family. The ones who married into non-alcoholic families did better. The ones who married non-alcoholics did better. The ones who married carefully thinking about these aspects of family life did better. Even the ones marrying into families more structured than the chaotic families they came from did better. Sometimes they made mistakes, but in general the statistics held up.

The fourth characteristic was the *family ritual* characteristic. We found [that families who focused on family rituals]—both the origin family and the [new families created by the kids when they were older]—did better. These families focused on a healthy dinner time, holidays, and celebrations without alcohol, and on routines set up so the family could count on it (one of the things that happens within alcoholic families is a tremendous destruction of all important ceremonies, ce-lebrations, and rituals). Those four characteristics were often in the minds of children of alcoholics and even in their healthy parent's mind as they tried to give a positive legacy to the younger generation.

> *"Whether you're a clinician, parent , teacher, or preventionist you can learn to talk about strength in ways you haven't before, which will make a meaningful difference in the life of a young person. To do that you have to believe there are strengths. This is mindset that we share."*

BB: Fascinating. You know that deliberateness/plan-fulness and spouse selection are exactly two of the major findings in two different studies Michael Rutter did in Great Britain.

SW: Yes. We chronicled a bunch of these in our book. The Beardsley study on children of depressed mothers showed that kids did better if they had a positive sense of the future, which is the same point again, this planfulness, and they didn't overly attribute to themselves their mother's depression. Some kind of independent deliberate position that occurs inside of kids is preventive for them.

BB: Are we finally moving to a more broad-based, strengths-oriented movement?

SW: I wouldn't say that the clinical activities are there yet, but I would say that I encounter lots of receptive audiences where the people are saying to me, "Oh, this is exactly what I do, but I didn't know there was a name for it, and I didn't know it was legit to do it." So there's a lot of affirmation that lots of therapists, when the door is closed, turn to the client's strength because that's basically what they have to work with.

BB: It also says something about their deep common sense and wisdom that in many ways, our institutions, and maybe a lot of our specialized programs, try to train us out of.

SW: We understand that there is a whole damage orientation that is not only in society, but in professional academies, and we understand where that comes from. One of the results of this is that there is very powerful language of damage that has risen up over the years, so that it's so easy to describe people and their "borderline personality disorder" and that they are "fragmented inner objects" and things like that. It sounds very deep and important when you talk about pathology.

But when you talk about a strength such as creativity or the various aspects of some-one's insight, it sounds almost pedestrian and banal. We need to get out there and push this vocabulary of strength so people really believe it's as valid, deep, and substantive as the other stuff. And, of course, it's a lot better in certain ways to work with.

I had a very interesting experience recently. I was on a panel at a substance abuse conference, and the man following me was a world-famous endocrinological expert with an expertise in fetal alcohol syndrome. He had always presented all the damage statistics and scary possibilities for mothers who drink in terms of what was going to happen with their babies. In my presentation before him, I had presented some of the statistics that showed that even in most situations there were a lot of people who were figuring out how to do things well. I showed that transmission of alcoholism in families wasn't the majority of circumstances, that in the majority of famlilies in fact, it was not transmitted. I didn't mean that it wasn't a problem, but people ought to know that they are not walking time bombs. They're not doomed.

So he got up at the end of my presentation, [looking] a little pale, and said [to the audience], "You know I don't think that I can present my presentation anymore as I would have done. Because, after listening to this guy, I realize that every one of my slides is going to be a scare statement to you about the dangers of drinking for mothers when, in fact, it's probably representing one tenth of one percent of deliveries, even with people who do exactly what happens when the bad things happen." He said, "It's not that these bad things don't happen, but I guess that I do have to tell you that it's by far the minority of cases where this will occur. We don't even know why it doesn't happen in the other ones. We've only studied the ones where it happens."

I think that for researchers to really be willing to shape their studies and their reports and give equal time to strength and the people who are doing well in the face of difficult things that happen—there's a lot of stuff they have to go through [to be able to do this], because they're afraid that they are going to lose their funding.

BB: That if you say there are strengths, the policy response is, "Oh, then we don't need to do anything. We don't need programs to help people." What message would you give to parents in light of all the research you've done?

SW: The main application of our work on resilience is talking about strength—talking to adults about strength. Our big push is that whether you are a clinician, parent, teacher, or preventionist you can learn to talk about strength in ways you haven't done before, which will make a meaningful difference in the life of a young person. In order to do that you have to *believe* there are strengths. This is mindset that we share.

But also, from our perspective, you have to have names for these strengths so that you can point them out to young people when they are using them. I do it all the time in my clinical work. I'd like to describe a couple of examples of how I do it in my clinical work with parents and with kids, because that's where I actively work with this stuff.

"I am very actively involved in psycho-educational practice in family therapy. I'll spend a lot of time teaching family members about their strengths… teaching parents to talk to their kids about their strengths…talking to siblings about the different strengths in each other."

For example, just last week, I did a case consultation at the local children's hospital with a mother and daughter. I won't describe to you the problems, but what was important was that I was able to get the daughter to talk about how she handled gossip in the school. This daughter was in a lot of trouble and was the recipient of a lot of malicious gossip. Girls were coming up and saying, "Oh, you're a whore," and boys were coming up to her and asking if she would agree to have sex with them. This kid is 14.

There also had been a lot of trouble between mother and daughter and a lot of accusations about how the daughter is not taking good care of herself. The mother is suspicious about everything that the daughter does, etc., etc. The daughter has run away a lot. As you can

imagine, it was a tense situation. In getting the daughter to talk about how she handled this malicious gossip, I was able to get her to focus on and identify what she evaluated in the social situation; that is, how she used her insight and independence, and how she was creative with her moral strength. I got her to actually say to her mother by saying to me, that she had the strength, that she was strong. And I said to the mother, "Well it's a very interesting set of things she's told us about herself. Have you ever heard it before?" She said, "No." She [said she] had never thought about her daughter as having those faculties that she used on the street and in the classroom when the girls were calling her names.

I [asked] the mother, "How about you? Have you ever been the victim and the recipient of malicious gossip?" [She] thought for a second, kind of turned a little pale, and said, "Well. Yes. There are some co-workers of mine who have accused me of being a lesbian behind my back." [The] daughter, who had not raised her eyelids to her mother probably in months, certainly not in the session, almost dropped her mouth and looked at her mother for the first time. I said to the mother, "Well that's pretty interesting. What did you do?" She described to me how she had gone to her supervisor, complained, gone over what the possibilities were, and decided to not tell certain people.

So I said to the mother, "How do you think you're handling it compared to your daughter?" She said, "Actually, I've learned a few things from [her]." She described how more sophisticated her daughter was in evaluationing these difficult gossip rumors than she had been. The daughter was, of course, tickled pink.

So I then closed this little sequence by pointing out the strength that this daughter had. Then the daughter said for the first time, "You know, mom, if you told me more about your life, I'll bet we could get along a lot better."

BB: What a wonderful story! Why do you think people have such a hard time—like the girl seeing her strengths, the mother seeing hers, as well as looking and seeing her own daughter's strength?

SW: To be focused on a strength is a stretch. It's unfortunately not natural. First of all we think it's bragging if we say we have one. We think it's kind of silly if we complement somebody because they have one. We are embarrassed by strength. We are embarrassed by the sort of confrontation about how hard life is and giving somebody a pat on the back for the good job they've done. It doesn't go well. Then between parent and child, we have certain expectations of our children even though we've not met them in ourselves. We think we can criticize them easily for the things they have not done perfectly rather than focus on the hard work that they've been doing.

BB: You've nailed a lot of the issues in parent/child communications right there. What do you see as the greatest challenges facing families during this time of transition, not traditional nuclear [families], but people who would define themselves as a family?

SW: Of course I see a lot of divorced families in my practice, so I have to believe that understanding strength in the face of fragmented, non-nuclear, non-traditional families—this is one of the great challenges of today—and being able to accept differences among each other [is useful].

It's very hard to be generous inside the family. It's a hard change to come by. Our lives are busy, we're struggling, and we have so few resources from the community to give us strength. It's very hard to feel filled up, very hard to feel like you have a lot to give. It's much easier to feel like you need a lot. So if everybody's walking around feeling needy and nobody is saying, "I have to give at least as much as I take in order for this family to be filled up," families will never be appreciated as positive institutions.

Here's a wonderful little example: A colleague of mine saw a family in which everyone was very self-centered. Everybody was bitching about what they weren't getting and at the end of the third session, a little eight-year-old girl pulls him by the sleeve and says, "Tell me the truth doc. Whose side are you on here?" And he said, "Well Suzy, to tell you the truth I'm against all of you. Because when I look around in this family, all of you are first for yourself, and it seems like I'm the only one of you whose on the side of the family."

I think it's true a lot. It's very hard to find people who are on [the family's side] as an institution and feel they have something to give it.

BB: I know I have always been in a position where I felt like I have all these expectations from my work life that are in direct opposition to my family—things like time. It's always amazing to me that people expect you to work weekends, nights, and so on.

SW: And that they don't realize that you have to be flexible. Things come up in families all the time. People get sick, they have an accident. You have to have flexibility in your life to be able to be an active member of your family. It's very hard to come by flexibility when people are saying, "You know we need this by yesterday," and fax machines, and so on, that require everyone to shape up . . . to be there at every moment.

That's why family members especially need to see their strengths in dealing with all this stress. I use the notion of resilience in talking about strengths very actively. Like the case I just described to you about the mother and the girl and the gossip, I am very actively involved in psycho-educational practice in family therapy. I'll spend a lot of time teaching family members about their strengths. I'll spend a lot of time teaching parents to talk to their kids about their strengths. I'll also spend a fair amount of time talking to siblings about the different strengths in each other.

My favorite session is the session where several adult children will get together and talk about what it was like growing up in their families. But they come often to tell horror stories. My goal in the session is to change them to talking with admiration about each other's strengths. I want them to say, "Oh, I didn't know that about you Suzy. I didn't know that you knew how to do that." The idea that each of the children have different strengths that they're using, and that, hopefully, I'm going to be able to find something in every kid, and certainly, you know, I expect I will—that's what I'm going to go for.

You do have to understand that as a therapist I'm aware that people come in pain, so I'm not just focused on strength. I'm always trying to balance it. Our model shows that there is an equal amount of time for the damage part of the story, for the hurt, for the pain. We conceptualize people as being damage-first people and strength-first people in terms of how we're going to approach them in a clinical setting. Sometimes you just have to approach first from the damage part of their story, the trauma, the trouble, the pain in order to get their trust.

If you only present solutions to them and talk about how fabulous they are, they'll simply leave and say, "Oh you're on some kick, and you don't really know me." So those are the damage-first people and eventually you get around to showing them that there is more to the story than their damage story.

Then there are others who come in quite willing to talk about their strengths because they are either aware of them or they are not voluntary patients. Or there are whole families often very eager to talk about something they've done well as a family. I like to think about clients as being either damage-first or strength-first, but, in any case, I'm going to be finding a way for them to be talking about their strengths in the family sessions and get the other family members to acknowledge that they have these capabilities.

BB: This is very powerful work. Do you feel your field of family therapy is moving more and more to a strength focus?

SW: Yes, I would say that my phone doesn't stop ringing. It's a very healthy practice. People know that I am interested in positive qualities. I think I have a good reputation around town for that approach. And then my clients are often very willing to joke with me about my focus on strengths. Sometimes they come in and say, "Oh, we had this horrible weekend. I dare you, Steve, to find the strength in this story." They're actually playing with me.

I don't know if it's a movement, but I think it's certainly comfortable for me. I also know that a lot of my colleagues like it and don't yet do it. So I don't know how to accept it on this sort of sociological level, but I certainly think that it's in my blood now.

I think the whole solution-focused approach has a lot of these characteristics. The only difference between me and some of the other solution-focused therapists is that we have this specific vocabulary of people in terms of their bouncing back from adversity rather than what the solution-focused folks are doing. They are always just inviting the family to describe what they did that works. I always find that a bit too loose for me. Maybe I'm a bit of a control freak that way. But I feel that words give tremendous power to people, and that if I can give a name to something, they can walk away with it.

BB: I find that even just giving people some information about resiliency research is empowering.

SW: Right. It's like translating it for them. That's why I think that the good therapy, the good counseling is very psycho-educational because you are teaching people something.

BB: What I see in the education field—especially brain research/cognitive science—with people like Howard Gardner, and his multiple intelligences research, and now Daniel Goleman and emotional intelligence is that schooling has really had a very narrow focus and we definitely need to broaden it. Schooling itself must move towards a strengths focus— so that students will be acknowledged and validated for their unique skills and abilities.

SW: Absolutely. People who have street smarts, who have creative smarts, language smarts, and emotional smarts—all smarts which don't show up on SATs— must be acknowledged. ☯

Bonnie Benard, M.S.W., has authored numerous articles and papers on resiliency and provides speeches and training on resiliency throughout the country. She can be reached at Resiliency Associates, 1238 Josephine, Berkeley, CA 94703 (510-528-4344), or by e-mail: (bbenard@flash.net).

Research Report

Promoting Resilience In Families

by Joan M. Patterson, Ph.D.

Most often we think of resilience in terms of individual behavior and functioning. However, the process of becoming a resilient individual happens in a social context. For children and youth, two primary social contexts shaping and influencing their growth and development are their families and schools. These social contexts can also be described in terms of their resilience. Children's competence and functioning are closely related to the quality of their social environments. Hence, competent, well-functioning families and schools are more likely to have children who are competent and function well. In this article, I will focus on the family system and discuss what we mean by *family resilience*, as well as ways in which service providers and policy makers can promote resilience in families.

What is Family Resilience?

All families encounter multiple tasks, needs, demands, and challenges, which they try to manage with their internal capabilties and the resources they are able to access in their communities. These family challenges and demands ebb and flow over a family's lifetime. Sometimes, the nature of the demands and/or the sheer number of them can place a family at risk and undermine their ability to maintain healthy functioning. However, many families are able to develop their strengths and abilities; they are able to "bounce back" from the stress and challenges they face and eliminate or minimize negative outcomes. This is what is meant by *family resilience* (Garmezy, 1991; Patterson, 1991; Walsh, 1997): It is the ability of the family to develop and/or maintain healthy functioning and successfully adapt to life's challenges and risks.

The challenge to those who provide services to families and establish policies that affect families is to do their work in a way that strengthens families' capabilities to successfully manage the multiple, ongoing demands of daily life. Just as a child's functioning is enhanced by living in a well-functioning family context, so too, the family unit's functioning is enhanced by living in a healthy, empowering community.

There are many different pathways that families can take in becoming resilient. Ways that helping professionals can facilitate this goal are discussed in this article.

What Do We Mean by "Family?"

Rather than using a narrow, culturally biased definition of family, helping professionals should think broadly about who constitutes a family, using a definition such as, "a group of people, living together or in close contact, who take care of one another and provide guidance for their dependent members" (Wood, 1995). This way of thinking validates diverse family structures, such as heterosexual and homosexual married or cohabiting couples, with or without children; separated, divorced, always single adults with children; fictive kin relationships (Fine, 1993); etc. Most important, for any given individual who comes for services, "family" should be whoever that individual says it is (for him/her).

Too often professionals judge families as dysfunctional, often without understanding what is meant by this phrase. *Family functioning* refers to the patterns of relationship connecting members of a family system (Bateson, 1972). In other words, it is the way family members are with each other in the day-to-day processes of living—getting things done, accomplishing their tasks, and trying to reach their goals. There are many different ways to get things done and hence, many kinds of relationship patterns that are effective. There are patterns for showing positive feelings, such as a hug, a kiss (on the lips, cheek, or in the air), verbal compliments, and smiles. Similarly, families have patterns for showing anger and conflict (yelling, ignoring, pouting, leaving the house, banging things, or denying feelings). There are patterns for getting things done such as earning family income, preparing meals, taking the kids to appointments and activities, disciplining children, solving problems, making decisions, etc. *The point is that there are many different relationship patterns that can work very well for families and outsiders need to be careful in hastily applying judgments of family dysfunction without understanding a family's culture, beliefs, values, and goals.* These relationship patterns are not static, however, but need to change periodically as family needs change. For example, disciplining a teenager is very different from disciplining a toddler. When professionals maintain a nonjudgmental attitude, family members themselves are more able to assess what is working or not working in their family when there is a need for change. They are much more open to considering change and alternative ways of relating if they do not have to be on the defensive against helpers' assessments and labeling of them.

Figure 1.
The Family Adjustment and Adaptation Response (FAAR) Model

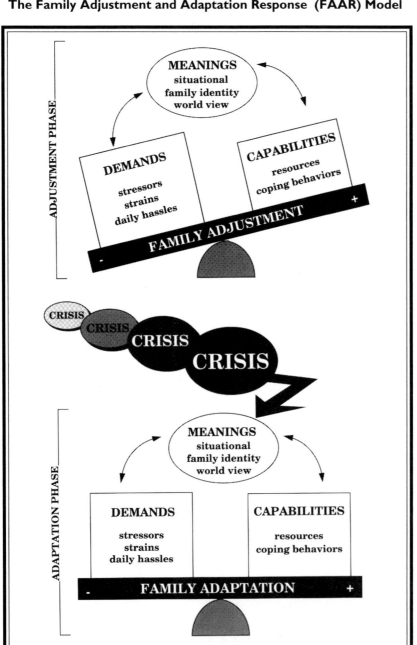

How Do Families Become Resilient?

Patterns of family functioning emerge over time as family members spend time together and interact in carrying out the activities of life associated with their ages, cultural context, socioeconomic position, and lifestyle preferences. As stated above, a family is faced with needs, demands, and challenges, which they try to meet with their capabilities. The family system strives for balance. Successfully achieving this balance, particularly in the aftermath of major demands and challenges, is what makes a family resilient.

This idea of a family "balancing demands and capabilities" is the essence of a family framework called The Family Adjustment and Adap-tation Response Model (Patterson, 1988), which is presented in Figure 1.

Family *demands* include (a) stressor events, both normal events like having a child and nonnormative events such as a child's death; (b) strains, which are ongoing tensions associated with carrying out one's roles in life; and (c) hassles, which are minor upsets of daily routines. Families are never dealing with a single demand, but rather, stressors, strains, and hassles accumulate, creating a pileup of demands. Some are associated with individual family members, others with the family as a whole, and other demands come from community/society needs (see Table 1 for examples).

TABLE 1

Stressors, Strains, and Hassles Contributing to Family Demands		
Stressors	**Strains**	**Hassles**
Death of a relative	Marital conflict	Child has temper tantrum in public
Acute illness	Trying to get a job	Losing car keys
Parent loses a job	Parent role overload	Appliance breaks down
Birth of a child	Inability to pay bills	Child refuses to eat
Child's school closes	Daily tx for chronic illness	Parking ticket
Divorce of parents	Meeting work deadlines	Child loses favorite toy
Child leaves home	Neighborhood violence	Family members' schedules conflict
Natural	Caring for an elderly parent	Running out of diapers

In assessing family stress, it is important to realize that it is not only major life events that cause stress; strains and daily hassles must also be considered. Service providers who help families recognize the strains and hassles in their lives and validate that indeed these are *real* and create tension contribute to families feeling empowered and more hopeful that they can take charge and manage better. This realization often helps members readjust their expectations, short and longterm, and also allows them to appreciate their accomplishments.

It is also important to remember that the demands contributing to the pileup are always changing. Families are continuously juggling new and old demands with their existing and acquired capabilities, in an effort to reorder priorities and maintain some semblance of balance. The balance is never absolute, but dynamic, like the movement of a balance beam.

The two types of *capabilities* for meeting demands are (a) resources, which are characteristics, traits, or competencies of individual family members, the family unit, or individuals or groups in the community; and (b) coping behaviors, which are specific efforts by an individual or a group to meet the challenges of a demand. Resources are what the family *has*; coping behaviors are what they *do*.

Identifying Family Resources

Many resources are acquired over time, usually in response to demands. In fact, this is the basis of the concept "eustress," which refers to how stress can be good (Selye, 1974). Individuals and families actually become stronger and grow and develop when they are faced with demands they can successfully manage—a premise documented by much of the resiliency literature. This point is key to understanding and promoting individual and family resilience. An infinite variety of resources exist within and between families as reflected in the diversity of families. It is the role of helping professionals to facilitate families discovering their own internal resources, as well as in finding and using formal and informal community resources. Examples of individual, family, and community resources are presented in Table 2.

TABLE 2

Resources: Individual, Family, and Community		
Individual Resources	**Family Resources**	**Community Resources**
Self-esteem	Family income	Health care services
Parent education & knowledge	Family cohesion	Quality schools
Physical & mental health of members	Shared interests and activities	Formal & informal recreation
Developmental status of children	Communication skills	Recreational facilities & youth groups
Practical skills & knowlededge	Family flexibility	Friendly & helpful neighbors
Social knowledge	Safe & adequate housing	Churches & synagogues
Personal flexibility	Good parenting skills	Support from friends
	Conflict resolution skills	Social services
		Safe neighborhoods

One of the ironies regarding many of these resources is that when families experience a pileup of demands, they often find it difficult to maintain and use these resources. In the face of prolonged imbalance and stress, self-esteem may be diminished, family cohesiveness may be reduced, family communications may be impaired due to constricted or angry emotional expression, and the family may become isolated in the community. At the very time when families most need resources, they may be accessing fewer and may be unaware of what resources are available. Helping professionals can play a critical role in empowering families by identifying individual, family, or community resources that they have utilized in the past or need to access in times of crisis. Most importantly, families have the best chance of managing stress and restoring balance by building on their strengths. Helping professionals can help set this process in motion by reminding families of these strengths and helping them reactivate them as they seek to restore balance.

Coping is what individuals and families *do* to manage stress and restore family balance. Families who have a broad and diverse array of coping behaviors that include some or all of the five coping functions that meet individual and family needs are more likely to have a good outcome (see Table 3). Relying on only one coping behavior (like exercising to reduce tension) may be helpful in the short run; however, given the diverse demands faced by families, one coping strategy may not be adequate.

Coping behaviors are learned. Children begin to learn how to manage demands and meet their needs by observing their parents and others, and later, by interacting with their peers. Parents can be encouraged to try new behaviors as a way to set an example for their children. One of the important benefits of support groups is learning new coping behaviors, such as thinking differently about life and about personal control, which is encouraged by groups like Alcoholics Anonymous. Helping professionals promote coping behaviors and contribute to family resilience when they observe and then point out positive parent and child characteristics. This acknowledgment of individual and family strengths from a trusted professional provides hope and encouragement to try other positive coping behaviors.

Looking For Meanings

In addition to demands and capabilities, the *meanings* the family attributes to their situation are a critical factor in achieving balanced functioning. Helping professionals who take the time to understand each family's unique meanings about their situation (i.e., demands and capabilities), who they are as a family, and their world view are truly "family-centered" and culturally competent in the way they provide services. Since meanings are subjective, usually implicit in behavior, and not something persons can necessarily articulate directly if asked, it takes important skills on the part of a professional to genuinely listen and hear what matters to families and how they see their lives. Yet there is little question that this is what families crave from those who are trying to help them. They need to be understood as a first step in discovering solutions to their unmet needs or problems.

Many demands only exist by virtue of their definition (such as role strain associated with unreasonably high expectations). Similarly, many capabilities are the result of subjective appraisal (such as self-esteem). In studies of families with a medically fragile child, many of these families developed positive meanings about their situation as a way to cope (Patterson & Leonard, 1994). They focused on the positive characteristics of their child (warmth, responsiveness, and the ability to endure pain), of other children (empathy and kindness), of themselves as parents (assertiveness skills in dealing with service providers), and of their family (greater closeness and commitment to each other from working together). What was so profound in understanding how these families adapted was observing that there were real limits on reducing demands because chronic illness (and the ongoing demands for care and management of acute crises) do not go away. Even after these families acquired resources available in the community, there was still an imbalance. Thus, many families coped by changing the way they thought about their situation, by changing their perceptions. They emphasized what they had learned and how they had grown as a family, rather than the hardships they had experienced.

TABLE 3

Family Techniques: Coping To Manage Stress and Restore Balance	
Coping Functions	**Examples**
Reducing family demands	• Parent declines job promotion that would require family move before son's graduation from high school • Family moves terminally ill grandmother into a nursing home
Increasing family resources	• Parent develops a sense of mastery from caring for a chronically ill child • Parent completes job training program and gets a better job
Maintaining and allocating resources	• Family does things together to maintain sense of closeness • Parents spend time with sick child in hospital
Managing personal, internal tension	• Family members exercise daily to release tension • Family watches funny movies together and laughs
Changing ways of thinking about the situation	• Parents develop more realistic expectations for child's school performance • Family views challenges as an opportunity to develop new skills

The Regulatory Process of Families

Families have a way of knowing what makes them feel a part of their own group, separate from other families around them. A family identity emerges from the spoken and unspoken values and types of relationships that guide family members in how they relate to each other. It is through routines (such as family mealtime, or children's bedtime) and rituals (such as holiday and birthday celebrations) that family values and identity are developed and maintained. However, when major stressors occur, these routines and rituals may be disrupted and changed and values may be modified. This disruption of family regulatory process threatens the development, maturation, and stability of the family system (Steinglass et al., 1987). The family's valued interactions may be subsumed by the problem, especially if the problem is chronic. Professionals working with families confronted by a problem in their child may unwittingly contribute to this distortion of family process when and if they encourage families to devote a disproportionate share of their time, energy, and other resources to meeting the problem. This is often noted in families whose children have a chronic illness, particularly one that requires extensive home care. When families don't or can't do what is prescribed, they are sometimes labeled "resistant" or "noncompliant." Professionals should provide information and offer methods for managing illness and other problems, because families want and need this support. However, families also need service providers to be more respectful of their choices, of the ways they prioritize competing demands, and to acknowledge that they cannot always carry out all that has been recommended. Good advice is better received when it is coupled with respect for the family's values and routines and recognition of their efforts and sacrifices.

Another kind of family meaning, the family's perception of and orientation toward the world, is based on how it interprets reality, what its core assumptions are about its environment, as well as its existential beliefs, such as the family's purpose in life. Cultural beliefs and religious beliefs, such as trust in a higher power, often contribute to the family's world view. The family's conception of its social world provides an overarching guide for how it deals with change around it, whether it believes in its own ability to master and solve problems, and how receptive it is to new information (Reiss, 1981).

Family Adaptation

The outcome of the family's efforts to achieve balanced functioning is called *family adjustment* or *family adaptation*, both ranging on a continuum from good to poor. Good outcomes are reflected in (a) positive physical and mental health of individual members, (b) optimal role functioning of individual members, and (c) maintenance of a family unit that can accomplish its life cycle tasks.

There are many periods of family life when the family follows a fairly predictable pattern of interaction and is able to remain balanced. However, there are times when the nature and/or number of demands accumulates faster than the family can effectively manage with their abilities (at least those of which they are aware). They are out of balance, feeling extreme disruptiveness and tension. This is a family *crisis*—not a pejorative descriptor of families, but a simple observation that there is a need for significant change in some aspect of family functioning. Because families in crisis are disorganized and often are functioning at less than their optimum, they are vulnerable to being labeled "dysfunctional" by outsiders. Since this is often the time families voluntarily or involuntarily encounter the professional helping system, it may, in part, explain the tendency to negatively label help-seeking families. What is important to remember is that many families in crisis are basically well-functioning families who would benefit more from a professional who helps them see their strengths than from someone who pathologizes them and focuses only on their deficits. This is not to negate that there are families who are almost continuously in crisis and whose instability is associated with family functioning patterns that are not adaptive. In the former instance empowerment strategies may help the family resolve the crisis and restore balanced functioning. In the latter case, a referral for family therapy may be warranted. It is important that a family in crisis should not feel stigmatized, dysfunctional, or that it has failed.

Family systems get stronger from successfully managing stress. This explains why some families voluntarily take on new challenges as a way to grow and develop. A level of stress that family members can successfully manage strengthens them by increasing their repertoire of resources, coping behaviors, and ways of interacting. However, if the pileup of demands is too great and sufficient capabilities cannot be found, the system is weakened and changed into a less functional or supportive social relationship. In family systems, the dissolution may take the form of divorce, child abuse or neglect, emotional problems, behavioral difficulties or school-related problems.

Figure 2
Circular sequence of effects between child functioning and family functioning

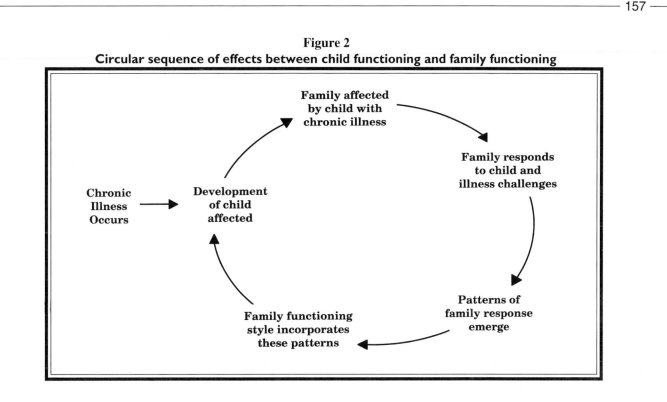

The Relationship Between Family Functioning and Individual Development

It is also important to recognize the relationship between family functioning (outcomes of adaptation), and individual development and functioning. For example, when a family experiences a major stressor like a child being diagnosed with a chronic illness, it has an impact on the family, leading to changes in its functioning patterns. This new style of functioning, in turn, affects the perception and care of the child, the course of the illness, and course of development of the child (Patterson, 1991). For example, it has been observed that a mother sometimes becomes overly protective of her child with a chronic illness—perhaps to assure that medical needs are met, or to show that she still loves the child despite the illness, or to try and compensate for the guilt, pain, suffering, and loss associated with the illness. Her overinvolvement with the child may be associated with father's pulling away from the mother and/or the child because the emotional demands of the illness are hard for him, or because he resents the mother's closeness to the child, or because he has to work harder to pay medical bills. The important point is that the stressor event (diagnosis of chronic illness in this case) has an impact on the family, changing their functioning patterns in some way. The reciprocal impacts on the individual and the family are circular and continuous over time, as depicted in Figure 2. It is counterproductive for the family or helping professionals to ignore this circular pattern of causality and instead to think that the child's problem alone has impacted the family, or to think that the family itself caused the child's problems. A change in one person has an effect on the whole system and bringing about improvement in the health or function of one person involves working with the whole family system.

Strategies for Promoting Resilience in Families

One of the major barriers to more effective work with children and families has been the failure to recognize, value, and empower families to discover and develop their own capabilities. Families often are unaware of their own strengths because they have been influenced by the tendency of professionals to narrowly focus on what they don't have (the deficit model). Too often, families approach helping systems in a "one down" position, believing someone else knows or has what they don't have and often feel they are incompetent, inadequate, or have failed. Unfortunately, bureaucratic policies within organizations have contributed to the over documentation of what's wrong with those who come for help as a way to justify expenditures for services.

Focusing on Families' Strengths, Competencies, and Successes

Promoting resilience calls for a different paradigm. It calls for a focus on each family's strengths, competencies, and successes. Many times these strengths are latent or dormant, outside the awareness of those who hold these abilities. The job of responsible professional helpers is to facilitate the discovery and conscious awareness of these latent capabilities. Empowerment is a process through which individuals or families increase their abilities to meet needs and goals and, at the same time, maintain their autonomy and integrity. The outcome of this process would, of course, be empowered individuals. Not only are those seeking help empowered, but the professional can and should be empowered as well. Openness on the part of professionals to being "changed" by those who seek our help is the best possible antidote to professional burnout. This process of working together, of being open to transformation, is the essence of the new paradigm in service delivery that emphasizes resilience.

Service providers are more likely to use empowering, resiliency-promoting behaviors if they (a) have self-awareness and self-respect, (b) are curious about what they can learn from families, (c) are genuine and accepting of the child and family, and (d) are egalitarian in their approach (versus hierarchical or paternalistic).

Promoting family resilience is first and foremost a set of attitudes and beliefs and a way of seeing others and believing in their inherent competence potential. The specific behaviors and skills flow from that. Just as there is a diverse array of latent strengths among families, so, too, there is a diverse array of resiliency-promoting helping skills embodied in professionals that will manifest themselves when the above philosophy of practice is embraced. The following are additional ideas of how an empowered and empowering professional might work.

> *Listen to the family's story.* Take the time to hear how they see their situation, including the needs and problems they have and how they have and are trying to deal with these. Informally, you are learning about their demands and capabilities as they see them. As you ask questions and listen, you should be learning something about how they see themselves as a family and maybe some aspects of their view of life, the world, and what matters to them. Be cognizant of who is doing more talking—you or them—and be sure you are creating space for them to tell their story.

> *Use the family's language and words as you interact.* The goal here is not to sound like a parrot, but rather to communicate respect and an effort to understand their world by using their language.

> *Acknowledge and validate emotions.* When emotions and feelings are apparent in the telling of their story, it can be helpful and empowering to a family when feelings such as loss, regret, hurt, guilt, sadness, etc. are acknowledged. When a family experiences empathic understanding from a professional they respect, it can have a powerful healing effect. When uncomfortable or painful feelings are ignored, denied, or treated as though they shouldn't exist, children and families are sometimes emotionally blocked from making needed behavior changes.

> *Ask questions versus providing answers.* Sometimes, families try to turn their life's problems over to professionals to fix because they feel powerless or incompetent. The deficit model of training tends to make professionals feel too powerful and as if they must have a ready answer for everything. When working with children and families, it is effective to ask questions that help the family discover their own strengths and solutions.

> *Provide information in a clear, timely, and sensitive manner.* Service providers should provide information to the family in language they understand, neither too technical nor too simplistic. How much information to provide, at what pace, with which sequence of priorities, and with which family members present are other factors that need to be assessed. When families are in crisis, out of balance, or experiencing considerable emotional distress, they are often unable to understand, remember, and accept factual information. In such cases, their emotions should again be acknowledged. Another time to present and discuss information might be negotiated. Too often, out of convenience, information is provided to only one family member,

precluding the opportunity for family support. In many instances, it would be wise to invite more family members to be present when information is shared and solutions are worked out. Working with the whole family is both a covert and overt way to recognize and support family problem solving, family support efforts, and other family strengths.

Co-create solutions with the family. True collaboration with children and families involves discovering the best solutions given the family's needs and circumstances. Professionals have a broad range of expertise about many different kinds of problems and ideas about the best solution(s) for these. Families, on the other hand, have specific, experiential expertise about their child, their family, their community, and their circumstances. Rather than fitting the child and family into predetermined solutions, professionals should guide families toward individized solutions.

Advocate for social policies that support families. Helping professionals are often well aware of social conditions that undermine families' abilities to develop and use their strengths. Policies that more equitably distribute society's resources and that provide greater flexibility for families to meet their needs would reduce the recurring crises many families experience and would reduce the need for so many one-on-one professional services. All professionals are encouraged to take an active role in advocating for family-supportive public policies.

Encouraging Family Resiliency

Balance is the underlying principle associated with successful adaptation to the challenges of life. Families can become resilient if they are encouraged to develop, maintain, and acquire resources and coping behaviors for managing demands. Given the diversity in family structure and functioning apparent in society today, helping professionals need to become more skilled in empowering families to discover and use their unique capabilities to find solutions congruent with their values, beliefs, and lifestyle. Professionals can communicate confidence and trust in families' diverse capabilities and support them in finding new ways to achieve balance. In the process, professionals will also achieve greater personal balance and perhaps improve their personal health and well-being. ☯

References

Bateson, G. (1972). *Steps to an ecology of mind*. New York, NY: Ballantine.

Fine, M. (1993). Current approaches to understanding family diversity: An overview of the special issue. *Family Relations, 42*(3), 235-237.

Garmezy, N. (1991). Resilience in children's adaptation to negative life events and stressed environments. *Pediatric Annals, 20*, 459-466.

Patterson, J. (1991). A family systems perspective for working with youth with disability. *Pediatrician, 18*, 129-141.

Patterson, J. (1991). Family resilience to the challenge of a child's disability. *Pediatric Annals, 20*, 491-499.

Patterson, J. (1988). Families experiencing stress. The family adjustment and adaptation response model. *Family Systems Medicine, 5*(2), 202-237.

Patterson, J., & Leonard, B.J. (1994). Caregiving and children. In E. Kahana, D. Biegel, M. Wykel M. (eds). *Family caregiving across the lifespan*. Newbury Park, CA: Sage.

Reiss, D. (1981). *A family's construction of reality*. Cambridge, MA: Harvard University Press.

Selye, H. (1974). *Stress without distress*. Philadelphia, PA: Lippincott.

Steinglass, P., Bennet, L., Wolin, S., & Reiss, D. (1987). *The alcoholic family*. New York, NY: Basic Books.

Walsh, F. (1997). The concept of family resilience: Crisis and challenge. *Family Process, 35*, 261-281.

Wood, B. (1995). A developmental biopsychosocial approach to the treatment of chronic illness in children and adolescents. In R.H. Mikesell, D. Lusterman, S.H.McDaniel (eds). *Integrating family therapy. Handbook of family psychology and systems theory*. Washington D.C.: American Psychological Association.

Joan Patterson, Ph.D., is a professor in the School of Public Health, Maternal and Child Health, at the University of Minnesota. She can be reached by writing her there at 420 Delaware St., S.E., Minneapolis, MN 55414, (612-625-5177) or by e-mail: (jasu@te.unm.edu).

Resiliency In Practice

Fostering Resiliency in Children and Youth: Four Basic Steps for Families, Educators, and Other Caring Adults

by Nan Henderson, M.S.W.

"Where do I _start_ in fostering resiliency in my children?" "What are the most important things to do?" "How long does it take?" "What if I only see them once a week (or once a month)?"

Parents and other family members, and educators and other helping professionals, all pose similar questions about resiliency. No one doubts that it is important, even crucial. Almost everyone agrees with my premise that resiliency—"the capacity to spring back, rebound, successfully adapt in the face of adversity, and develop social, academic, and vocational competence despite exposure to severe stress or simply to the stress that is inherent in today's world" (Henderson & Milstein, 1996, p. 7)—is needed by every child alive. Yet often feeling too stretched as it is, family members and helping professionals alike can't imagine fitting one more thing into their already time-pressured interactions with children.

After reading dozens of resiliency-focused studies and books, and after talking with hundreds of kids about their resiliency, I have identified four basic steps to fostering resiliency in children and youth—steps that can be used by every adult, whatever their role in children's lives.

The good news is this: _To a large degree, fostering resiliency occurs by integrating certain attitudes and behaviors with kids into the interactions we already have with them._ This is because fostering resiliency is a _process_ that occurs first and foremost in relationships.

When I ask young people who and what contributed to their resiliency (as defined above), they always name individual people first . . . then go on to mention activities, opportunities, classes, or—occasionally—programs. Their relationships with the individuals they name are characterized by the following recommendations:

1. Always communicate "the resiliency attitude." Fostering resiliency begins with an attitude, expressed verbally and non-verbally, that communicates, "I see what is _right_ with you, no matter what you have done in the past, no matter what problems you currently face. Your strengths are more powerful than your 'risks.' And whatever risks, problems, and adversity you are facing are steps on the road to bouncing back—they are not the end of the road!"

The Resiliency Attitude is also one in which caring and support is expressed in as many ways as possible—in word and in deed. Listening with compassion, validating the pain of a child's problems while conveying his or her ability to overcome, and providing thoughtful and nurturing gestures—great or small—are all part of this attitude. "She talks to me. She encourages me. She helps me a lot [with my baby]. She lends me money when I need it. She praises me. She tells me she is proud of me," is how Loretta Dejolie (see "Faces of Resiliency" on page 175) described her mother—the embodiment of the resiliency attitude.

L.W. Schmick, now finishing his freshman year in college, described the attitude of the teacher he credits most with his resiliency in this way:

> In my sophomore year, I had an English class with Brian Flynn . . . . A lot of teachers when they see an "at risk" student, they automatically distrust and they don't give them some of the responsibilities they would give other students. But Brian Flynn showed me respect and trust. He gave me a lot of power to take responsibility. He said, "If you want an inch, take an inch. If you want a mile, take a mile." I wasn't set apart as different. He saw me as just another person, not as an "at risk" student (Henderson, 1996a, p. 30).

2. Focus on strengths with the same or an even greater meticulousness as you use in cataloging weaknesses. Steve Wolin (see interview with Benard on page 145) believes that focusing on strengths goes against human nature. I believe it would be easier to do if we lived in a strength-reinforcing culture (that is possible to create), which viewed discussing one's capabilities and talents, goals and achievements as positive. A part of this culture would be a good news-reporting media focused equally on all the ways people help, support, sacrifice for, and care for one another. Whether it is because of "nature or nurture"—that old debate!— all adults interacting with young people need training in focusing on strengths, in "cataloguing . . . capabilities with the exquisite concern we normally reserve for weaknesses" (Higgins, 1994, p. 320). I have used a process called The Resiliency Chart outlined in Figure 1 to train myself and others in identifying, reinforcing, nurturing, and using strengths in personal and professional interactions with children and youth.

Figure 1. The Resiliency Chart

For each particular child, draw a t-chart as shown below. On the left-hand side of the chart, list all the concerns—internal, in terms of the attitudes and behaviors of this child, and external, in terms of environmental risks and stressors—that you have about the child. Try to limit your list to a handful of the most pressing problems. On the right-hand side of the chart, list every positive you can think of both within this child and within his or her environment. Think in terms of attitudes, behaviors, personality characteristics, talents and potential talents, capabilities, and positive interests. Think also in terms of the child's environment: List every person, place, organization, or structure that provides positive interaction and support for this child. Referring to Table 1, lists of individual and environmental characteristics that facilitate resiliency, can help with this strength-identification process. Don't limit your thinking, however, to these lists. Include anything you think of as a strength or positive support.

Child's Name_____

Problems/Challenges	Strengths/Positive Supports

Table 1. Individual and Environmental Characteristics that Facilitate Resiliency

Individual Characteristics	Environmental Characteristics
1. Gives of self in service to others and/or a cause 2. Uses life skills, including good decision-making, assertiveness, impulse control, and problem-solving 3. Sociability/ability to be a friend/ ability to form positive relationships 4. Sense of humor 5. Internal locus of control 6. Perceptiveness 7. Autonomy/independence 8. Positive view of personal future 9. Flexibility 10. Capacity for and connection to learning 11. Self-motivation/initiative 12. Is "good at something"/personal competence 13. Feelings of self-worth and self-confidence 14. Personal faith in something greater; spirituality	1. Promotes close bonds 2. Values and encourages education 3. Uses high warmth/low criticism style of interaction 4. Sets and enforces clear boundaries (rules, norms, and laws) 5. Encourages supportive relationships with many caring others 6. Promotes sharing of responsibilities, service to others, "required helpfulness" 7. Provides access to resources for meeting basic needs of housing, employment, health care, and recreation 8. Expresses high, and realistic, expectations for success 9. Encourages goal-setting and mastery 10. Encourages pro-social development of values (such as altruism) and life skills (such as cooperation) 11. Provides leadership, decision-making, and other opportunities for meaningful participation 12. Appreciates the unique talents of each individual

(Richardson et al.,1990, Benard, 1991, Werner & Smith, 1992, Hawkins et al.,1992, Higgins, 1994, Wolin & Wolin, 1993)

Adapted from the book, Resiliency in Schools: Making It Happen for Students and Educators by Nan Henderson and Mile Milstein, published by Corwin Press, Thousand Oaks, CA (1996).

The way The Resiliency Chart might look at two different points in one child's life is diagrammed in Table 2 and Table 3. Last fall, I wrote about Juanita Corriz, a 15-year-old ninth grader in Santa Fe, New Mexico, who—after a two-year wait—was matched with a Big Sister, Sharyn Obsatz, when she was 14 (Henderson, 1996b). When I talked with Juanita, it became clear that her life has changed significantly for the better in the two years since she met Sharyn—that her strengths evident at age 12 have been nurtured, that others have emerged, and that many of the "risks" in her life have been *mitigated* by this growing list of positive personal and environmental characteristics.

Table 2. Juanita, age 12

Problems/Challenges	Strengths/Positive Supports
1. Single-parent mom who must work every night, and who has several children to care for	1. Mom who gives message, "Become something better for yourself" and, recognizing her children's need for more quality adult time, contacted Big Brothers/Big Sisters
2. No father in her life—has never known her dad	2. Example set by mom of getting off of welfare
3. Lots of unsupervised time on her hands	3. Oldest of four children, recognition that "I am a role model for the others"
4. Family history of many people—"including about 20 cousins"—not graduating from high school	4. "Required helpfulness" role (see Werner, 1996) in helping with younger children
5. Family history of poverty	5. Desire to do well in school
6. Struggling with some of her schoolwork	6. Very giving of self to mom and younger siblings
	7. Sociability—outgoing, friendly, enthusiastic
	8. Interest and ability in foreign languages
	9. Insight about what she needs to do well

It is important to note that families often *simultaneously* contribute risks and strengths in a child's life—a point almost entirely overlooked in the dysfunctional family model. In Juanita's case, her mother is a high-school drop out, who got pregnant as a teenager, and who survived for many years on welfare—and now works nights as a custodian to support her family. But this same mother communicates to her children by example and by word, "Make a better life for yourself." Recognizing her own time limitations, she made the call to Big Brothers/Big Sisters that provided both Juanita and one of her younger brothers with mentors.

Two years later, as a result of weekly interactions with her Big Sister Sharyn whom Juanita describes as "a best friend . . . I've grown to love, who gave me the belief, 'I'm going to try to do good because I know I can do good'" (p. 19), I would modify Juanita's chart as shown in Table 3.

Table 3. Juanita, age 15

Problems/Challenges	Strengths/Positive Supports
Delete # 3 above Delete # 6 above	Add the following: 10. Weekly interaction for several hours with a Big Sister who conveys The Resiliency Attitude 11. A certain belief by Juanita that she will go to college 12. Over a 1.5 raise in G.P.A. 13. Increased time reading, due to Big Sister's influence 14. Expansion of altruism to include goal of one day being a Big Sister herself

It is not possible, nor even desirable in preparing a child to successfully cope with life, to eliminate 100% of the risks, stresses, challenges in his or her life. What can be done, through interactions with family members and other caring adults, is to increase "the right hand side of the chart" by focusing on and adding to strengths and environmental supports, which *mitigate* the impact of risk factors and stress. The balance is thereby shifted: The power of the risks and problems are reduced and the strengths—including talents, competencies, resiliency characteristics, and environmental supports—grow.

3. Build a Resiliency Wheel around each child. After communicating a resiliency attitude, after assessing and figuring out how to reinforce, nurture, and expand on strengths, the next step—which can happen simultaneously with the first two—is to build a web of resiliency-fostering environmental conditions around each child. This web is diagrammed in The Resiliency Wheel shown in Figure 2. This wheel is in actuality a web of protection, support, and nurture of each child's "self-righting tendency" (Werner & Smith, 1992) and capacity for resiliency. No child can have too many strands in his or her web and most today have far too few.

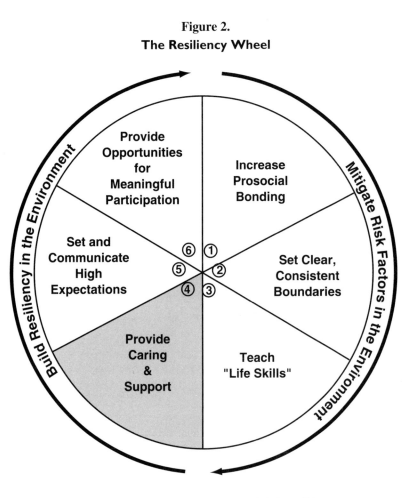

Figure 2.
The Resiliency Wheel

Reprinted from *Resiliency in Schools: Making It Happen For Students and Educators*
by Nan Henderson and Mike Milstein, published by Corwin Press, Thousand Oaks, CA, 1996.

Risk factor research, which encompasses hundreds of studies over several decades, (Hawkins, Catalano, & Miller, 1992) suggests three main strategies—elements one, two, and three of The Resiliency Wheel—for mitigating the impact of risk in the lives of children and youth, in effect moving them towards resiliency (Hawkins & Catalano, 1990). These are:

Increase Bonding. This involves increasing the connections between young people and resiliency-fostering peers and adults and between young people and any prosocial activity (such as sports, art, music, drama, community and/or school service, and reading and other learning).

Set clear and consistent boundaries. This involves the development and consistent implementation of family rules and norms, school policies and procedures, and community laws and norms. These expectations should be developed with input from young people, clearly communicated (in writing is ideal), and coupled with appropriate consequences that are consistently enforced. My experience as a clinical social worker working with families has shown me that often parents believe that their children know the family rules and what consequences to expect if they are broken, when in the children's minds there is no clarity or consistency about them. Recent experiences with groups of young people in schools has emphasized that here, too, kids *often* experience inconsistency and a laxness—which they complain to me about in our meetings!

Teach "life skills." These include cooperation, healthy conflict resolution, resistance and assertiveness skills, communication skills, problem solving and decision making, and healthy stress management. When these skills are adequately taught and reinforced they help young people successfully navigate the perils of adolescence, including resisting the use of cigarettes, alcohol, and other drugs (Botvin & Botvin, 1992), and successfully dealing with hurtful peer or adult behaviors.

The life-span focused resiliency research yields three additional steps (synthesized by Benard, 1991)—elements four, five, and six of The Resiliency Wheel—that are consistently shown to help young people "bounce back" from risk, stress, and adversity. These are:

Provide caring and support. This includes providing unconditional positive regard and encouragement. Because it is the most critical of all the elements that promote resiliency, it is shaded on The Resiliency Wheel. In fact, it seems almost impossible to successfully "overcome" adversity without the presence of caring. This caring does not necessarily have to come from biological family members—though that is ideal. Optimally, every child should have several adults he or she can turn to for help (Benson, Galbraith, & Espeland, 1994). Educational reformers are recognizing the criticalness of a caring environment as the foundation for academic success. Noddings (1988) notes, "It is obvious that children will work harder and do things—even odd things like adding fractions—for people they love and trust" (p. 32).

Set and communicate high expectations. This step appears consistently in both the resiliency literature and in the research on academic success. It is important that expectations be both high and *realistic* to be effective motivators. In reality, however, many children, especially those stuck with one or more of the myriad of labels used in schools and agencies, experience unrealistically low expectations and adopt low expectations for themselves.

Provide opportunities for meaningful participation. This strategy means providing opportunities for problem solving, decision making, planning, goal setting, and helping others, and involves adults sharing power in real ways with children. This resiliency builder is also increasingly showing up in school change literature with expectations that teaching become more "hands-on," curriculum more "relevant" and "real world," and decision making site-based, actively involving all members of the school community (Cooper & Henderson, 1995).

One way that a family member or other concerned adult can use The Resiliency Wheel is by filling in the grid shown in Figure 3, The Resiliency Web, for each child. Again, the goal is to weave as many "strands" in each area, recognizing that due to an individual's circumstances, most of the strands in one or several of the six elements of the Wheel may come from the family, or the school, or the community—rather than being equally distributed across each of these environments.

Figure 3. The Resiliency Web

Child's Name_____

	Prosocial Bonding	Clear, Consistent Boundaries	Life Skills Taught/ Practiced	Caring and Support Provided	High Expectations Communicated	Opportunities for Meaningful Participation/ Contribution
In the Family By whom/what? How?						
In School By whom/what? How?						
In the Neighborhood By whom/what? How?						
In the Community By whom/what? How?						

Once this grid is complete, where should a parent or other adult start in making use of this information? Start where you see the greatest need and/or start wherever you can. Often, as in the case of teacher Brian Flynn, who guided L.W. Schmick and his peers through a community service project, one action will embody many of the elements of The Resiliency Wheel. It is important to recognize that there is no way to know just how much of this web is needed by any one individual to assure "shifting the balance" to a resilient outcome. Most resilient kids who have been studied didn't have a strong web in their family, school, *and* community environments. Some have only a few strands in just a few places. So, start wherever you can based on your assessment of what would help an individual child the most and based on available resources.

Children do need both quantity and quality of resiliency-fostering interactions. Yet, feeling they don't have enough time to give, parents and other adults often underestimate the power of what they can do. As Higgins (1994) notes:

> Several subjects in [my] study [of the resilient] strongly recommended that those of you who touch the life of a child constructively, even briefly, should *never* underestimate your possible corrective impact on that child . . . . In fact, one of the strongest leitmotifs rippling through the interviews [I conducted with resilient survivors] was the reparative power of simple, open availability . . . . Remember, too, that the surrogates [caring adults outside the immediate family] of the resilient were generally available for only small amounts of clock time, and some faded after a limited developmental exposure. Yet their positive impact persisted for life (pp. 324-325).

4. Never Give Up! Resiliency is a life-span process and it ebbs and flows throughout an individual's life. Many resilient survivors of difficult childhood circumstances share how crucial persistence by caring people around them was in their ability to both become resilient and maintain their resiliency. Leslie Krug, now 17 and nearing high school graduation from an alternative school, went through ninth grade in a traditional high school three times before succeeding on the fourth try in her alternative school. She, too, credits her mother as a major source of resiliency. "She just kept making me go to school. She wouldn't let me drop out," Leslie said in an interview last year. She reported that during years of skipping school and "hanging out" her mom got mad at her for her behavior but she never gave up on her. No matter what, her mom was "just always there" (Henderson, 1996c, p. 13).

Phil Canamar's story (Henderson, 1996d) shows how each of the four steps discussed in this article helped him change from a gang and drug-involved 16-year-old school dropout to a 19-year-old nearing high school graduation, and currently soliciting grants from companies such as Honeywell to help "multicultural youth." Phil, too, had a single-parent mother who worked overtime to support her three children. He began getting into trouble in middle school when he experienced a void of caring, supportive adult interaction. This void, he said, contributed to his gang involvement, which he initiated at a time when he said to himself, "No one is here for me. I'm sick of it." He said "I turned toward the gang to find support" (p. 14). Eventually, he dropped out of school and he ran away from home.

His life began turning around when he reconnected with Joe, a former male friend of his mother's who had told him if he ever needed help to contact him. He eventually moved in with Joe and Joe's parents, all three of whom he considers his family. He reports that they give him love and care, support, and encouragement. Phil also contacted an alternative school he had heard about years before. On the day of his initial contact, the principal encouraged Phil to attend, telling him "I know you are a good kid."

"The structure of the school"—which is built around adult and student cooperative teams, experiential activities, identifying and nurturing strengths, finding real-world work placements as part of learning— "the environment here, and last—but not least—my teacher Kathryn who always [for several years] gave me encouragement to take it one day at a time," (p. 14) are the reasons Phil says he is still in school and working in a community agency grant-writing to help other kids. His goal after graduation is to own his own video production company.

"Facilitating resiliency is more a matter of orientation than specific intervention," writes Higgins (1994, p. 319), based on her study of resilient survivors of childhood trauma. It is clear that fostering resiliency doesn't happen as a result of putting kids through a program, though many programs such as Big Brothers/Big Sisters, as well as families, provide the caring adults that provide this crucial "resiliency orientation." A "resiliency orientation" is something all caring adults, how ever and where ever they interact with children, can convey—through an attitude of optimism and encouragement, a focus on strengths, a commitment to weaving strands from The Resiliency Wheel into children's lives, and persistence, for decades if necessary, in these approaches. ☉

References

Benard, B. (1991). *Fostering resiliency in kids: Protective factors in the family, school, and community.* Portland, OR: Western Regional Center for Drug-Free Schools and Communities.

Benson, P., Galbraith, J., & Espeland, P. (1994). *What kids need to succeed: Proven, practical ways to raise good kids.* Minneapolis, MN: Free Spirit Publishing.

Botvin, G., & Botvin, E. (1992). Adolescent tobacco, alcohol, and drug abuse: Prevention strategies, empirical findings, and assessment issues. *Journal of Developmental and Behavioral Pediatrics, 13* (4), 29.

Cooper, C., & Henderson, N. (1995). *Motivating schools to change: Integrating the threads of school restructuring.* Tasmania, Australia: Global Learning Communities.

Hawkins, J., & Catalano, R. (1990). *20 questions: Adolescent substance abuse risk factors* (Audiotape). Seattle, WA: Developmental Research and Programs, Inc.

Hawkins, J., Catalano, R., & Miller, J. (1992). Risk and protective factors for alcohol and other drug problems. *Psychological Bulletin, 112* (1), 64-105.

Henderson, N., & Milstein, M. (1996). *Resiliency in schools: Making it happen for students and educators.* Thousand Oaks, CA: Corwin Press.

Henderson, N. (1996a). L.W. Schmick: Challenging the "at risk" label. *Resiliency In Action, 1* (3), 29-30.

Henderson, N. (1996b). Juanita Corriz: A relationship with a big sister taught her to "want everything there is good for me in life." *Resiliency In Action, 1* (4), 19-20.

Henderson, N. (1996c). Leslie Krug: "I've been in so much trouble and I'm still here." *Resiliency In Action, 1* (1), 12-13.

Henderson, N. (1996d). Phil Canamar: "I feel the pain and anger in everybody's heart that joins a gang." *Resiliency In Action 1* (1), 13-15.

Higgins, G. (1994). *Resilient adults: Overcoming a cruel past.* San Francisco, CA: Jossey-Bass.

Noddings, N. (1988). Schools face "crisis in caring." *Education Week,* December 7, p. 32.

Richardson, G., Neiger, B., Jensen, S., & Kumpfer, K. (1990). The resiliency model. *Health Education, 21* (6), 33-39.

Werner, E., & Smith, R. (1992). *Overcoming the odds: High risk children from birth to adulthood.* New York, NY: Cornell University Press.

Werner, E. (1996). How children become resilient: Observations and cautions. *Resiliency In Action 1* (1), 18-28.

Wolin, S., & Wolin, S. (1993). *The resilient self: How survivors of troubled families rise above adversity.* New York, NY: Villard Books.

Nan Henderson, M.S.W., is a national and international speaker and consultant on fostering resiliency and wellness, alcohol and other drug issues, and on organizational change. She has co-authored / edited five books about resiliency, and is the president of Resiliency In Action. She can be reached at Nan Henderson and Associates, 5130 La Jolla Blvd., #2K, San Diego, CA 92109, p / f (858-488-5034), or by e-mail: (nanh@connectnet.com).

Resiliency In Practice

Selecting Parenting Programs that Foster Resiliency

by Nancy Sharp-Light

My interest in writing parenting programs began in early 1978 while living on the Zuni Indian Reservation in Zuni, NM. As a teacher and a counselor, I worked with many students and their families to assist with a variety of issues, including poor school performance, behavior problems, and issues relating to family alcoholism. I found that most of the materials available did not address some very basic parenting issues and didn't relate to Zuni culture and tradition. I have since heard similar comments from parents and facilitators from around the country. Below, I share the basics of what I have learned about elements to avoid and elements to include in parenting curricula which either hinder or help the process of fostering resiliency in families.

In 1991, counselors from the Gallup Schools in NM asked me to write a program for parents that would include not only basic information about parenting but one that honored the personhood and culture of the parents. The curriculum overviewed in this article is the result of that request.

The awareness that parents need support, information, and skills, just like their children, is increasing. As a result, parenting curricula abound. The process of selecting one that fosters resiliency while being appropriate for cultural diversity can be overwhelming. It needn't be. Below are some guidelines to facilitate the selection process. An overview of one parenting curriculum that fosters resiliency called, "We're Doing The Best We Can," is included. This program is designed specifically to help parents recognize their own resiliencies, provide them with new information and skills, and honor cultural diversity.

The Heart of Resiliency-Building Parenting Programs

The heart of an effective parenting curriculum begins with nurturing the parents. The same factors that foster resiliency in youth—caring/bonding, high expectations, meaningful participation and contribution, and life skills—foster resiliency in adults. If parents do not know how to nurture themselves, acknowledge their strengths, value their own accomplishments, accept themselves unconditionally, and forgive themselves for mistakes, they will be less likely to model and teach these behaviors to their children. If a program concentrates too heavily on information and skill-building, it will not be as effective as one which begins with sessions focused on fostering the inherent resiliency in the parents and continues to support and reinforce this throughout the program.

Look For Balance

The most helpful curricula for parents have three points of balance: self-esteem building versus information-giving/skill-building; attention to a variety of individual learning styles; and the amount of time for facilitator presentation versus time for interaction among participants.

Do individuals perform better when they feel better, or feel better when they perform better? The answer to this is not either/or, but both. A heavy focus on either building self-esteem or information-giving/skill development can cause frustration. In fact, the two are complimentary. It is important to learn ways to improve self image. However, it is practice and skill development that helps to internalize and manifest positive self-esteem. Therefore, when assessing programs, look for those which have a good mix of self-esteem-building activities and skill-building activities.

Additionally, look for a program in which all three learning styles are used: auditory, visual, and tactile. Everyone—including adults—learns best in one of these ways. A curriculum must incorporate all three in order to accommodate each person's best learning style. Beware of a format that concentrates heavily on any one method, i.e. mostly lecture, whether by a facilitator or on a video, or multiple worksheets. The best format is "say it, show it, do it."

Finally, look for a balance between how much the facilitator is required to speak and how much time is allowed for participants to share and interact. Parents must be allowed ample opportunity to share their "stories" with one another. In this way, they learn they are not alone, that their experiences have value, and that they have the inner wisdom to create solutions appropriate for their families.

Guidelines For Selection

It is just as important to know what doesn't work as what does in selecting a parenting program. Assumptions upon which some parenting programs are based which can unintentionally sabotage resiliency fostering for parents is provided in Table 1. These assumptions can hinder parents' recognition and development of their strengths, capabilities, and capacity to do well.

Table 1

Assumptions That Sabotage Parenting Programs

1. There must be a problem or the parents wouldn't be there.
2. All that parents need is information about skills (rules and consequences, what to say, and when to say it, etc.).
3. Once parents have more information they will be able to put it into practice.
4. Parents know the resources available to them and how to use them.
5. There is a common language.
6. There is a shared level of education.
7. There is a common culture.

1 Many parents are tired of being blamed and shamed for the troubles of society. There is currently a great deal of negative publicity about parenting. If their child gets into trouble, even good parents are made to feel like bad parents. This attitude is a major reason why many parents will not attend parenting classes.

2-3 These two assumptions can actually create a sense of frustration, shame, and hopelessness rather than nurture self-honor, respect, confidence, and responsibility. An effective parenting curriculum must help parents realize their own resilience while learning new skills—exactly what they need to do for their children.

4 It is rarely the case that parents are aware of all the resources available. Even when they are, it does not mean that they are comfortable or skilled at asking for help. Discussions about resources

and opportunities to practice asking for help (role playing, pairing up and reading a script, etc.) are useful.

5-6 The assumption that all participants use English as their first language, are proficient in their use of it, or that all participants have the same level of education is simply inaccurate. Much information, even when presented with the best of intentions, may not be understood by many. A rule of thumb relating to the level of language used is if "language" is being taught, the use of an expanded vocabulary, with definitions, is appropriate. However, if a concept is being taught, such as parenting and nurturing, the simpler the vocabulary the better. In one facilitator training a participant summed this up by saying, "Why use 'dollar' words when 'dime' words will do!" Participants, regardless of first language or level of education, shouldn't have to struggle with terminology. Rather, they should be able to focus on the concepts.

7 This country has a variety of rich and wonderful cultures. To present only one culture's methods of parenting or set of values can feel shaming or disrespectful to those whose lifestyles are different. During my 13 years on the Zuni Reservation and my subsequent work with families from other cultures, this has been the most commonly expressed reason for not attending parenting classes.

Elements which foster resiliency and should be in any parenting curriculum are listed in Table 2. Parenting curricula should also work from a strengths perspective just like resiliency building for youth. It is important for parents to have the opportunity to identify their own postive behaviors, strengths, and successes, rather than only concentrating on possible deficits and failures.

Table 2

Elements That Empower Parents

1. An initial focus on nurturing the parents.
2. Opportunities for dialogue, interaction, and sharing of experiences.
3. Opportunities and encouragement to practice new skills, through experiential activities.
4. Basic information on developmental stages, behavior management, and local resources.
5. In general:
    - a positive approach,
    - simple language,
    - sensitivity toward differences,
    - a sense of fun.

1 The best resource for a parent is another parent. The most effective parenting programs provide numerous opportunities for parents to share and interact. Any program offers information, but the ultimate value and benefit to the parents occur when they are in community with one another, sharing their experiences, hopes, dreams, problems, and solutions. Diverse cultures can learn from one another and those with similar backgrounds can provide support, "normalization," and pride for one another. Discussion time allows for meaningful participation, contribution, and a sense of belonging.

2-3 Opportunity for and encouragement to practice is critical to the learning process. This can be accomplished through a variety of practice activities including participant role-playing, interactive teaching "games," and suggested home-based activities between sessions. It is more likely that parents will be able to utilize new skills if they have, first, had a chance to internalize them through practice in a nonthreatening, non-critical situation. Activities which don't work for parents are as valuable a learning tool as those which do. Helping parents realize that mistakes are not a sign of failure, but of progress, reduces potential shame and teaches an important resiliency building characteristic—persistence.

4 Most parents agree with the saying, "children don't come with operating manuals." Therefore, it is important to include information on the normal stages of childhood development. This information provides parents with a reference of what behaviors to expect at any given age. Such knowledge can reduce anxiety and fear that something is "wrong" with either them or their child. It is particularly important for first-time and teen parents to have this kind of information. Sessions on how managing misbehavior and encouraging positive behavior are also vital for any parenting program. Facilitators can present techniques, but the content and context of the application should come directly from the parents.

5 Even though parenting is "serious" business, opportunities for fun, camaraderie, networking, and socialization are as important as the information. Humor is a great relaxer and can help break down walls of defense. Refreshments allow time for socialization, bonding, and networking. Small and large group discussions encourage acceptance, meaningful participation, and the creation of local support networks among parents.

Each of these elements of fostering parent resiliency model what parents should do to foster resiliency for their families and children.

"We're Doing the Best We Can"

The curriculum, "We're Doing the Best We Can" is one example of a resiliency-building parenting program. It is based on the tenant that every parent is already doing some things "right" and builds on this to expand parents' knowledge and skills. It is currently implemented in several multicultural settings by a variety of organizations, including schools, social service agencies, and medical doctors who provide parent education. Two consistent comments made about this curriculum are how easy it is for facilitators to implement and how easy it is for participants to understand and utilize.

The program consists of six two-hour sessions. There are three sections—Your Self, Your Child, and Your Family—with two sessions devoted to each topic. All sessions include review/preview and short lecturettes followed by interactive learning activities. Suggested processing questions, and frequent opportunities for parents to discuss and share their ideas and experiences are included. Masters for all handouts and overheads are provided.

Curriculum Goals and Design

Part One: Your Self includes two sessions designed for parent self-reflection. Parents explore ways that they do/don't take care of themselves and how this affects their family relationships. Participants examine the methods their parents used to raise them, and possible reasons why—i.e. rapid changes in society, family, and education since World War II— what worked for their parents may not be working for them now.

Part Two: Your Child (sessions three and four) is designed to teach parents normal childhood development. They learn about what behaviors to expect from their children at different ages and examine how culture and the media affect the normal developmental process. They learn about the importance of consistency in their own behavior— setting and enforcing rules, consequences, rewards, and punishments—and explore techniques for managing and correcting misbehavior without shaming their children.

Part Three: Your Family (final two sessions) focuses on ways to encourage and support positive behaviors, how to schedule quality time, and ideas for activities to do during this time. Parents share their family and cultural traditions and discuss creating "new" traditions. Included is a video that shows parents of different ages and culture, sharing their stories of family traditions, the challenges, and the joys of their parenting experiences. It summarizes and exemplifies all the points of the program and is recommended viewing during the last session.

Curriculum Features

The following list describes some of the features of this curriculum.

User-Friendly: "We're Doing the Best We Can" is designed to provide facilitators with all the information needed in a simple, bulleted, list fashion. Very little prep time is required. No outside research is necessary.

Choose and Use Design: There is more information than can be presented within any two-hour session. So, facilitators can select what is most appropriate for their population. Charts and graphs are normally provided in two ways: an expanded English version and one appropriate for the language needs of English as a Second Language (ESL) participants.

Cultural Relevancy: An appendix demonstrates how the curriculum can be adapted for different cultures. The included sample lesson is based on the child-rearing practices of the Navajo Indians of the Southwest. However, throughout the curriculum, sessions are designed so that the participants can, quite naturally, share their cultural traditions.

Activities and "Try-outs:" All sessions include activities that are fun and teach at the same time. Each session ends with participants choosing one new thing to work on for one week called "try-outs"—simple activities such as having one sit-down meal with their family, self-care activities, making a point to say, "thank you" to a child for putting the top back on the toothpaste, etc. The purpose of the "try-outs" is to gently build positive habits, rather than force drastic, immediate changes. At the beginning of the next session, they share what worked and what didn't.

Flexibility: "We're Doing the Best We Can" is flexible and can be adapted to a variety of needs and populations. For example, one facilitator needed more time to examine childhood developmental stages with a particular group because there were many first-time and teen parents participating. Other facilitators have either expanded the program to eight or ten weeks, or divided the program into parts one and two.

Observations and Comments

In Albuquerque, NM, the program is used as part of a Parents Anonymous support group working with issues of child abuse/neglect. The director says, "It [the program] emphasizes the empowerment of the parent in relation to his/her parenting. It's concrete and fun. In use with several 'macho, taciturn' men, particularly one Native American man, it was wonderful to see their efforts in writing/drawing something for their children." A parent who has taken the class twice says, "I could never get my kids and husband to do anything around the house. This class helped me realize that I was demanding their help, getting mad, and then doing everything anyway. Now I ask politely and wait and make sure to say, 'thank you.' They're actually helping me now. It works!" The facilitator for a program in progress through one of the Gallup schools says her current group of parents ranges from a 16-year-old boy, to a teen mother, to a set of Native American grandparents. About the 16-year-old boy she says, "I knew him in grade school. He had a lot of behavior problems. Then he started using drugs. He's now in recovery and volunteered for the class. He says he wants to make sure he gives his kid what he didn't get." Another parent reports, "I didn't realize how much I was putting myself down in front of my kids and how it upsets them and makes them act bad. Now, I'm trying to catch myself and we all feel better." Parents of all backgrounds and levels of education comment that they appreciate the positive, simple, down-to-earth approach of "We're Doing the Best We Can." They also express appreciation for the opportunity to share and network with other parents. They report a sense of confidence, pride, and well-being as a result of being involved in this program.

Improving the Parenting Experience for All

A parenting program should include a nonthreatening, caring, and supportive atmosphere in order to create the environmental conditions that will foster resiliency. It must provide opportunities for parent networking, meaningful contribution and participation as well as basic parenting skills. It must help parents identify not only their personal strengths but those of their children and family as a whole. When parents feel good about themselves, and feel capable and knowledgeable, the parenting experience improves for both themselves and their children. ℮

Nancy Sharp-Light has been in education since 1972 in a variety of capacities including teacher, counselor, and district coordinator for substance abuse prevention programs. In 1984, one of her programs won a state award and in 1988, she won the award for outstanding teacher of the year in New Mexico. She has authored 11 curricula and currently provides trainings and workshops nationally. She can be reached at Sharp-Light Consulting, p/f (505-891-1600) or by e-mail: (nslight@aol.com).

The Faces Of Resiliency

Loretta Dejolie: A Teen Mom Builds
a Better Life for Her Daughter

by Nan Henderson, M.S.W.

Emmy Werner reported in the first issue of this journal that life-span studies that have followed teen-age welfare mothers into later life have found they "do not end up permanently taking Aid For Families of Dependent Children." There are only three such research studies, she said; "very few people have bothered to study them over time." In her own longitudinal research of over 40 years, "less than five percent [of teen-age moms on welfare] were still on some kind of government support when we saw them in their mid-30s. They moved up the socioeconomic ladder as they got more education and more vocational skills, and in their mid-30s were people who had decent and well-paying jobs. Over time, teen-age mothers do work themselves out of the dependency on AFDC, given two things: one, access to continued education, and the other, access to child care." (see "How Children Become Resilient: Observations and Cautions" by Emmy Werner, Ph.D., on p. 11).

Loretta Dejolie is a living example of Emmy Werner's findings. With the help of her mother, who is providing the child care, and access to a school that provides an accessible and caring opportunity for learning, Loretta will no doubt follow in the footsteps of other teen moms who have gotten off welfare and are now doing well on their own.

Loretta Dejolie dropped out of school at age 16 when she was pregnant and had a baby girl, Amber, at age 17. Before she dropped out, Loretta was skipping school, getting Ds and Fs, driving around, drinking, and "being wild"—behaviors she had begun in junior high school.

At age 17—two years ago—Loretta went back to school, is now getting all As and Bs, and planning to go to college. She is considering a career in nursing.

Loretta credits two family members with changing her life: her mother and her baby daughter.

Loretta said her daughter changed her life even before she was born. "I quit drinking and smoking months before I got pregnant, because I knew it was going to happen," Loretta explained. "And then as soon as I got pregnant, I knew that I had to stay quit because I might be having fun, but she

might be paying for it. I knew I wasn't the only one anymore. I really wanted to make a better life for her."

Loretta said that she had no idea how hard being a teen parent would be. If she had to do it again, "I would have Amber later so I could give her a better life than I'm giving her now—a house, a better environment. I should have waited."

She said she had tried not to think about getting pregnant, "but I should have thought about it... Now, it is way too much." Amber's dad moved almost 200 miles away and he and Loretta have had an on and off relationship since Amber was born. He occasionally helps Loretta financially "a little bit."

She survives, for now, by receiving welfare. But she is determined to get off. "I get AFDC but I don't like it," Loretta said. "My goal is to get off... to get a good paying job. I went back to school right after Amber was born because I felt like I had to or we'd all be stuck here forever in the same old place. I really didn't want that for Amber. I know a lot of people that do that and they're not really happy with their lives. I don't want to be like that." Loretta believes that the children of the people she knows on welfare pay a price. "I know how their kids feel," she said. "They feel bad. I can see anger and frustration in their faces."

**Loretta Dejolie and
her daughter, Amber**

She has a different goal for her daughter. "I want her to be happy. I want her to have everything she needs and maybe some things that she wants. I don't want to be incredibly rich. I just want to be comfortable. And I hope she'll go to college and be whatever she wants."

When asked who else—besides her daughter—helped her grow from a wild teenage girl, ditching school, and flunking to a serious student getting As and Bs and planning to attend college, Loretta quickly answered, "My mother."

"She talks to me. She encourages me to go to school. She helps me a lot with Amber. She lends me money when I need it, if she has it. If I do something good, she praises me. She tells me she is proud of me."

Loretta's mother also wants something better for her daughter than she experienced, having dropped out of high school herself, and becoming a young single mom when Loretta's dad died when Loretta was just a baby. She has lived on her husband's social security, supported three daughters, and moved frequently. Today, Loretta, her mom, her two sisters, and Amber all live in a motel.

Loretta, however, is working with her school counselor in researching scholarships and federal aid available for her to attend college. She also credits the school—an alternative high school— with her success. She said she was directed to try it by a counselor when she went back to re-register for school after she had Amber. The principal persuaded her on the spot to attend.

That was two years ago. And Loretta says she doesn't think she would have made it in the traditional high school she started in. Instead, she thrives in the alternative school.

"It is smaller. Everybody knows each other. The teachers are really nice . . . you can talk to them, too, if you are having problems—not just to the counselors. They pay more attention to you. They help you get through the assignments."

Loretta offered this advice to other teenage girls that are hanging out "and being wild" and ditching class: "If you want something better you have to try . . . you have it do it. Nobody can do it for you." It's a message she is role-modeling for her daughter. ☺

Commentary

Parenting for Resiliency: How My Second-Born Child Taught Me to Use the "Power of the Positive"

by Tim Duffey, M.Ed.

One memory of my young fatherhood is emblazoned in my mind. The picture, as clear as if it were yesterday, is of me standing in the hallway of our home holding our screaming second-born child, a boy 30 months of age. This child held a special place in our hearts after having survived a serious bout with spinal meningitis when he was just five months old. Two days in Pediatric Intensive Care and eight additional days in the hospital pressed our family to new levels of endurance and tested our own resilience. That medical emergency bonded his mother and me to him in ways we had never encountered previously or since.

However, it was not our son's medical history that caused the image I remember so accurately. It was his behavior. In parenting seminars we had attended as young parents, we heard Dr. Charles Dobson, in his *Focus on The Family* video series describe this child's profile as "strong willed." On this particular day, "strong willed" was an understatement.

It had been clear from the beginning that this child had a personality distinct from our firstborn. He had a high need to be in close personal contact. Tantrums were a common occurrence. Within the first two years of life it was already evident that, in his view, limits were suggestions only— things to be tested. We established boundaries, he challenged them. If the answer was "no," he did it anyway. All of our parenting skills were being taxed to the limit.

I'd thought we had a pretty good bag of tricks as we approached parenthood. I'd earned a degree in sociology and psychology;

my wife had a degree in child development. I had also received a masters degree in counseling and human development and had begun working in a large high school counseling center. Beyond that, we'd done our "homework"—utilizing parenting books, courses, tapes, etc. We'd discussed our parenting philosophy in depth before we started our family. We'd enhanced this philosophy through a parenting course at the local university, which focused on the writing of Dreikurs & Grey (1970). Through professional events, we came to know the work of Barbara Coloroso (1983) whose audio tape *Discipline: Kids are Worth It* has been played so many times by us and a myriad of friends and acquaintances that I am amazed the message is still audible. Following her guidance, we provided clear expectations, followed through with logical consequences, always strove to provide choices—an opportunity to "save face," and worked hard to encourage development of skill areas (gifts) we saw each child possess. These skills supported the parenting philosophy we had developed and were particularly important for this child's—our son Aaron's—excitement for life!

In my relatively short tenure in the school counseling center where I was working at that time, I had come to see a pattern of students with energy like our Aaron's. Frequently, they had frustrated nearly everyone near them with their approach to life. They steadily challenged rules and limits and were perceived to regard what applied to others as having little bearing on *their* behavior. Often, their parents had decided it was better to back off and give them room to make their own choices than to continue fighting to draw the line and enforce expectations. Too often, I saw these kids referred to as "juvenile delinquents," "troubled kids," or "high risk." The result often was a lowered expectation for performance and/or behavior; one they frequently lived down to.

That day in the hallway with screaming Aaron in my arms, I remember these thoughts racing through my mind. My son screamed because I would not allow him to continue throwing toys. I did not want my son to end up facing the same challenges I saw young people in my school facing. I knew then that we, as parents, had a choice. We could focus on the risk that his personality and energy held. We could talk about how, if he didn't change, he would end up in trouble with the law, be a juvenile delinquent, end up on probation, and be "no good." Or, we could find ways to direct that energy—to challenge him to use his strong sense of direction to his favor. *His* future options would likely depend in some large degree on *our* current attitude and choices. It was also clear that this would be hard work.

We renewed our efforts to set clear limits and consistently enforce them. We sought regular opportunities to show him our care and support in the endeavors of his choosing. We looked for means of directing his energy and enthusiasm for life, drawing from his natural gifts and talent. We continued to utilize consequences that we believed were fair and respected his ability to choose whether or not to encounter them. We sought periodic reprise and recreation for ourselves as a couple. We committed and recommitted to give it the best we had.

Some twelve years have passed since then. Just a few months ago, I watched this same child walk on stage as The Artful Dodger in our community theater's production of *Oliver!*. My eyes filled with tears as I struggled to comprehend where the years had gone. Where was my "little boy?" This young man, presuming to be my son, took the stage with a presence and strength that I sensed to my core. Theater has been one of the directions in which, with our guidance and support, he directed his incredible energy. He is a natural for it. The spotlight has attracted him for years, providing a positive time commitment and an amazing outlet for the creative energy housed in that young body.

Similarly, sports, public speaking, voice lessons, positive friendships, other caring, principled adults, family responsibilities, and participation in our congregation's youth group have contributed to shaping the raw materials I held in my arms some twelve years ago. Today I marvel at his ability to lead, his immense social awareness and sensitivity, and his gift for placing people at ease. We certainly did not do it alone. On the path to his current life success, contributions were made by many.

In the past few years as I have become immersed in the resiliency and positive youth development research, I have recognized that the thoughts running through my head on the day I held our screaming son in my arms were thoughts of the power of the positive—the power of resiliency. I knew then what I now have the language to communicate with others—that our attitudes and choices as adults are powerful determining factors for the future of our youth. The belief system and research base from which resiliency and positive youth development has grown affirms what I have long believed regarding our support of children and youth. Through Aaron, I have seen its impact first hand and I thank him for the lesson. ℮

References

Coloroso, B. (Speaker). (1983). *Discipline: Kids are worth it* (Cassette Recording). Boulder, CO: Barbara Coloroso.

Dreikurs, R., & Grey, L. (1970). *A parents' guide to child discipline*. New York, NY: Hawthorn/Dutton.

Related References

Parents today can benefit from many resources built upon resiliency and positive youth development research. Among them:

Benson, P., Galbraith, J., & Espeland, P. (1995). *What kids need to succeed*. Minneapolis, MN: Free Spirit Publishing.

Bluestein, J. (1993). *Parents, teens, and boundaries: How to draw the line*. Deerfield Beach, FL: Health Communications.

Faber, A. & Mazlish, E. (1980). *How to talk so kids will listen & listen so kids will talk*. New York, NY: Avon Books.

Leffert, N., Benson, P., & Roehlkepartain, J. (1997). *Starting out right: Developmental assets for children*. Minneapolis, MN: Search Institute.

Seligman, M. (1995). *The optimistic child*. New York, NY: Harper Collins.

Tim Duffey, M.Ed., is Past President of the National Association of Leadership for Student Assistance Programs, cofounder of the New England consulting group, Common Ground In Prevention, and a former Feature Editor of Resiliency In Action. *He can be reached at Common Ground In Prevention, (207-839-6319) or by e-mail: (tduffey47@aol.com).*

Speeches, Presentations, and Training From The Editors of Resiliency In Action

Bonnie Benard, M.S.W.: *Resiliency Associates, 1238 Josephine., Berkeley, CA 94703, t/f(510) 528-4344; bbenard@flashnet.com*
- "Fostering Resiliency in Kids"
- "Fostering Resiliency *is* Violence Prevention"
- "Working from a Resiliency Framework (in Families, Schools, and Communities)"

Nan Henderson, M.S.W.: *Nan Henderson and Associates, 5130 La Jolla Blvd., #2K, San Diego, CA 92109, t/f(858) 488-5034; nanh@connectnet.com*
- "How Families, Schools, and Communities Foster Resilient Children"
- "Resiliency in Schools and other Organizations: Making it Happen"
- "Teaching Youth and Adults About Resiliency"
- "The Resiliency Training Program™" Training of Trainers

Craig Noonan, Ph.D.: *Alternatives, 5130 La Jolla Blvd., #2K, San Diego, CA 92109, t/f (858) 488-5034; wnoonan@popmail.ucsd.edu*
- "Creating the Resiliency Relationship"
- "How People Change Problematic Behavior"
- "How to Motivate Positive Change in Clients, Students, Parents, and/or Colleagues"

Nancy Sharp-Light: *Sharp-Light Consulting, 602 San Juan de Rio, Rio Rancho, NM 87124 (505) 891-1600; nslight@aol.com*
- "Team-Building for Resilience"
- "We're Doing the Best We Can: A Resiliency-Building Parenting Program"
- "Classroom Techniques for Moving Students From Stress to Success"
- "Teaching Optimism"

ORDER FORM

MAIL WITH YOUR *PO* TO:
RESILIENCY IN ACTION
P.O. BOX 90319
SAN DIEGO, CA 92169-2319

OR *FAX* TO:
(858) 581-9231

OR *CALL TOLL FREE:*
(800) 440-5171

OR ORDER *ON-LINE* AT:
WWW.RESILIENCY.COM

PLEASE SEND *# COPIES:* _____ OF:

THE BOOK: RESILIENCY IN ACTION: *Practical Ideas for Overcoming Risks and Building Strengths in Youth, Families, & Communities*

COST:	1-10	COPIES:	$28.95 + 15% S/H
	11-25	COPIES:	10% DISCOUNT
	26-50	COPIES:	20% DISCOUNT
	51+	COPIES:	25% DISCOUNT

FED. ID #85-0438768

(PLEASE PRINT!)

(SEND TO)

NAME/ORGANIZATION _____
ADDRESS _____
_____
CITY _____ STATE _____ ZIP _____
TELEPHONE ( )-_____ FAX ( )-_____
E-MAIL _____
ORGANIZATION _____
POSITION _____

(PAYMENT METHOD:) TOTAL: $_____ *(REMEMBER TO INCLUDE 15% FOR SHIPPING AND HANDLING TO U.S. DESTINATIONS)*

☐ CHECK ENCLOSED ☐ PURCHASE ORDER ATTACHED
☐ CREDIT CARD (MASTER CARD/VISA)

NAME ON CARD _____
CC# _____ EXP. DATE_____
SIGNATURE _____

ORDER FORM

MAIL WITH YOUR **PO** TO:
RESILIENCY IN ACTION
P.O. BOX 90319
SAN DIEGO, CA 92169-2319

OR **FAX** TO:
(858) 581-9231

OR **CALL TOLL FREE:**
(800) 440-5171

OR ORDER **ON-LINE** AT:
WWW.RESILIENCY.COM

PLEASE SEND # COPIES: _____ OF:

THE BOOK: **RESILIENCY IN ACTION:** Practical Ideas for Overcoming Risks and Building Strengths in Youth, Families, & Communities

COST: 1-10 COPIES: $28.95 + 15% S/H
             11-25 COPIES: 10% DISCOUNT
             26-50 COPIES: 20% DISCOUNT
             51+   COPIES: 25% DISCOUNT

FED. ID #85-0438768

(**PLEASE PRINT!**)

(SEND TO)

NAME/ORGANIZATION _____

ADDRESS _____

_____

CITY _____ STATE _____ ZIP _____

TELEPHONE (___)- _____ FAX (___)- _____

E-MAIL _____

     ORGANIZATION _____

     POSITION _____

(PAYMENT METHOD:) TOTAL: $ _____ (REMEMBER TO INCLUDE 15% FOR SHIPPING AND HANDLING TO U.S. DESTINATIONS)

☐ CHECK ENCLOSED   ☐ PURCHASE ORDER ATTACHED

☐ CREDIT CARD (MASTER CARD/VISA)

     NAME ON CARD _____

       CC# _____ EXP. DATE _____

     SIGNATURE _____